ART DECO
CERAMICS
IN BRITAIN

ANDREW CASEY

ART DECO
CERAMICS
IN BRITAIN

ANTIQUE COLLECTORS' CLUB

©2008 Andrew Casey
World copyright reserved

ISBN 978-1-85149-544-3

The right of Frank Ashworth, Peter and Brenda Aspinall, Paul Atterbury, John Barter, Stella Beddoe, Hilary Calvert, Andrew Casey, Dan Dunlavey, Ann Eatwell, Linda Ellis, Sharon Gater, Miranda Goodby, Clive Hillier, Michael Jeffery, Julie McKeown, Helen Martin, Steven Moore, Harvey Pettit, Susan Scott, Greg Slater, Greg Stevenson, David Steventon, Sue Taylor, Ian Turner and Vega Wilkinson to be identified as authors of contributions to this work has been asserted by them in accordance with the Copyright, Designs and Patents Act 1988

British Library Cataloguing-in-Publication Data
A catalogue record for this book is available from the British Library

Printed in China
for the Antique Collectors' Club Ltd, Woodbridge, Suffolk

Frontispiece: *An earthenware ginger jar and cover decorated with the Moon and Mountain pattern designed by Susie Cooper for A.E. Gray & Co Ltd, c.1927/1928. Height of jar 9¼in. (23.4cm).*

The Antique Collectors' Club

FORMED IN 1966, the Antique Collectors' Club is now a world-renowned publisher of top quality books for the collector. It also publishes the only independently-run monthly antiques magazine, *Antique Collecting*, which rose quickly from humble beginnings to a network of worldwide subscribers.

The magazine, whose motto is *For Collectors–By Collectors–About Collecting*, is aimed at collectors interested in widening their knowledge of antiques both by increasing their awareness of quality and by discussion of the factors influencing prices.

Subscription to *Antique Collecting* is open to anyone interested in antiques and subscribers receive ten issues a year. Well-illustrated articles deal with practical aspects of collecting and provide numerous tips on prices, features of value, investment potential, fakes and forgeries. Offers of related books at special reduced prices are also available only to subscribers.

In response to the enormous demand for information on 'what to pay', ACC introduced in 1968 the famous price guide series. The first title, *The Price Guide to Antique Furniture* (since renamed *British Antique Furniture: Price Guide and Reasons for Values*), is still in constant demand. Since those pioneering days, ACC has gone from strength to strength, publishing many of today's standard works of reference on all things antique and collectable, from *Tiaras* to *20th Century Ceramic Designers in Britain*.

Not only has ACC continued to cater strongly for its original audience, it has also branched out to produce excellent titles on many subjects including art reference, architecture, garden design, gardens, and textiles. All ACC's publications are available through bookshops worldwide and a catalogue is available free of charge from the addresses below.

For further information please contact:

ANTIQUE COLLECTORS' CLUB

www.antiquecollectorsclub.com

Sandy Lane, Old Martlesham, Woodbridge, Suffolk IP12 4SD, UK
Tel: 01394 389950 Fax: 01394 389999
Email: info@antique-acc.com
or
Eastworks, 116 Pleasant Street - Suite 18, Easthampton, MA 01027, USA
Tel: 413 529 0861 Fax: 413 529 0862
Email: info@antiquecc.com

An advertisement for Era Pottery Co. showing the latest products, 1934.

Contents

Foreword

Eric Knowles

PRIOR TO 1972 my understanding of the Art Deco style was mostly limited to the treacle coloured furniture that graced the homes of many, a then, grandparent, not forgetting the ubiquitous glazed chalk figures of leggy ladies restraining sleek hounds that had pride of place on the window sill of many a terraced house in my part of north-east Lancashire.

Fortunately a clearer understanding of all things Deco arrived that year when the, still much lamented, Victoria and Albert Museum's circulation department's 'Art Deco' travelling exhibition arrived at Burnley's Towneley Hall Museum and Art Gallery. Here, in this magnificent Tudor building, the former family home of the Towneley family, I was introduced to such names as René Lalique, Gérard Sandoz, Jean Puiforcat, Gabriel Argy-Rousseau, Edgar Brandt, Georges Fouquet and Jean Goulden, to name but a few.

As these names might suggest, the emphasis of the exhibition concentrated on the French contribution to a style whose very name was derived from the Paris Exposition des Arts Décoratifs et Industriels Modernes held in 1925. The ceramics on display included the wax resist and crackle glazed wares of René Buthaud and Primavera alongside the interesting matt glazed pots of Emile Decoeur and the stylish figural designs favoured by Jean Mayodon.

Now I may well be the victim of a failing memory but, apart from a single Keith Murray designed Wedgwood vase and a Clarice Cliff sugar sifter, British ceramics from those inter-war years appeared to have been largely ignored by the organisers at the V&A

It is, however, important to remember that back in 1972 the interest in British ceramics from the inter-war years was only just beginning to awaken prompted by later exhibitions of Clarice Cliff and the pioneering work of Martin Battersby and Bevis Hillier aided and abetted

(Opposite and above) A rare vase decorated with a hand-painted 'hunt' theme designed by Susie Cooper, 1931. This piece was probably produced for display purposes. Height: 12¼in. (31cm).

by dealers such as John Jesse and Richard Dennis operating from London's Kensington Church Street, not forgetting Victor Arwas in nearby Mayfair.

Fast forward to today and the insatiable appetite for all things Deco and an age where the collectors can arm themselves with a veritable arsenal of reference books and attend the various specialised fairs and galleries that offer today's busy marketplace. The most recent exhibition to concentrate on the output of British ceramic manufacturers from 'The Jazz Age' was held at the Walker Art Gallery in Liverpool providing a benchmark in terms of a present-day understanding and appreciation of the British approach and innovation in decorative ceramic design.

Over the ensuing three decades, since my interest was first kindled, British ceramics from this period can now lay claim to a following of not only dedicated but also increasingly educated collectors all with a growing thirst for more and more information. Enter Andrew Casey and his team of highly respected authorities.

Art Deco Ceramics in Britain is a bold step forward in providing a consolidated reference work that examines in great detail the responses of a multitude of British potters to the influences and trends experienced by all those who lived through this turbulent age of progress and change.

This is unquestionably a 'Benchmark' reference work in its own right by virtue of being the collaboration of so many respected authorities who collectively share not only a deep understanding but also an obvious passion for their specialised subjects.

Within these pages you will find an explanation as to how the Art Deco style developed in Europe and how new and radical motifs and patterns permeated their way into British mainstream ceramic design. This reference work also examines why such established and world famous factories as Josiah Wedgwood and Sons Ltd, Minton and Royal Doulton all had to accept the popularity of Art Deco and were left with little option of having to give the public what they wanted. More importantly, the book deals with the smaller, often family owned, potteries and how they were able to respond and compete by providing a vast range of 'Deco' wares that incorporated colourful hand-painted decoration with inventive forms at a price to suit those of lesser means.

Andrew Casey and his team have also managed to acknowledge a significant number of previously lesser-known makers whose praises have until now been unsung. Add to all this welcome knowledge the many new and splendid colour illustrations and you have a reference work that should grace the library of any self-respecting Art Deco crackpot.

As one such crackpot I have no hesitation in commending *Art Deco Ceramics in Britain,* but may your pots never be cracked.

Eric Knowles F.R.S.A.

1.

The European Background

Stella Beddoe

ART DECO is a shortened form (adopted in the 1960s) of *Arts Décoratifs et Industriels Modernes*, the title of the International Exhibition of Modern Decorative and Industrial Art held in Paris in 1925 (Plate 1.1). The organisers of the event hoped to emulate the success of the great Paris exhibition of 1900, which had marked the peak of art nouveau and reinforced the French domination of contemporary style. They aimed not only to promote innovative design for industry but also to celebrate modern life and the many opportunities offered by new technologies. Electricity, automobiles and telephones were becoming common and leisure time could be spent enjoying radio, cinema and foreign travel. Art deco, known at the time as the *Moderne* style, was developed for the French luxury market after World War I and relied on the high standards of traditional French craftsmanship. It also borrowed from great French style periods of the past. Just as art nouveau had revived interest in the mid-eighteenth century rococo of Louis XV, so art deco put a new spin on the neo-classical style of the French Directoire and Empire periods of the 1800s.

Art deco was fascinated by antiquity; it borrowed motifs from the exotic cultures of Ancient Egypt, Africa, China and Japan, while production designs for Diaghilev's *Ballets*

Plate 1.1. The interior of a country dining room for the Maîtrise Pavilion (Galeries Lafayette) at the Paris Exhibition, 1925, designed by Malvine Tcherniack.

Plate 1.2. A female figure made by Lorenz Hutschenreuther, Selb, Bavaria, c.1910.

Plate 1.3. **Serafin,** *designed by Georges Guiard, Paris, 1913.*

Russes made the Turkish and Persian styles popular. It was also influenced by avant-garde art movements, taking bold colour from the Fauves, geometrical forms from Cubism and images of speed from Futurism. As the style trickled down, certain shapes and motifs appeared regularly. Some designers experimented with new geometrical shapes such as the cubes and cones introduced by Cubism, while others revived antique forms like urns and cornucopias. Speed and energy were implied by weather symbols such as asymmetrical sunbursts, clouds and thunderbolts or elegant, swift animals like antelopes and greyhounds. The neo-classical taste was reflected in the use of human figures wearing classical robes, portrayed in antique architectural settings hung with swags of stylised flowers.

The Paris exhibition was a triumph for the French designers who arranged the opulent interiors of grand pavilions with furniture crafted from fine and rare materials, including tropical woods decorated with ivory, gilding and lacquer. In general the style was too exclusive and over-decorated for austere post-war Germany, where Modernism was evolving within a left-inclined society, and in Britain the design establishment remained hostile to what they saw as French decadence. But it did provide a rich source of ideas for the popular market, particularly designs for ceramics, glass and textiles.

A radical reassessment of ceramics took place in Europe in the late nineteenth century regarding the relative status of porcelain, earthenware and stoneware. Hitherto stoneware had been a hardwearing but banal material, used largely for storage containers and domestic pipe-work. After fine stonewares arrived from Japan and pioneers of art pottery developed high-temperature glazes, it became a favourite medium for sculptural work by respected makers. In Britain these included Doulton artists and in Belgium Hector Guimard designed some imposing architectural pieces. In Germany Richard Riemerschmid revived the sixteenth century stoneware traditions of Westerwald and Sieburg and in France Chaplet, Delaherche and Paul Gauguin were leading practitioners of the medium.

By the 1920s stoneware was still dominant in art pottery. Paul Gauguin's son Jean had continued his father's interest in sculptural ceramics and produced powerful and original animal figure pieces for the Danish firm Bing & Grøndahl's stand at the 1925 Paris Exhibition. The discovery of Persian and Islamic pottery by Andre Méthey led him to abandon faience for the vibrant coloured glazes of central Asia. He executed designs supplied to him by painters such as Bonnard, Derain, Matisse and Vuillard. Stoneware specialists Emile Decoeur and Emile Lenoble were particularly drawn to the ceramic traditions of the Far East and were as interested in Korean and Chinese work from the Tang and Song dynasties as they were in Japanese. Bernard Leach, having spent over ten years studying ceramics in Japan, returned to England in 1920. Together with the Japanese potter Shoji Hamada, he established his influential studio at St Ives in Cornwall and produced a range of stoneware and *raku* pottery which won praise at the 1925 exhibition. From this period onwards studio ceramics and quality production ceramics tended to divide and develop along separate paths.

A number of ceramicists, however, became involved in running design studios, producing ceramic editions for some of the great Paris department stores. In 1921 the designer Maurice Dufrêne was appointed head of the 'Maîtrise' studio for Galeries Lafayette. Another ceramicist, René Buthaud, devised broad simple vessel shapes for his own work, which he treated as canvases on which to paint his large figurative subjects (Plate 1.4). In 1923 René Guilléré, who had founded the 'Primavera' design studio for another store, **Au Printemps**, offered Buthaud the job of technical and artistic director of a new factory near Tours. He later worked for Galerie Georges Rouard who had designs for ceramics by artists such as Robert Bonfils and Marcel Goupy made by Haviland of Limoges.

In 1920 the great Sèvres porcelain factory, always an innovator in the field, appointed Maurice Gensoli head of their new faience department to produce designs by eminent artists from a variety of other disciplines. They carved translucent porcelain-like cameo shell to create lamps and covered the surfaces of elongated ovoid vases with stylised swags of fruit and flowers and abstract starbursts of pyrotechnic colours. Contemporary French enterprise inspired Wedgwood to commission designs from French artists Marcel Goupy and Paul Follot, before putting British designers under contract.

The French design establishment had been alarmed at the development of design and manufacture in Germany under the Deutsche Werkbund in the 1900s. The 1925 exhibition was mounted partly to counter this perceived threat to France's status as style leader. In the event, German production collapsed after World War I and neither Germany nor the United States mounted displays at the 1925 exhibition. Bolshevik Russia, despite the recent revolution, did participate. It showed porcelains from the former St Petersburg Imperial Porcelain Factory decorated with Constructivist geometric designs and revolutionary slogans, symbols and heroic workers. Ironically these

Plate 1.4. A covered stoneware urn depicting a female figure wearing a hat and floral motifs, designed by René Buthaud, Bordeaux, France, about 1925. Height 11in. (27.9cm).

exquisitely hand-painted products for the proletariat proved far too expensive for their intended market. Lenin, when quizzed in 1918 about the factory's dilemma, replied evasively that:

> ...our industry, for an initial period at least, can make such services for the large gatherings of Soviets, for major celebrations, and then, when our economy is developed, that is when the workers and peasants can buy them.[1]

In Weimar Germany, experimental workshops such as the Bauhaus were establishing the basis for Modernism, where the form of objects, made from new materials

Plate 1.5. Two stoneware vases designed by Charles Catteau for Boch Frères, Belgium, about 1925. Height of tallest item 10½in. (26.7cm).

using new technology, should reflect their function in modern life. Modernists aimed to produce clean, sleek forms without ornament, which they considered redundant in an advanced civilisation. Nevertheless, German ceramic production was not immune to decoration. Fräulein Milli Merkel, the former chief secretary of the earthenware factory at Grunstadt, described how a cake stand in the style of the Russian

Suprematist artist, El Lissitzky, was decorated:

The patterns were chosen at craftsmen's meetings and in the end even by the charwomen who, after all, accurately reflected the taste of the buyers. The board of directors did not, to my knowledge, participate in the design.[2]

Abstract geometrical patterns in bright colours, stencilled

Plate 1.6. A part tea set designed by Grete Heymann-Marks for her Hael-Werkstätten factory, 1930.

with a spray-paint gun, were particularly favoured. The distinctive conical forms and solid bi-concave disc handles of Margarete Heymann-Marks' best-known tea service for her 'Hael' ceramic factory (Plate 1.6) and Eva Stricker-Zeisel's designs for the Schramberger factory also demonstrate the influence of Russian Constructivism.

The Rosenthal factory in Bavaria produced a wide range of high quality porcelain in the art deco taste. There were jazzy ginger jars and sparsely decorated tea services, applied with elegantly scrolled and sharply angled handles. Ornamental figures included gilt and polychrome Asiatic dancers, inspired by the *Ballets Russes*, and the stylised attenuated figures sculpted in 1926-27 by Gerhard Schliepstein in biscuit-glazed, white porcelain. Major porcelain factories elsewhere in Europe produced similar services to those from Rosenthal. Joachim and Arno Malinowski's designs for Royal Copenhagen, Edward Hald's for Rörstrand in Sweden and Gio Ponti's for Richard-Ginori in Italy all demonstrate the same delicacy and restraint in their tablewares, adorned with tiny classical figures or abstracted plant forms. Wilhelm Kåge's unusual *Argenta* range for the Swedish firm of Gustavsberg involved inlaying figures and motifs in silver on to green-glazed stoneware (Plate 1.7). It is one of the most lyrical expressions of Arcadian art deco, evoking a vanished Golden Age.

Plate 1.7. An earthenware vase decorated with the **Argenta** pattern, designed by Wilhelm Kåge for Gustavsberg Pottery, Stockholm, 1930. Height 6¼in. (16.5cm).

1. Tamara Kudryavtseva, *Circling the Square, Avant garde Porcelain from Revolutionary Russia*, exh. cat., Somerset House, London, 2004-05, p.25.
2. Tilman Buddensieg, *Keramik in der Weimarer Republik 1919-1933*, exh. cat. Victoria and Albert Museum, London, 1986, p.10.

2

The British Background

Stella Beddoe

At the present time we have a number of very capable architects and designers working in England. We also have some excellent makers of furniture, designers of textiles, papers, etc. half a dozen painters of originality skilled in mural painting, and a small army of decorators and assemblers. But we have nothing to show which expresses unity or a national style...[1]

So WROTE a disillusioned Paul Nash in 1932, a time of transition in the history of design in Britain. The Arts and Crafts movement, the dominant force in design until well into the twentieth century, would eventually give way to Modernism; the role of the designer-maker evolved into that of the industrial designer; Nash himself was an example. The 'assembler' to whom he referred (the French *ensemblier*, a respected designer of integrated contemporary interiors), never found a place in Britain.

The establishment in the late nineteenth century of the Arts and Crafts movement, led by William Morris, with its unshakable belief in the superiority of the hand-made over the mass-produced, highlighted the strengths and weaknesses inherent in the British tradition. On the one hand craftsmen employed technical skills refined to the most exacting standards on the highest quality materials, whilst remaining visually under-educated and resistant to new ideas. Leading designers and cultural critics expressed horror at the new construction methods demonstrated by the French art nouveau furniture selected by Sir George Donaldson from the Paris Exposition Universelle of 1900 and bequeathed to the Victoria and Albert Museum. The anonymous author of an article published in the *Architectural Review*, entitled 'Pillory: L'Art Nouveau at South Kensington', pronounced most of the items to be 'pretentious trash' and went on to refer to the examples of

furniture, ceramics and glass as the product of this 'fantastic malady'.[2]

Frustration at similarly hostile, reactionary attitudes within the glass industry was expressed thirty years later by Keith Murray (Plate 2.1), the most renowned freelance designer in British industry since Christopher Dresser, who addressed the Society of Glass Technology in 1935:

Such complacency is found in the fetish, 'English Crystal is the best in the World'. Who cares?... Other people make crystal, Baccarat, Moser, Orrefors, Lalique, Lobmeyr and others, but does the reputation of those forms depend on the fact that their glass is lead crystal? Of course not... It rests on good design and workmanship.[3]

One unfortunate consequence of the success of the Arts and Crafts movement was that Britain, as world style leader for a time, was content to rest on its reputation rather than attempt further innovation. The inter-war years in twentieth century Britain were a period of brief economic boom and social euphoria, followed by financial gloom and manufacturing slump, during which public taste was marked by nostalgia for earlier styles which were associated with periods of power and prosperity in Britain. In the eighteenth century Ravenscroft's development of lead crystal, together with Wedgwood's innovations in ceramics,

Plate 2.1. Four examples of the Keith Murray 3801 shape vase decorated with matt glazes: moonstone, matt green, blue and grey, Josiah Wedgwood and Sons Ltd., 1933. Height 5⅞in. (15cm).

meant that Britain had led the world in material technology and design. Indeed the Modernist critic Nikolaus Pevsner, writing in 1937, reported that:

> Wedgwood's [sic] are still producing their 18th-century shapes, and some of them are so perfect that it would be unjustifiable to abandon them.[4]

The eighteenth century was popular with the middle classes who displayed their collections of Chelsea and Derby porcelain in imitation Chippendale cabinets. The medieval flavour of Arts and Crafts products had also caught the public imagination and generalised Tudorbethan or Jacobean styles evoked 'Merrie England'. But Paul Nash exclaimed in exasperation:

> …There exists in the English character an extraordinary sentiment which, baldly stated, is that everything new is ugly and everything old is beautiful.[5]

In 1907 the Deutsche Werkbund was founded to promote good design in German industry. Seven years later it led to the formation in Britain of the Design and Industries Association, pledged to promote W.R. Lethaby's Arts and Crafts maxim of 'fitness for purpose' and to improve the standard of design for mass production. Founder members included Ambrose Heal, the enterprising director of his family store, Frank Pick, then a rising manager on the Underground Railways, and the metalwork designer Harold Stabler, one of the three founders of Carter, Stabler & Adams. Other members involved in ceramics included Gordon Forsyth, the influential ceramic designer and teacher, and Charles Noke of Royal Doulton, an artist-potter who designed for Josiah Wedgwood and Sons Ltd.

Heal and Stabler had visited a Werkbund exhibition in 1914 before the outbreak of war and were very impressed by the standard of design. Misunderstanding the anti-German propaganda intentions of the Board of Trade's 1915 exhibition of shoddy German goods, they demanded to redress the balance with a display of Werkbund products exhorting British industry to similar standards of excellence. When British production resumed after the war, however, owing to low manpower, poor supplies of raw materials and other factors, the wholesale price of goods such as ceramics had risen by over 200% from the pre-war period and the public would require considerable inducements to buy good design.[6]

In Paris in 1911, following a visit to the Wiener Werkstätte in Vienna (whose workshops had been inspired by C.R. Ashbee's Guild of Handicraft), the French couturier Paul Poiret set up the Atelier Martine. This was an art school where working-class girls were encouraged to draw spontaneously from nature, free from academic preconceptions. The school's success led to the establishment of the Maison Martine, which produced exotic theatrical schemes for interior decoration as well as startlingly original designs for fabrics and furniture, prompting the setting up, in 1912, of the Primavera Design Studio at the Au Printemps department store.

The writer and painter Roger Fry must certainly have visited Martine when he organised an exhibition of English painting at the Galerie Barbazanges in July 1912, for the two buildings were adjacent in the rue St Honoré.[7] It must have spurred his resolve to set up a design studio and the Omega Workshops were duly opened at 33 Fitzroy Square in London in July 1913. The painters Duncan Grant and Vanessa Bell, together with Fry, went on to create and produce designs for furniture, textiles and pottery throughout World War I until the venture was liquidated in 1919.

They regarded themselves as artists rather than makers and, with the exception of Roger Fry, who studied with a potter at Mitcham and later at the Poole Pottery, remained indifferent to manufacturing skills. Eventually pottery blanks were made at Poole for them to decorate. Despite their crude execution the bold, colourful designs of Omega products came nearest to the spirit of innovation discernible elsewhere in Europe at this period. In general, however, the Omega venture met with hostility and venom from other British designers. Dedicated as it was to free self-expression, it was totally antipathetic to the Arts and Crafts principles of moderation and morality. The craftsman designer C.R. Ashbee considered Omega 'Too awful, simply a crime against truth and beauty...'.[8]

In 1924 the British Empire Exhibition was held at Wembley in West London. It was conceived on a very ambitious scale and the famous stadium was built to designs by architect Maxwell Ayrton and engineer Owen Williams with further contributions from Oliver Hill and Clough Williams-Ellis.[9] It housed pavilions representing commerce, industry, agriculture and the arts throughout the Dominions and was such a success in terms of numbers of visitors that it reopened again in 1925 but had to be closed prematurely as it became too costly to run.

The 1925 Paris Exhibition of *Arts Décoratifs et Industriels Modernes* was, for the British participants, visitors and critics, an anticlimax and a disappointment after Wembley. Government expenditure did not match that at Wembley and many firms were unable to afford the expensive independent exhibition space, while those who did exhibit did not show their latest work. The excuse given was that there was a fear of designs being stolen and copied, but manufacturers did not want to waste money exhibiting in France, which had always been a poor market for British goods.

The British Pavilion, a flimsy, lightweight edifice, was unfortunately placed opposite the Italian, which was twice the size and constructed of permanent building materials. A solemn tome, comprising *Reports on the... Industrial Arts, as indicated...at Paris,* was published by the Department of Overseas Trade. The reviewers tried to encourage but the overall tone was depressed and deflated. There was a preponderance of church art, textiles showed little originality compared with French examples and none of the British furniture bore comparison with modern French work. Among the best work on display were stage designs and decorative painting, but many of the exhibits had already been shown at Wembley.

In his review of the pottery section, Gordon Forsyth expressed admiration for some of the established manufacturers and emerging studio potters, such as William Staite Murray. He complimented Wedgwood on their experimental work, Doulton for individual exhibits and praised Carter, Stabler & Adams at Poole for their Della Robbia faience tiles. In general, however, his critique of the British contribution to pottery was fairly damning:

> the British Section as a whole was inclined to be staid and dull. There was in the pottery section a real lack of the spirit of adventure on the artistic side... a little virility in the treatment of clay by our distinguished potters would have created a sensation.[10]

He concluded:

> Pottery has always exercised a great fascination for many of our greatest English artists, both sculptors and painters, and it is a thousand pities, as far as English pottery is concerned, that this particular fascination is not translated into practical application of their great talent.[11]

With a few exceptions, such as Poole Pottery (and even their centrepiece 'The Bull', Plate 2.2, had been designed by Harold and Phoebe Stabler in 1914, paying tribute to Viennese ceramics of that time), manufacturers showed

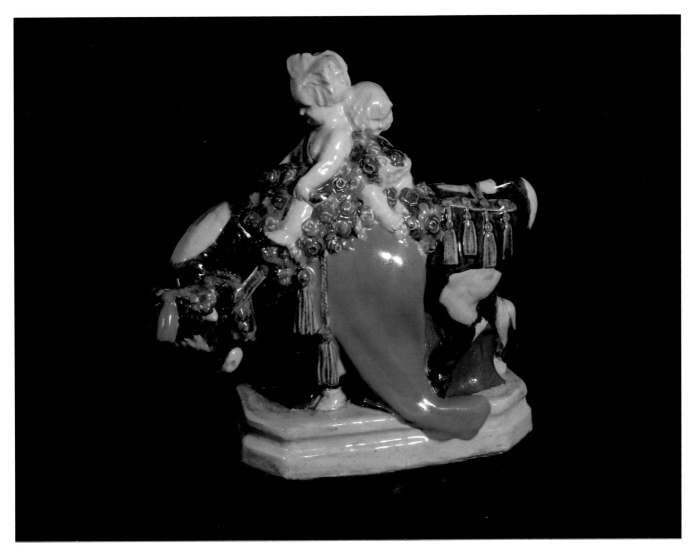

Plate 2.2. An example of 'The Bull' designed by Phoebe and Harold Stabler in 1914 and made at Poole Pottery from 1922 to the early 1930s. Height 13in. (33cm).

little awareness of modern design, however high the quality of their goods. In spite of the alarm bells which sounded at the Paris exhibition and the poor showing made by British exhibitors, designers were slow to react. Instead there was a renewal of interest in rural workshops. Bernard Leach, having returned from prolonged study in Japan in 1920, launched the studio pottery movement from St Ives in Cornwall where he taught Michael Cardew and Katherine Pleydell-Bouverie. He also visited the burgeoning craft community at Dartington Hall in Devon.

After the 1925 exhibition French art deco designs began to permeate the British ceramic industry, particularly at the cheaper end of the market. While preparing his 1937 report into the state of industrial art in England, Nikolaus

Pevsner noted, with evident distaste, that such decoration was of two discernible types, 'Modern Floral' (Plate 2.3) and 'Banded' (as described by retailers). Clarice Cliff, working at A.J. Wilkinson's Royal Staffordshire Pottery, is perhaps the best-known designer and populariser of ebullient, 'Modern Floral' patterns. Her designs also embraced new geometric forms but with little understanding of the function of the vessels to which they were applied.

In 1932 the findings of the Gorell Report on the state of design in industry led to a series of exhibitions of current products, notably the *Exhibition of Industrial Art in Relation to the Home* held at Dorland Hall in 1933 and *British Art in Industry* at the Royal Academy in 1935. It also encouraged

Plate 2.3. Examples of 'Modern Floral', a hand-painted pattern by Susie Cooper for the Susie Cooper Pottery Ltd, 1932.

the active participation of fine artists in designing for industry. The most ambitious of these projects was undertaken by E. Brain & Co, Foley China, together with the Royal Staffordshire Pottery and Stuart Crystal, culminating in an exhibition of artist-designed ceramics and glass held at Harrods in 1934 (see Chapter 5). Gordon Forsyth had expressed the hope that:

> manufacturers and artists will come together and thus produce for England pottery which will be unsurpassed....[12]

Here at last was a project which aspired to that ambition. It was a critical success but a marketing failure. In trying to analyse why the British public was still so resistant to good modern design Pevsner interviewed the managing director of one of the leading pottery works. He was surprised to be told that young people from the wealthier classes lived in small London flats and preferred to spend their money on motor-cars and leisure pursuits while their parents' generation had decidedly conventional tastes. This was in stark contrast to Continental Europe where established manufacturers like the Meissen and Berlin porcelain factories produced modern lines.[13] It is also implicit that Europeans were far better visually educated.

1. Paul Nash, *Room and Book*, 1932, p.27
2. *Architectural Review*, 10 (1901), pp.104-107.
3. 'Some Views of a Designer' by Keith Murray, read at the London Meeting of the Society of Glass Technology, Burlington House, 8 January 1935. Reprinted in: *British Glass Between the Wars* (exh. cat.), Broadfield House Glass Museum, Dudley, 1987, p.107.
4. Nikolaus Pevsner, *An enquiry into Industrial Art in England*, Cambridge, 1937, p.81.
5. Paul Nash, *op. cit.*, 1932, p.36.
6. Frances Hannah, *Ceramics*, 1986, p.30
7. Isabelle Anscombe, *Omega and After: Bloomsbury and the Decorative Arts*, 1981, p.13.
8. Ibid., p.31.
9. The stadium was finally demolished in 2002 to make way for a modern sports arena.
10. Gordon Forsyth, 'Pottery', *Reports on the Present Position and Tendencies of the Industrial Arts, as indicated...at Paris, 1925*, HMSO, 1925, p.131.
11. Ibid., p.135.
12. Ibid., p.135.
13. Pevsner, *op.cit.*, 1937, p.76.

3.

New Ceramics for the New Way of Living

Greg Stevenson

IT ISN'T SURPRISING that the inter-war years saw a renaissance in British ceramic design. The industry was struggling to survive, pot-banks were closing every week, and the top end of the market collapsed when the 1929 Wall Street crash effectively destroyed the export market to the United States. If the British hadn't innovated then the industry might well have died out completely, swamped by cheap imports from Europe and Asia.

But it wasn't just the 'change or die' mentality that drove the innovation in form and decoration that we have now come to term art deco. British life was changing too, and these new ceramics found a niche in the new lives that people were building in newly built homes across our shores. When people look back on the period they think of the Depression, and it is true that times were hard, very hard, for many. Yet behind this poverty the middle classes were growing quickly in the inter-war years and a new generation was fast becoming the home-owning society that we recognise today.

It was in these inter-war years that the people of Britain underwent something of a technological revolution. For the first time the whole nation was connected via new technologies such as the wireless, the cinema, and also the massive growth in popularity in national (rather than regional) newspapers and magazines.[1] Housewives were bombarded with scenes of domestic bliss and how they could be achieved through the new consumerism. Interest in the home and how it was decorated and presented for guests increased ten-fold as having the latest fashions became ever more important to the new middle classes. Snobbery was rife and having the right consumer goods became an easy way of sending out the 'right' messages about being with the latest styles and the new, modern way of living. For the first time a significant proportion found themselves knowing about the latest fashions, motivated to buy them, and with the

Plate 3.1. Of the four million homes built between the two world wars, the majority were strictly traditional in style.

capital to exercise their shopping desires – all this in an era that is now infamous for its hardship and poverty.

It is difficult to know if reports on the Depression were exaggerated, but people talked about those in isolated communities, such as the valleys of South Wales, being close to starvation. Certain towns which had grown with gusto in the industrial rush of the mid- to late nineteenth

21

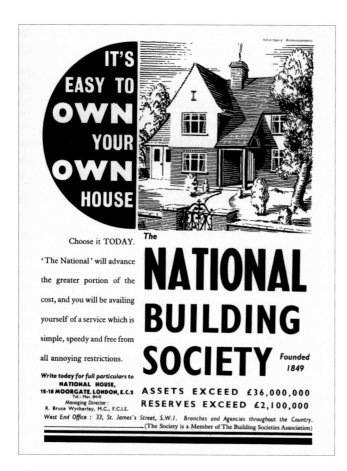

Plate 3.2. *Increased availability of affordable mortgages meant that more couples than ever before could buy their first home.*

century found themselves high and dry when the tide of industry receded, and thousands found themselves living in towns miles from available work. We can be sure that there wasn't a great deal of art deco design being bought in places like Brynmawr, South Wales in the early 1930s, yet at the same time there was a consumer boom happening in many of Britain's towns and cities. Improved transport meant that people could move out into suburban areas where new houses could be built on relatively large plots at relatively affordable prices (around £350-£750 for many homes in the 1930s). Out went the necessity to build cramped terraces and in came the fashion for semi-detached homes with a front door for guests and a side door for tradesmen.[2]

Improved transport also meant that the inter-war years were a great period in standardisation in building materials and consequently building styles. The last remnants of vernacular traditions were lost as builders erected cookie-cutter copies of homes across Britain.

Some four million homes were erected in Britain between the two world wars and most of them were built in the new style, the 'semi'.[3] These weren't architect-led designs statements, rather a pedestrian interpretation of a cottage style that appealed to the mass market. Stuck-on pine timber framing was tarred black to give the appearance of an ancient timber-frame structure and cottage style leaded-lights (sometimes even with contrived 'repairs') were fitted to the ubiquitous bay windows. A few gnomes and a concrete wishing well in the front garden completed the picture. Suburban Britain had arrived; people wanted the cottage look and this was what they got in their newly built homes, in the pictures that hung from the picture rails, and on the tea-sets that they used on a Sunday afternoon (Plate 3.1).

Mortgages were more readily available and cheaper than they had ever been before (Plate 3.2), and the movement into home ownership grew at a remarkable pace. Whereas many had been content (or forced) to rent 'rooms' in town centre terraced homes, now they could afford to move out to the suburbs and buy a home through small, regular payments. Hence there was a huge movement of young couples, often just married, moving into newly-built suburban homes, and with no furniture to furnish them as they were moving from rented homes that were supplied ready furnished (Plate 3.3). This, I would argue, created the consumer boom that fuelled the new designs in home furnishings, including ceramics. People of limited means needed new furnishings, were looking for new styles, but had little money to spend on them. The Potteries responded by churning out tonnes of cheaply produced on-glaze enamelled ware in brilliant colours to brighten up the homes of the newly-wed generation. Art deco ceramics, or rather a very British interpretation of them, were now available in china stores alongside traditional designs that had remained unchanged for generations.

When we look at inter-war homes we can see a reflection of British society of the time. Council housing was commonly well laid out and influenced by the Garden Village movement. Here sash-hung neo-Georgian windows were favourite, as a rejection of the so-called vulgar designs of the Victorians. Speculatively built housing for the new middle classes had to look different and so cottage style casement windows were usually adopted, or metal frame Sunray windows, such as those provided by Crittall for those who preferred something a 'bit more modern'. And 'a bit more modern' is about as modern as Britain got during the

Plate 3.3. *House builders boasted that every house was different, revealing that home owners wanted to be seen to display individual styles in their homes. In the event most opted for one of the thousand variants of the 'Tudorbethan' semi.*

period, whether we are reviewing homes, furniture or even ceramics. The antiques trade has focused attention on the brilliant and innovative designs that you will see in this book (and who can blame people for wanting to collect them?), but let us not forget that eighty per cent[4] of the output of the Potteries was as traditional as it had been for decades. Critics such as Herbert Rhead, who wrote for *The Times* newspaper,[5] and Nikolaus Pevsner were frustrated about the lack of demand for what they felt was 'good' design,[6] but the simple fact was that most of Britain wanted something traditional (Plate 3.5). One could argue that the situation hasn't moved much from this position today.

Britain went for traditional homes (Plate 3.6.), the cottagey look with leaded-light windows, traditional furnishings (remember those ghastly 'Tudorbethan' oak dining tables?), and traditional ceramics (think of Blue Willow and the thousands of boring transfer patterns). Even when customers wanted new pottery they went for new ceramics that were still preoccupied with traditional cottage imagery and floral images interpreted in a modern manner. So why do we think of the names Clarice Cliff and Susie Cooper when people mention 1930s ceramics? Their designs, and all those like them, stand out from the masses of traditional, plain, banded and generally nondescript material that was being produced at the time.

Imagine walking into a china shop on a British high street in the early '30s. You are about to get married and you are choosing a dinner service for your new life in a suburban home. The shop has pots from a much greater variety of manufacturers than you would see in a similar shop today, but most are selling traditional shapes produced from Victorian moulds and decorated in

Plate 3.4. *Lydia Watson standing proudly at the gate of her brand new semi at Kidbrooke in south-east London in 1936. Soon she would be buying ceramics to display in the bay window.*

Plate 3.5. We are so used to seeing reconstructed 'art deco' interiors that we forget that most British interiors of the 1930s were traditional in inspiration, such as this 'Blenheim' room set for Drages department store. The veneered sideboard nods to the deco styles.

monochrome transfer-printed floral and Oriental patterns. If money was tight you could opt for an undecorated service or, if you were feeling just a little bit modern, then there would have been a variety of banded ware. But in one corner there might be some of the output of A.J. Wilkinson under the Clarice Cliff label, or a selection of ziggurat vases by Myott & Sons. These designs must have sparkled among their drab contemporaries and it is no surprise that they created a niche in the ceramics market. Yes, the designs were shocking and yes, they would probably go out of fashion in no time at all. But they were exciting and seemed to capture the essence of the new Jazz Age. For those who fancied taking a risk on something new and different and which made a strong statement on the fashion sensibilities of their owners, these were just the ticket.

Just as the work of the pot-banks seen in these pages stands out from the majority of what was being produced at the time, there was a small hard-core of 'Moderne' designs (those that aspired to be Modernist) in British housing. That isn't to say that there weren't any truly Modernist houses built between the wars; some one-off luxury Modernist villas were built in the south-east of England, along with a sprinkling of social

Plate 3.6. Traditional 'cottage' dining rooms such as this were popular in the 1930s, yet owe more to the Arts and Crafts movement than art deco. Familiar symbols such as the elongated trees in the painting on the wall and the galleon in the window were borrowed from this earlier design movement and recycled on ceramics in the 1930s. The popularity of cottage imagery on inter-war ceramics belongs to the same tradition.

housing. These, however, were the exception rather than the norm. If they had an equivalent in the ceramics of the time we could compare them to the work of Keith Murray for Josiah Wedgwood and Sons Ltd – masculine, modern and exactly the kind of new 'good taste' that the upper middle classes of the time aspired to. These architectural masterpieces sparked Moderne homes, cheaper imitations of Modernist architecture that looked modern without following the Modernist tenet of form following function. Haute couture always loses something when it is watered down for mass-market high street stores, and architecture is no different. Flat-roofed white-painted villas with steel windows began to be built in small numbers across Britain and most commonly in seaside resorts. Traditional red brick walls were rendered to appear as if concrete, cantilevered balconies were added as signatures of the contemporary style and flat roofs were poorly designed and often leaked. They looked great, owed much to Hollywood, but didn't quite achieve the design philosophy that inspired them. Not that this mattered, as the minority who wanted such villas were looking for something that *looked* contemporary rather than truly being the product of a modern design process (Plate 3.7). And this was just

Plate 3.7. Many 1930s homes were designed to look modern without following Modernist design principles. This 'Allustre' enamelled fireplace, for example, is in a contemporary design yet burns coal. Most house builders were slow to take advantage of new technologies such as electricity when supplying fixtures. Many ceramics were also designed to look modern without being the products of a genuine modern design process.

what the new art deco ceramics of the period were also all about: surface over substance, 'all fur coat and no knickers'.

It can't be denied that British art deco ceramics are, in design terms, a pale shadow of the Continental originals that inspired them. They weren't necessarily produced in modern ways and they adopted the new angular handles and spouts without really thinking through their practicality. Designers such as Clarice Cliff bought French fashion magazines, translated what they saw into earthenware designs which could be mass-produced, and these then inspired a host of other manufacturers to follow suit, copying the British designs that sold well rather

than returning to the original design source. Before long we had created something new and, in my opinion, something utterly marvellous. British art deco ceramics *shouldn't* be worthy of the interest they attract today, being largely ill thought-out copies of Continental designs that had *meant* something. But their charm is undeniable, their designs are incredibly decorative, and they tell us more about Britain in the 1920s and 1930s than any officially 'good' design ever could. It didn't matter that in most cases the only thing art deco about these ceramics were the motifs that were painted on them.

The British ceramic industry did a wonderful job in mimicking Continental art deco design, something that

Plate 3.8. Only the most modern interiors, such as displayed here in Bowmans department store, London, would have used truly modern ceramics. Here a matt-glazed bowl designed by Keith Murray for Wedgwood joins a typically 'boxy' sofa and armchair.

was intended to be the ultimate refinery of surface and decoration for the new elite. British factories, most of them working without a designer of any description, distilled French art deco into a handful of iconic images such as the ziggurat form, Egyptian motifs, and the use of bright enamel colours. Design critics at the time poured scorn on this new output and we can understand why, but with hindsight we can see the true value of these pots. These were the pots that the people of Britain wanted, the new generation of newly-weds moving out into suburbia into their new homes. These were the ceramics that they chose to place in the bay window, or in the china cabinet, to tell the world that they had arrived and that they were familiar with contemporary design. Today we don't complain when IKEA produces a watered-down version of a Philippe Starck design and

produces it at a fraction of the cost, so we shouldn't look down at the ceramics equivalent of this from the inter-war years.

British designers interpreted art deco designs to such an extent that they created something new and something that reflected the social changes in Britain at the time. A new generation was looking for a new way of living and they found it without wholeheartedly embracing Modernism and the design elite of the time (Plate 3.8). This is the story that the ceramics from the period tell us; they look modern, but they weren't quite modern. No matter, because this is exactly what was happening in British homes between the wars. So next time you look at the wonderful and sometimes exotic designs that you see in this book, take note, for each of these pots is a little piece of social history.

1. For further reading see A. Thorpe, *Britain in the 1930s*, Blackwell, 1992.
2. For further reading see G. Stevenson, *The 1930s Home*, Shire, 2000.
3. For further reading see P. Oliver, I. Davis & I. Bentley, *Dunroamin – The Suburban Semi and its Enemies*, Pimlico, 1991.
4. According to a survey by N. Pevsner. See his 1937 article 'Pottery: Design, Manufacture, Marketing' in *Trends in Design* journal No. 2:9-18.
5. See H. Read, *Art & Industry. The Principles of Industrial Design*, Faber & Faber, 1934, and also H. Read, *The Practice of Design*, Faber & Faber, 1936.
6. See N. Pevsner, *An Enquiry into Industrial Art in England*, Cambridge University Press, 1937.

4.

The Real Thing or Impostors?

Dan Dunlavey

IT IS HARD TO THINK of an artistic movement that drew on as many stylistic cues as art deco – it was informed by new developments in fields as diverse as Egyptology, African ethnography, popular music, technology and the performing arts. Like any other style, it has waxed and waned in popularity over the years. Following its first flush of favour in the inter-war period, it was laid to rest following the outbreak of renewed hostilities at the end of the 1930s. However, such a rich background naturally provoked some exceptional pieces of work and it was always inevitable that public taste would rediscover art deco at some point. A major re-evaluation came in the 1960s when the term 'art deco' was first coined, adapted from 'Paris Exposition Internationale des Arts Décoratifs et Industriels Modernes', the 1925 exhibition that first brought the style to an international audience. Since that time art deco has attained a canonical status whereby it may not always be fashionable, but is perennially considered stylish. Ceramics represent an affordable way to acquire a stake in this popular field and, with such a wide range available, interest has burgeoned in recent years.

Although lacking a distinct label – a banner under which they could march to a unifying beat – artists working in the art deco style from c.1918-1939 did subscribe to a series of tenets to a greater or lesser extent. Central among these was the rejection of 'art for art's sake', a thesis that would soon become a cornerstone of the Modernist movement. As a direct reaction against the sinuous, organic lines of the art nouveau style, straight lines and flat, clean surfaces were held up as an ideal. In terms of decoration, 'high style' art deco – the most expensive pieces sold at the very best Paris boutiques – was unashamedly exclusive (Plate 4.1). Rare materials such as ivory, marble and woods like ebony were manipulated using complex and costly specialist techniques.

By the late 1920s this high style aesthetic had been appropriated by the new world of industrial design. Embracing the possibilities presented by mechanised manufacture to produce good quality design for the masses, many British pottery companies attempted to cater

Plate 4.1. An earthenware vase designed by Charles Catteau for Boch Frères, about 1925.

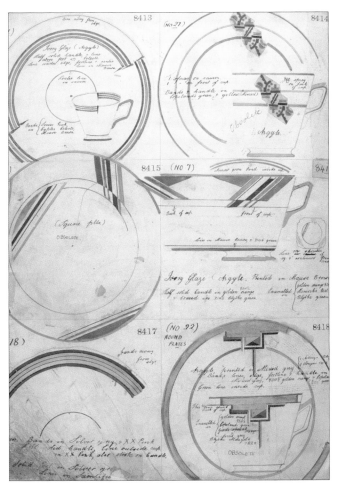

Plate 4.2. A pattern book entry, thought to be from the Jackson and Gosling factory, showing a selection of proposed art deco patterns, about 1930.

to the contemporary taste for what was known as the 'Moderne', 'Jazz' or 'Cubist' style. They achieved this with varying degrees of success and today's collector has to contend with a dizzying array of period ceramics, some of which pay little more than lip service to the ideals and aesthetic of the art deco movement. Following the Wall Street crash of 1929 many firms were unable to invest in the new range of shapes needed to make true art deco ceramics and so employed artists to paint deco designs on generic or outmoded forms. At the other end of the spectrum, a few factories retained the services of a new breed of industrial designers and artist decorators who produced ranges rooted firmly within the idiom (Plate 4.2).

The venerable Staffordshire firm of Josiah Wedgwood and Sons Ltd makes an interesting case study of how a large British firm balanced financial constraints with the need to cater to changing public taste. Tellingly, Wedgwood used the *Globe* range of shapes designed by Norman Wilson in 1935 – for both deco and non-deco lines during the '30s. While the firm did not subscribe wholeheartedly to the art deco style, it did score some notable successes. Millicent Taplin, employed as a painter from 1917, produced a pattern called *Sunlit* during the 1930s featuring brightly coloured stylised foliage and geometric designs and *Falling Leaves* featuring stylised green leaves (Plate 4.3). Better known is the work done by Keith Murray and Eric

Plate 4.3. A part bone china set decorated with the Falling Leaves pattern, designed by Millicent Taplin for Josiah Wedgwood and Sons Ltd, about 1934.

Plate 4.4. A tall hand-thrown shoulder vase (shape 3805) decorated with a matt straw glaze. Designed by Keith Murray for Josiah Wedgwood and Sons Ltd, 1933.

Ravilious, both commissioned by Wedgwood's artistic director, Victor Skellern. Unfortunately, Murray's designs for hand-painted patterns did not sell well and much of Ravilious' work was thought too outré for public consumption and so was held back from production. In fact Murray's work was modern rather than art deco (Plate 4.4). As an early pioneer of Modernism, Murray felt that form should be allowed to express itself without surface decoration getting in the way.

The Newport Pottery struck commercial gold through the efforts of Clarice Cliff (Plate 4.5), who remains the most well-known British art deco ceramicist. Her *Bizarre* range of earthenware in particular combined sleek and functional deco forms with stylised geometric decoration in vivid orange, blue, yellow and a host of other bright colours, defined by simple black borders. The line encompassed everything from tableware to massive decorative chargers and the low cost made possible by intensive factory production techniques made it a firm favourite with consumers.

Susie Cooper, working for A.E. Gray & Co as a designer from 1922, found comparable success with her softer colours and is also avidly collected today. Inspired by the success of peasant pottery imported from Czechoslovakia, Gray encouraged Cooper to emulate

Plate 4.5. An earthenware Coronet shape lemonade set decorated with a Café au Lait Bobbins pattern design by Clarice Cliff for A.J. Wilkinson Ltd, 1931-1933.

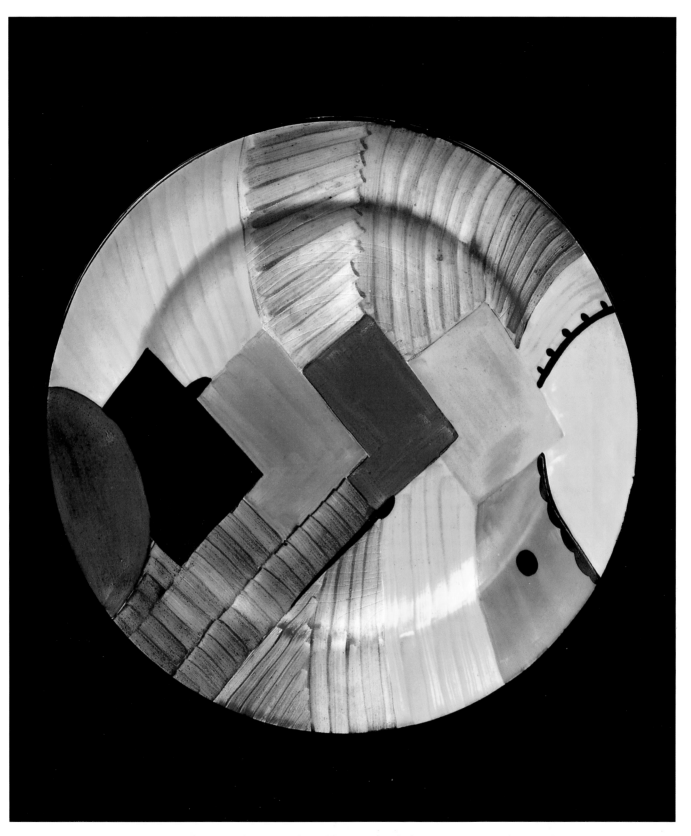

Plate 4.6. *A large earthenware plaque decorated with the Cubist pattern, designed by Susie Cooper for A.E. Gray and Co. Ltd, c.1928.*

Plate 4.7. A bone china Vogue shape coffee set for two decorated with the Blocks pattern, designed by Eric Slater for the Shelley Pottery, 1932.

the crude painting style and bright colours of peasant pottery in her decorative work for his company (Plate 4.6). This resulted in some celebrated geometric patterns in vivid colours, such as *Cubist* and *Moon and Mountain* (see Frontispiece), but Cooper was frustrated at being unable to design her own shapes and launched her own business in 1929. By 1932 she was sourcing her whiteware from Wood & Sons Ltd, another Staffordshire firm that sold tableware decorated with stylised foliate designs superficially art deco in appearance but lacking

the sympathetic relationship between form and decoration so admired in the work of Cliff and Cooper.

Another giant of the British ceramics industry during the 1930s was Shelley. Two ranges in particular – *Vogue* and *Mode* – were quintessentially art deco in style. The *Queen Anne* range, first sold in 1926, represented a bridge between this bold new direction and the Victorianate shapes and designs that had preceded it. The *Vogue* cup consisted of a steep conical bowl with a solid triangular handle and a large foot that sat in the

Plate 4.8. An earthenware coffee pot and sugar basin (lid missing) decorated with art deco patterns designed by John Guildford for Barker Brothers Ltd, 1929.

well of its accompanying circular saucer (Plate 4.7). Companion side plates had straight edges with rounded, recessed corners. Both the *Vogue* and *Mode* shapes were sold in dozens of different decorative styles, the majority of which featured geometric abstractions and angular floral motifs. In 1932 Shelley unveiled the *Eve* range, which jettisoned the stylish yet undeniably impractical solid handle. The decoration, too, was toned down from the highly stylised deco motifs of the *Vogue* and *Mode* ranges to a more traditional floral look.

True art deco shapes should represent a departure from florid Victorian and art nouveau style lines. Straight edges, perhaps combined with curved corners, and pure geometric forms – triangles, squares, circles – are things to look for. Motifs should reflect the roots of the movement: tribal masks, silhouettes, galleons in sail, lightning strikes and stylised fountains and sunbursts are all classic examples. Stylised landscapes, depicting natural forms in a Cubist style, are another quint-essentially art deco theme, probably best exemplified in

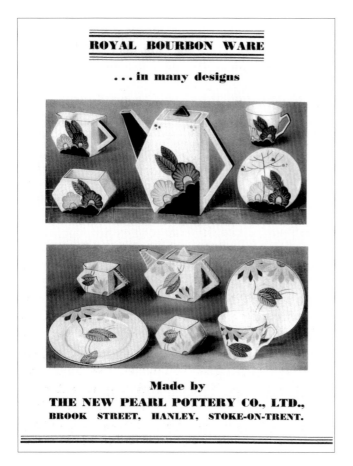

Plate 4.9. A Royal Bourbon trade advertisement illustrating the latest shapes and patterns, 1935.

Plate 4.10. A company advertisement for the Decoro Pottery showing the latest examples of pottery, February 1936.

the work of Clarice Cliff. Colour tended to veer between two extremes – monochrome black and white on the one hand and bold splashes of vivid colour on the other (Plate 4.8). Pastel shades were also used by more restrained designers such as Cooper. Drab browns are anathema to the vivacity inherent in the movement, as are naturalistic representations of figures and flowers.

Notable successes were scored by many other firms, including Hollinshead & Kirkham, whose 'less is more' approach to certain of their lines resulted in a clean, pared-down deco look set off with simple, symmetrical finials and handles in the form of lightning strikes. The New Pearl Pottery's *Royal Bourbon Ware* was certainly bold, featuring lozenge-shaped bowls, square lids and chunky handles and spouts (Plate 4.9). Others still appeared largely derivative – Albert Jones of Longton, for example, entered the fray with a range called *Landscape* that was more than faintly suggestive of Clarice Cliff's *Bizarre* ware.

Then there were the companies whose approach to the deco style was confused at best. Lovatt's Potteries advertised a matt-glazed range with delicate ribbing reminiscent of Keith Murray's work, let down only by the overly fussy relief mouldings of animals and plants that detracted from the clean lines and surfaces of the vessels. The Decoro Pottery Co went even further, combining abstract geometric designs with almost naturalistic floral motifs on a mottled ground – the result of which was simply an unappealing muddle (Plate 4.10). Only a select few firms had the requisite understanding of and confidence in the burgeoning art deco style to invest sufficient resources in developing ranges that could truly be described as such. Too many were content to fudge the issue, decorating outmoded forms with new designs or fretting about public reception instead of commissioning and marketing genuinely exciting products.

5

Modern Art for the Table:

An Experiment to unite Artists with Industry

Ann Eatwell

ON 22 OCTOBER 1934 an exhibition of ceramics and glass opened at Harrods in London.[1] It was the culmination of a project spearheaded by Thomas Acland Fennemore, sales director of the Staffordshire firm E. Brain and Co Ltd, trading under the name of Foley China. In consultation with designer Milner Gray and painter Graham Sutherland, Fennemore conceived the idea of inviting contemporary artists to design for industry in an attempt to improve standards in English tableware.[2] To begin with only a handful of the more avant-garde artists were invited to submit designs, but the criteria were relaxed to broaden public appeal. So the avowedly modern Barbara Hepworth, Paul Nash and Ben Nicholson produced designs alongside establishment figures such as Academician Laura Knight and Frank Brangwyn. Of the final list of twenty-eight artists and designers, some, like Freda Beardmore, Ludwig Kny and Thomas Acland Fennemore, who designed under the name of Thomas Acland, already worked in the pottery and glass industry. Others worked in related areas of manufacture. Allan Walton and Michael Wellmer were textile designers. Many of the fine artists

Plate 5.1. View of the 'Contemporary Art for the Table' exhibition at Harrods in 1934.

Plate 5.2. An example of the Laura Knight Circus candlestick.

Vanessa Bell, Frank Brangwyn, Clarice Cliff, Eva Crofts, John Everett, Gordon Forsyth, Moira Forsyth, Duncan Grant, Milner Gray, Barbara Hepworth, Laura Knight, Ludwig Kny, Paul Nash, Ben Nicholson, Dod Procter, Ernest Procter, Eric Ravilious, Anne Riach, W.P. Robins, Albert Rutherston, Graham Sutherland, Allan Walton, Billie Waters, Michael Wellmer.[3]

Three firms took part: E. Brain and Co (bone china for breakfast, tea and coffee sets); A.J. Wilkinson (earthenware for breakfast, dinner and dessert services); Stuart and Sons (glass for cocktail sets, beer, wine and sherry glasses). Responsibility for production within the companies rested on Thomas Acland Fennemore, Clarice Cliff[4] (Art Director for A.J. Wilkinson) and Geoffrey Stuart (a director of Stuart and Sons). Clarice Cliff and Geoffrey Stuart also helped the artists realise their designs on the new materials and Freda Beardmore took this role at E. Brain and Co. Only Eric Ravilious and Ludwig Kny (a designer for the glass firm) produced designs solely for glass. A fee of £10 was paid per design plus royalties. In the two years before the exhibition at Harrods all the artists were invited to the factories to learn about the production processes. Some, like Albert Rutherston and Laura Knight, took advantage of the offer.

Although the artists were free to determine subject, treatment and colour for the ceramic designs, these had to fit standard factory shapes.[5] The expense of providing new shapes for all would have been prohibitively expensive in an industry where a good shape might be expected to last for thirty years. Laura Knight's work was the only exception; her *Circus* wares were individually modelled (Plate 5.2). Designs were in some cases altered with the artist's approval to meet commercial or technical concerns. In contrast, Stuart and Sons allowed their artists to design both shape and decoration. The glass was inevitably more expensive. The designs were drawn to scale by the artists, some of whom, on the ceramics side of the venture, tested their ideas by decorating straight on to ceramic shapes. This approach was favoured by designers in the industry itself such as Susie Cooper. Drawing on paper could never be as effective as seeing the design develop in the round. An example of Ben Nicholson's prototype design for a pattern on a bone china factory shape is in the collection of the Victoria and Albert Museum; the artist produced two patterns for E. Brain and Co. Some, like Laura Knight, designed for all three firms with five designs for the bone china company alone.

had experience of designing for industry: Frank Brangwyn had designed ceramics; Vanessa Bell and Duncan Grant, as part of the Omega Workshops (1913-20), had experimented with designs for textiles, pottery and furnishings; Paul Nash, through an association with Omega and the Footprints Workshop in the 1920s, had designed for the decorative arts.

The complete list of artists comprised: Thomas Acland, John Armstrong, Freda Beardmore, Angelica Bell,

Plate 5.3. Another view of the 'Contemporary Art for the Table' exhibition at Harrods in 1934.

Twelve sets of each of the final selection of ceramic designs were made and marked as 'First Edition'. These cost exactly the same as subsequent services and it was expected that the popularity of the 'First Edition' sets would determine the scale of production of each pattern. Over sixty-five ceramic patterns are known to have been produced and about eighty glass designs still survive. It is not known how many of the latter were made.[6] Thomas Acland Fennemore had wide advertising experience and it is probably to him that credit for the limited edition of ceramic designs must be given. The idea was not unknown in the Potteries and manufacturers like Josiah Wedgwood had used such schemes to conjure exclusiveness and excitement around their products.

In the same way the opening exhibition at a top London store such as Harrods created a useful splash of publicity as well as selling directly to the public and missing out the conservative wholesalers and store buyers. This, it was hoped, would give adventurous shoppers a chance to buy something new and persuade the store buyers that modern design could sell. Similar displays at leading shops throughout the country and abroad continued to distance the experiment from the usual launch of ceramics and glass at trade fairs. Opened by Sir William Rothenstein, Principal of the Royal College of Art, with 1,000 guests, the exhibition at Harrods was judged a success both commercially and critically. Writing in his memoirs, *Since fifty*, Rothenstein commented, 'So successful were the exhibits that for a time, I was told, they affected the sale of Harrods' usual wares'. The event was reviewed by over thirty newspapers and periodicals from national and regional daily papers to specialist journals like *Design for Today*. Later, the leading books on design in industry, for example, Nikolaus Pevsner's *An Enquiry into Industrial Art in England* published in 1937, felt the project worthy of discussion and a selection of pieces were shown at the prestigious 'British Art in Industry' exhibition at the Royal Academy in 1935.

In contemporary photographs of the exhibition at Harrods the layout of the displays shows that each artist had paper designs exhibited with the finished goods for sale (Plate 5.3). This reinforced the message of an

Plate 5.4. A collection of dinnerwares decorated with the Chaldean or Chevaux pattern by John Armstrong for A.J. Wilkinson Ltd.

important and identifiable designer. Unlike the glass, the ceramic prices were considered to be reasonable for the middle market, although one of the cheapest dinner services, *Chaldean* or *Chevaux* by John Armstrong, retailed at £3.5s.0d. for twenty-six pieces (Plate 5.4). This was more expensive than Susie Cooper's dinner services (£2.12s.6d. for a set for six in 1935) which might be expected to have appealed to a similar consumer. The *Chaldean* or *Chevaux* pattern was a best seller and over twenty services were sold during the exhibition. Hand

painted after Armstrong's design, the horse is reminiscent of prehistoric cave art, in blue, black and old gold, bordered by a brown banding and black broken lines.

Hand painting, revived in the potteries in the '20s through the efforts of Gordon Forsyth and A.E. Gray, was economically viable due to the skills and low wages of the paintresses. Hand painting gave the customer the veneer of an individually crafted object although the process was on a more industrial scale. Quite a number of patterns in the experiment used this form of

Plate 5.5. A part coffee set decorated with a design by Ben Nicholson for E. Brain and Co.

decoration from Vanessa Bell's sketchy floral and foliage designs to Paul Nash's stylised foliage, abstract lines and geometric shapes and Allan Walton's more classical but modern reworking of an egg and dart motif. Ground laying (dry colour dusted over a thin layer of oil ground) was used to good effect in Ben Nicholson's designs (Plate 5.5). Varying the widths of the bands and the colours his patterns demonstrate an understanding of the possibilities created by the decorating techniques in use at the time. The patterns fit very pleasingly on to the simple, functional shapes with which he had been supplied (Plate 5.6). While these received acclaim from Modernist critics. Nicholson's designs are rather derivative of the banding already on the market from the Susie Cooper Pottery and numerous copyists. However, Anthony Blunt in *The Spectator* remarked:

dare we say, finally, that in his exquisite breakfast set in dove grey and crimson Mr Ben Nicholson has at last found his cup of tea?[7]

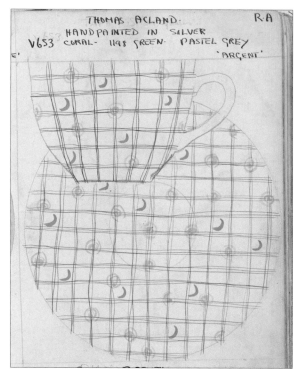

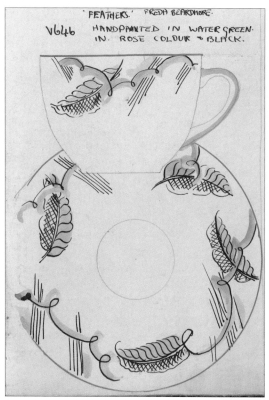

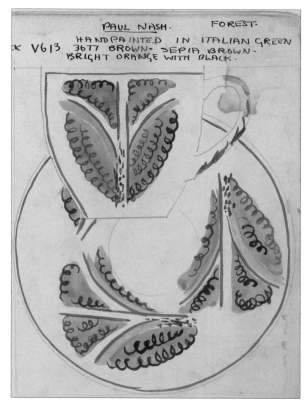

Plates 5.6-9. Several patterns from the E. Brain and Co pattern books. Clockwise from top left: a banded design by Ben Nicholson (see Plate 5.5), a pattern by Thomas Acland, the Feathers pattern by Freda Beardmore and Forest by Paul Nash (see Plate 5.11).

A combination of hand painting and transfer printing was used on some designs to reproduce a complex pattern but retain some element of the individual touch of the hand painting. Laura Knight's *Circus*, an example of this, was widely admired although some critics felt her designs were over elaborate and merely painted on the pottery.[8] It may be that Albert Rutherston and Milner Gray in particular saw the artistic potential in transfer printing as the sole means of decoration, although this decision could have been at the discretion of a factory designer such as Freda Beardmore. *Old Mayfair* by Milner Gray used six topographical scenes of Mayfair, printed in black (Plate 5.10). Decorating with views on pottery has a long and distinguished lineage. The service delivered by Josiah Wedgwood to Queen Catherine of Russia in 1774 was painted with scenes of English country houses and countryside. Milner Gray's designs are also precursors of the 1950s patterns of Staffordshire firms like Midwinter and Swinnertons. It is to the credit of the experiment that transfer prints of such high quality were produced. The common practice at the time was to buy in bulk lithographs designed by the printers.[9]

The variety and the wide style spectrum of the designs were praised by contemporary commentators. Those designs singled out most especially were: *Marine* by Dod Procter, *Chaldean* by John Armstrong, *Circus* by Laura Knight, the larger beer set (in glass) by Ernest Procter and Ben Nicholson's ceramics. Critics of the venture tended to fall into predictable groups, some favouring more traditional treatments such as topographic or floral patterns while others championed a modern look. The trade press emphasised the importance of commercial application and misunderstood the free approach of some patterns as merely bad drawing. The best designs were attributed by them to local designers. Certainly, Thomas Acland's ground laid border with the pattern scratched out uses the paintress's skills in sgraffito to good effect. The designs of Freda Beardmore, for example, are successful, if unadventurous, contemporary treatments of feather and leaf themes.

While the experiment led some critics to rejoice that ceramics was no longer the monopoly of 'little art-potteries run by high minded individuals in the South Downs', the venture can claim only a qualified success. Commercially, even if the products sold well at Harrods and raised a certain public enthusiasm, it was not enough to convince the conservative buyers. Few stores would take a chance on new design. Only a limited

Plate 5.10. *One of six topographical scenes of Mayfair from* Old Mayfair *by Milner Gray for E. Brain & Co, printed in black.*

number of patterns in ceramics and glass were produced during the years following the exhibition.

It is not easy to say what went wrong. The reluctance of the buyers may have been crucial but the venture itself was not without flaws. Some of the work shown could be fairly criticised for demonstrating a lack of appreciation of the interdependence of shape and decoration. More rigorous selection of the patterns themselves, Thomas Acland Fennemore later admitted, should have taken place.[10] The overall effect of the experiment on the Staffordshire pottery industry was very limited. Manufacturers may have gained an increased respect for their own designers but few looked outside the industry for artists as Fennemore had done. An exception to this may have been the commissioning of Eric Ravilious to work for Josiah Wedgwood and Sons on the strength of his designs for the Stuart glass works. Generally, it was left to the smaller more progressive firms such as The Susie Cooper to produce radical design.[11]

Today the experiment should be remembered and admired for its breadth of vision, its scale, the quality of many of the designs, their variety, strength and unique style, as well as the adventurous spirit of the designers, manufacturers and retailers who took part.

Plate 5.11. An example of the Forest *pattern designed by Paul Nash for E. Brain and Co.*

1. The first re-evaluation of the whole venture can be found in Ann Eatwell, 'A Bold Experiment in Tableware Design', *Antique Collecting*, November 1984, pp.32-35. A detailed discussion of the designs produced by E. Brain and Co is in R. Pelik, 'The Harrods Experiment', *Ceramics*, August 1987, pp.33-41 and for the glass in Hester Bury, 'Designs for Glass by Eight British Artist, 1934', *The Journal of the Decorative Arts Society,* 1977, No. 10, pp.36-43. The project is also discussed in Judy Spours, *Art Deco Tableware,* London, 1988, pp.173-180.
2. The quality of design in industry, for many years a matter of concern in the Potteries, came under particular scrutiny in the 1930s. The Gorell committee report of 1932 for the Board of Trade recommended, amongst other things, a more prominent role for the artist in industry. The exhibition 'British Art in Relation to the Home' held at Dorland Hall in 1933 was a direct response to the report. Two patterns by Milner Gray, one for A.J. Wilkinson and one for E. Brain and Co, were shown here as well as two by Clarice Cliff for A.J. Wilkinson. The initiative led by T.A. Fennemore was very much part of this campaign for better design.
3. In the advertising leaflet for the exhibition at Harrods, 'Exhibition of Contemporary Art for the Table', only twenty-six artists are mentioned. Ludwig Kny and Eric Ravilious (both designing for Stuart and Sons) are not acknowledged.
4. Milner Gray described Clarice Cliff's involvement with the scheme as follows: 'I think she has been given greater credit than deserved for her part in the so-called Harrods experiment, certainly as regards its conception and inception. Neither Fennemore, Sutherland nor I were much enamoured of her work, we did not include her in our original list, but in a way it was I suppose typical of the period, a style that we were trying to improve upon. It was of course heavily pushed by the firm in the event of its inclusion.' Letter from Milner Gray to Ann Eatwell, 4 October, 1983.
5. Freda Beardmore, interviewed by Ann Eatwell in about 1986, thought that examples of the factories' shapes may have been sent to artists who did not visit the factories so that they could design with a shape in mind.
6. The designs for a large number of the patterns for both ceramics and glass survive. The Stuart and Sons designs are now at the Wedgwood Museum as part of the Stuart and Sons archive. The A.J. Wilkinson designs are in the Horace Barks Reference Library as part of the A.J. Wilkinson archive PA W-N/80 Decoration Description Book. The E. Brain and Co designs are in the Wedgwood Museum in the form of pattern books for the company.
7. A. Blunt, 'The Crafts delivered', *The Spectator*, no. 5, 26 October 1934, p.619.
8. Noel Carrington, 'Artists and Industry at Harrods', *Design for Today*, December 1934, pp.461-464.
9. According to Freda Beardmore, the E. Brain and Co factory had its own in-house copper plate engraver and printers at the time, which enabled high standards (interview with Freda Beardmore recorded in about 1986). The printed designs of Milner Gray and Albert Rutherston were praised by critics such as Noel Carrington.
10. '...the writer, originator of the idea [for the Harrods show] frankly admits that a number of designs were produced which were unworthy both of the artist and the producer.' T.A. Fennemore, 8 March 1958.
11. Comparatively few designers were employed in the pottery industry of the 1930s.

6.

Wedgwood

Sharon Gater

WHEN THE PARIS EXPOSITION opened in 1925 it was visited by Kennard L. Wedgwood, head of Josiah Wedgwood & Sons, New York, together with J.E. Goodwin, the company's Art Director. The event won for Josiah Wedgwood & Sons the Grand Prix while J.E. Goodwin was awarded the Diplome d'Honneur and Mabel Tatton, Marcel Goupy and Anna Zinkeisen obtained silver medals.

In 1925 the gulf between the Paris Exposition and Josiah Wedgwood & Sons Ltd was really quite vast. The first was heralded with much excitement as the first successful attempt to bring together the countless characteristics and styles which would in later years find the common heading of 'art deco'. The second was an old established family firm, working in premises which were becoming rapidly obsolete and with a regard for manufacturing ceramics which had more to do with keeping its workforce in employment than with producing up-to-the-minute fashion items or fulfilling requirements set for it by a passing artistic movement (Plate 6.1).

The settings for the displays in Paris were sumptuous and evidently heavily influenced by contemporary cinema. Wedgwood's advertisement in the exhibition catalogue, on the other hand, describes themselves in most modest terms, simply as: 'Manufacturers of china ware, Queen's Ware, earthenware, Jasper ware, Black Basalt, China lustre ware, mortars and pestles etc.'.[1]

Significantly, Anna Zinkeisen's award winning plaques in blue and white Jasper depicting Adam and Eve, while

Plate 6.1. The Art Studio at Wedgwood, Etruria, about 1890.

Plate 6.2. A page from the album 'The Etruscan Breadwinners 1898', featuring Thomas Allen, Frank Wedgwood and Harry Barnard.

Plate 6.3. A blue jasper plaque with white bas-relief of Adam, by Anna Zinkeisen, 1925.

executed in what is arguably the most traditional of Wedgwood's bodies, have become the epitome of the company's contribution to the art deco style. It is furthermore surprising that, to design *Adam* and *Eve* and also *Sun and Wind,* Anna Zinkeisen had carefully studied the work of one of the earliest exponents of Jasper, John Flaxman (Plate 6.3).

It is clear that, even motivated by such diverse objectives, there were still areas in which Wedgwood's output fulfilled perfectly the requirements of 'art deco'. Some were a deliberate attempt by designers to create ceramics in the contemporary style while others simply fulfilled certain prerequisites of art deco purely by coincidence.

Most notably, Wedgwood had always maintained the production of traditional lines even though they were supplemented by more avant-garde, fashionable designs. 'Tradition' was synonymous with craftsmanship on which Wedgwood's reputation had been firmly based since the founding of the company in 1759 (Plate 6.4). In 1902 Wedgwood had written on the subject of Jasper ware to one of its travellers, emphasising the importance of their more traditional lines:

This speciality should be the plum of your whole trade, and

should be used by you to obtain orders in other lines when they would not otherwise be procured.[2]

In contrast, the masculine angularity of art deco found expression in the uniformity of mass-produced factory objects, often enhanced by geometric surface patterns. Mechanisation was seen for once as being complementary to design rather than injurious to aestheticism. History has tended to confirm that design trends derive to a greater or lesser extent from the prevailing social climate. The idea that the exuberance of colour and form central to the art deco style was a reaction against the muddy, khaki hues and the desolation of the 1914-1918 war was certainly one with which Wedgwood's managers and employees alike could identify. Inevitably, the Continental market had been lost through enemy action during this time and in 1914 the factory began to close down for two days each week. Managers took reductions in their salaries and yet still the general fear was expressed:

We cannot say what the future has in store for us and our action with regard to the workpeople must depend on circumstance.[3]

Plate 6.4. The Il Penseroso pattern by Thomas Allen, 1883.

Plate 6.5. The Tours shape as illustrated in the 1927 sales catalogue.

Worse still was the loss of many potters while on active service and the death of Company Chairman, Cecil Wedgwood, as he led a battalion of the 8th North Staffordshire Regiment into battle on the Somme in 1916. For Wedgwood this was the reality which would provide the foundations for an artistic trend which is usually associated with the glamour, vitality and explosive colours of the Jazz Age.

For their part, the French wished to establish a national style, separate from that of Germany. Even before the groundbreaking exhibition of 1925, contemporary design possessed a marked French element – one which was also echoed in Wedgwood's output during the first thirty years of the twentieth century.

Before the outbreak of the Great War, Cecil Wedgwood was a frequent visitor to Europe where he would find authentic examples of Dutch, German and French ceramics to deliver to the company's Art Director, John Goodwin, on his return to the works at Etruria. It

was then Goodwin's task to reproduce the pattern which would be manufactured for sale in Europe. Designs such as *Vieux Rouen, Poterat* and *Personages* proved to be best sellers at outlets including Rouard, Pannier Frères and Damon et Delente, for example.

Trips to France by Cecil Wedgwood and John Goodwin also resulted in direct contact with French designers – most notably Marcel Goupy (Art Director to Rouard) and Paul Follot who would eventually fulfil the same function at Le Bon Marché and Waring and Gillow.

Factory records indicate that in April 1914 special payments made to Paul Follot amounted to £100 (factory minutes 19 May 1914). Again, wartime conditions made it impracticable for Follot's designs to be produced but in 1921 it was reported:

> The exhibition held at Mr. Rouard's shop in Paris, of the various table sets and ornamental pieces designed by Mr. Paul Follot and carried out by Messrs Josiah Wedgwood & Sons took place in the second week of April. Miss Mary Wedgwood and Miss Audrey Wedgwood represented the firm, and the exhibition was considered by all concerned to have been a success.[4]

Later in the year the designs were on display at Wedgwood's own London showrooms. Follot's delicate floral patterns – *Sylvia, Genie* and *Jacquiminot* – on his bone china *Tulip* shape (Plate 6.6) are a perfect reflection of the artist's style as applied previously to

Plate 6.6. A bone china coffee can and saucer, Tulip shape, decorated with the Sylvia pattern designed by Paul Follot. Date of introduction c.1922.

Plate 6.7. A covered vase decorated with the Jewelled Tree pattern by Daisy Makeig Jones, c.1920.

furniture and in the design of rugs and textiles. However, using Queen's Ware and Black Basalt, Follot could express his ideas in a much more robust way and created the *Pomona* range of ornamental pieces with its applied fruit and leaf motifs. In his notebooks Bert Bentley (1878-1937, an exceptionally skilled modeller and ornamenter who worked at Etruria) reveals that the modelling of this important French designer's work was left only in the most capable hands although, again, the prevailing situation prevented their production until the early 1920s.

Marcel Goupy is represented in factory pattern books by a range of toilet and tableware named after him and introduced around 1916.

The foreign influence introduced to art deco, even in its infancy, a strong element of Bohemian exoticism, the unlikely source of which can be traced to the founding of the *Ballets Russes* by Sergei Diaghilev in 1909. Too avant-garde for the Russian public, the company made its debut in Paris and throughout the 1920s its lavish costumes were in themselves works of art, designed by such artists as Léon Bakst, Pablo Picasso, Henri Matisse, André Derain and Giorgio De Chirico for example. The influence of the *Ballet Russes* was disseminated not just throughout other art forms but also through interior design and contemporary fashion for example.

In her studio at Etruria, designer Daisy Makeig-Jones, famed for her extensive range of *Fairyland Lustre* patterns and shapes, absorbed the decorative possibilities inherent in the multifarious cultures which now came into play in current art forms (Plate 6.7). Just as Orientalist ballets such as *Scheherazade* had drawn on Indian, Persian and Near Eastern culture for inspiration for lavish sets and exotic costumes, so Daisy's ceramic patterns began to reflect similar influences. The *Nizami* series of 1929 derives its name from the earliest Persian poet while *Lahore,* reminiscent of the erotic interior of a nomad tent, creates a style which is clearly at the hub of the art deco trend. However, it is *Silenus* with its elfin-faced dancing girls garbed in vivid colours, watched over by a red-faced devil, which best conveys the unexpected relationship between ceramics and the performing arts (Plate 6.8). So all-embracing was the art deco movement, however, that it spilled over into countless aspects of real life, popularising various forms of amateur dramatics including pageants and theatrical tableaux.

By 1930, what should have been purely a celebration of the birth of Wedgwood's founder, Josiah I, became a

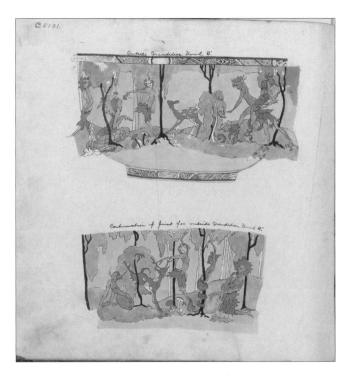

Plate 6.8. A pattern book entry of the Silenus pattern (C5131). 1923.

desperate attempt to advertise and sell the wares of a company which, like so many others, had been plunged into financial disaster by the Wall Street crash. Sir Francis Joseph, President of the North Staffordshire Chamber of Commerce, claimed at the close of the extensive programme of events organised to mark the bicentenary: 'This week we have made history, next week, orders will follow'.[5]

In fact it would take several years and drastic reassessment for Wedgwood to regain its status as the vanguard of ceramic design and technology. Nevertheless, the events staged in 1930 to draw international attention to the company are in themselves worthy of scrutiny as they serve to illustrate the extent to which Wedgwood had become entrenched in the whole ethos of art deco. Most notably, for a week in May, a pageant regaling the entire history of the Potteries from the Druids to the present day was held in Hanley Park. 640 Wedgwood employees took part in the extravaganza and roles were also played by members of the Wedgwood family. Particularly memorable are the Portland Vase figures, played by Wedgwood's

Plate 6.9. An illustration from the Veronese sketch book, about 1930. Veronese wares, introduced in the 1930s, were mainly ornamental shapes decorated with a number of glaze colours and decorated with simple motifs in silver lustre.

Plate 6.10. A Wedgwood Veronese Ware vase (model D57). Height of vase 2in. (5cm). 1930.

Plate 6.11. The Grafton Galleries exhibition, 1936, showing unique pieces by Norman Wilson.

handpaintresses and the 'Widow Finial' played by Daisy Makeig-Jones. The spectacle even earned the praise of a man who never feared to damn, George Bernard Shaw:

> It is on occasions such as this that one sees the enormous possibilities of dramatic art in this country – not carried out by small bodies of professionals... but coming right out of the love of the people of art.[6]

Gordon Forsyth, Superintendent of Art for Stoke-on-Trent, in his role as Master of Designs for the occasion, enlisted the help of the local art schools in the creation of costumes, the drawings for which he later donated to the Wedgwood Museum. Studied in isolation, the costume designs are extraordinary and elevate the pageant beyond provincial amateur theatricals. Such avant-garde figures as Princess Petroleum, for example, hark straight back to the days of the *Ballets Russes* and its revolutionary treatment of costume.

Further afield in London, a Wedgwood Ball (a charity event) was held at the Park Lane Hotel on 29 May. Debutantes and aristocrats gathered together to create living tableaux of traditional Wedgwood bas-relief subjects such as the *Dancing Hours*. Set-designer Oliver Messel assumed the pose of the central figure in the

Apotheosis of Virgil while Peggy Ashcroft, Lady Lever, Lady Armstrong and others dressed in white muslin, chiffon and latex to resemble Wedgwood's classical figures. It was reported that:

> Flaxman's famous Dancing Hours was one of the successes of the evening and might as well have been re-christened the Debutantes Frieze as a tribute to the pretty young things who took part in it.[7]

One year previously, artists were invited to submit their designs for a commemorative vase with which to mark the bicentenary of Wedgwood's birth in the most contemporaneous style. Again, however, even on such a unique occasion, when the entrants were invited along to the factory, it was the Jasper body they were urged to study in order to make their vases. Sadly, very few of the original entries are extant. Working with white reliefs on a blue Jasper body, the designs submitted by John Skeaping and Barbara Hepworth acknowledge Wedgwood's tradition and at the same time reflect an awareness of contemporary decorative motifs. The latter artist was commended for her designs but her then husband, John Skeaping, was awarded 2nd and 3rd prizes amounting to £100. The winning entry was by Danish glass artist, Emmanuel Tjerne, for an elliptical vase decorated with stylised figures of the four elements – Earth, Fire, Air and Water. The vase, while pre-dating Norman Wilson's matt glazes by two years, was none the less decorated with a matt jade green glaze and matt white reliefs. This and the uncomplicated shape of the vase anticipate the gradual departure from art deco and the transition to the more simplified lines of Modernism.

Artistic movements seldom come to a rapid conclusion – this is especially true when a particular trend exists within the confines of a manufacturing environment since orders need to be fulfilled and new lines originated. Yet in this case the demise of art deco coincided with circumstances which did speed up its disappearance from general production. Most shocking was the sudden death of Frank Wedgwood in October 1930. His successor, Josiah Wedgwood V, a brilliant young economist, came to the helm at a perilous time and immediately began to activate cutbacks – first of all in the number of patterns produced and then with personnel. Casualties included Daisy Makeig-Jones, Harry Barnard and artistic adviser, Charles Holmes. The last's *Sunbirds* pattern, stark in its red and black against a Queen's Ware background, provided a vivid contrast with Wedgwood's traditional patterns.

The decisions made by Josiah throughout his career are testimony to his willingness to take risks. Most notable was his decision to relocate the entire Wedgwood company from Etruria to Barlaston, even though war threatened to halt the entire process. More significantly, he actively involved himself in the area of design. His was the final decision to translate Eric Ravilious' graphic style on to Wedgwood ware, thus creating a unique ceramic style.

The retirement of John Goodwin and the appointment of Victor Skellern in 1934 coincided with the general move away from the vibrant colours and angularity of art deco to a style which was altogether softer in form and colour. Two years later, Skellern's leadership qualities and the development of design at Wedgwood under his tutelage were given a public arena at the Grafton Galleries exhibition between April and May in 1936. Given the luxury of hindsight, this event is the common factor which unites a number of different elements towards the end of the art deco era. It provides a showcase for all of the contrasting facets of contemporary Wedgwood design, an opportunity to inspect the multifarious strands of such a far-reaching style.

Plate 6.12. A pedestal earthenware bowl with a matt black exterior with midnight blue interior, by Norman Wilson with NW monogram. Diameter of bowl 8¼in. (21cm).

Plate 6.13. A Queen's Ware bowl and cover by Norman Wilson decorated with a grape and vine design by Millicent Taplin in silver, with NW monogram. Height 5in. (13cm).

Plate 6.14. A harlequin bone china coffee set designed by Louise Powell, 1936.

The initial purpose of the exhibition was to show the result of experiment in new design at Etruria, to illustrate the marriage between art and industry and to reaffirm Wedgwood's strong links with tradition, each of which was equally applicable to the art deco movement. The Grafton Galleries catalogue pays tribute to those responsible for creating new designs for Wedgwood in 1936 – namely Victor Skellern, Millicent Taplin, Star Wedgwood, Alfred and Louise Powell, Keith Murray and Norman Wilson (Plate 6.11). Such a variety of contrasting styles was at the same time striking in its modernity and yet firmly grounded on the Wedgwood tradition of fine craftsmanship and excellent quality. Also on display were modern reproductions of eighteenth and nineteenth century shapes and patterns still in current production. As it was phrased in the catalogue: 'There is no conflict between the best of the new and the best of the old'.

Victor Skellern, in his capacity as Art Director, evidently had the skill to fuse the work of resident and freelance designers while for the most part remaining out of the limelight. The exception to this was his collaboration with Norman Wilson for the production of a range of sgraffito ware with experimental glazes under the title: 'Stoneware and earthenware vases in special glazes' which were 'unique pieces which will not be repeated'.

While the Grafton Galleries exhibition doubtless gave more recognition to individual artists than had hitherto been given, arguably the richest display of contemporary art deco design is to be found in Wedgwood's handcraft pattern books. The Handcraft Department grew out of the tuition given to the hand-paintresses of Etruria by Alfred and Louise Powell. It opened in 1926 under the supervision of their prize pupil, Millicent Taplin. The books carefully recording each new pattern abound in the work of Milly herself, the Powells, Star Wedgwood, Victor Skellern and Keith Murray, together with freelance designers such as Leonard Bucknall, Ruth Ellis and Wyndham Goodwin. Some artists, however, remained anonymous despite the stylishness of their patterns.

As with most artistic movements, there is no definitive end to art deco. Instead there are, for a number of years, subtle indications that change is on its way. None too subtle, however, was the letter received from John Skeaping in 1926 which he began: 'I wish to introduce myself to your firm. I am an Academy Gold medallist and a Prix de Rome Scholar'.[8]

The animal figures he goes on to describe were eventually put into production in 1927 as a set of ten,

Plate 6.15. *An example of the work of John Skeaping. Duiker in cane ware body. Height 7in. (18cm).*

based on studies made by the artist while working at the London Zoological Gardens. The stylised, simplified forms with which Skeaping embodies his figures are a definite transition from the angularity of art deco (Plate 6.15). Ultimately, the departure would be made complete with the addition of Norman Wilson's matt glazes. Indeed, Wilson's matt glazes, first introduced in 1932, can be credited with the transformation of much of Wedgwood's modernistic output and hence the re-attainment of the company's reputation in the field of ceramic design.

It is significant that Wilson's glazes evolved in the same year that Keith Murray was first employed by Wedgwood on a freelance basis. While Murray's surface patterns undoubtedly reflect the final phase of art deco's popularity, his architectural shapes epitomise the simplicity and subtlety of an evolving design trend (Plate 6.16). The collaboration between Murray and Wilson is a perfect example of the coming together of an artist and a technician – both brilliant in their fields – to ensure the successful representation of constantly changing artistic styles.

Plate 6.16. *A Moonstone coffee set with platinum detail, designed by Keith Murray, 1934. Height of coffe pot 7¼in. (18.4cm).*

1. Catalogue: International Exhibition of Modern Decorative and Industrial Art, Paris. British Section, April-October 1925.
2. Josiah Wedgwood & Sons Limited to R.W. Lea, 24 October 1902.
3. Wedgwood Company Minutes, 26 August 1914.
4. Ibid., 4 May 1921.
5. *Staffordshire Weekly Sentinel, 31 May 1930.*
6. Ibid., 24 May 1930.
7. *Dublin Evening Herald,* 4 June 1930.
8. John Skeaping to Josiah Wedgwood & Sons Limited, 5 December 1926.

Spode Copeland

Vega Wilkinson

COPELAND was a classic example of a traditional manufacturer bringing in new blood to cope with new trends. In the 1930s W.T. Copeland & Sons Ltd at the Spode works in Stoke-on-Trent, Staffordshire was owned and managed by the fourth generation of the Copeland family, the grandsons of Alderman William Taylor Copeland. They were Richard Ronald John (Plate 7.1), who marketed the product, and Arthur Gresham, who was responsible for the manufacture and quality. Mr Ronald, as he was affectionately known on the site, recognised early that this new style which had been initiated in France would become the fashion, and immediately directed his art department to design new shapes and patterns.

Spode Copeland, always known for traditional designs, developed new designs in the art deco style with geometric lines and bright colours. The first of these patterns was *Luxor* in 1923 (Plate 7.2) and *banded patterns* (Plate 7.3) consisting of simple coloured lines that were totally different from the normal product range and sold well (Plate 7.4). The first true art deco pattern, however, was *Stop and Go* designed in 1926 (Plate 7.5). Mr Ronald believed that wherever there was a market Spode Copeland should be seen to be part of it, even if it demanded products outside the usual range. He believed that Spode Copeland advertisements and promotional leaflets should emphasise how the product could be used in the home and many show fine floral arrangements. He had acquired the reputation in the art department for selecting the new patterns; if he gave them his seal of approval the design would sell well and he was rarely proved wrong. In the early 1930s he designed *Autumn* (Plate 7.6); *Request* and *Mimosa* (Plate 7.7), still based on a floral theme, were designed by Thomas Hassall, then Art Director.

In 1931 Ida, Ronald's wife, stood as the Conservative parliamentary candidate for Stoke-on-Trent and Arthur Edward Hewitt (Mr Ted), then owner of the fine china factory Jackson & Gosling, became her agent. She was elected and served until 1935. Mr Ronald was impressed by Mr Ted's innovative ideas and enthusiasm for modernisation. His factory, trading as Grosvenor China, had won an order to supply the liner *Queen Mary* with a Cube tea set (Plate 7.8). The two factories amalgamated

Plate 7.1. Richard Ronald John Copeland (1884-1958), CBE, DL, JP, High Sheriff of Staffordshire 1939.

Plate 7.2. Luxor, an example of one of the first art deco patterns by Spode, 1923.

Plate 7.3. Spode Copeland group of band patterned ware featured in Modern Home, 1937.

Plate 7.4. Advertisement in Modern Home, September 1927, showing a room of the period and a selection of Spode banded pattern ware.

Plate 7.5. A dinner plate decorated with the restrained Stop and Go pattern, 1926.

Plate 7.6. A range of earthenwares including a tureen and cover, toast rack and coffee pot decorated with the Autumn pattern designed by Ronald Copeland in the early 1930s.

in 1931 and Mr Ted became managing director of W.T. Copeland & Sons Ltd.

By 1934 Thomas Hassall was surprised and rather put out to find Mr Ronald had engaged, unknown to him, Harold Holdway, a young designer who had trained at the Burslem School of Art under Gordon Forsyth and Harry Tittensor. Harold, previously employed by George Jones at the Crescent Pottery, had seen the post of designer advertised and applied. Mr Ronald recognised his talent and appointed him. This was a wise move as this young man brought new ideas to the art department. Holdway's first designs were *Reindeer* (Plate 7.9) and *Lauristan* (Plate 7.10), a more traditional pattern. By the late 1930s his pattern, *The Little Fisherman* (Plate 7.11), influenced by Chinese design, brought a new design to the marketplace.

In 1935 Mr Ted decided that a freelance artist, not previously associated with the ceramic industry, would not only improve design but also bring a competitive element into the design department. Agnes Pinder Davis was appointed to design watercolour sketches that would then be produced on sample plates and shown to the company representatives for their opinions as to whether they would sell. However, when the patterns

Plate 7.7. A period image of the Mimosa pattern designed by Thomas Hassall, Spode Copeland Art Director until 1940, from The Studio, 1940.

were chosen, she insisted that she had the final choice and that her name was included in the factory backstamp. Thomas Hassall was appalled, as designers had never been given this privilege at Spode, but the policy worked well. One of her well-known patterns was

Plate 7.8. An article on Stoniers of Liverpool, a famous retail house which had secured orders from various potteries for the Queen Mary. Jackson & Gosling Grosvenor China Cube tea set. From The Pottery Gazette, 2 March 1936.

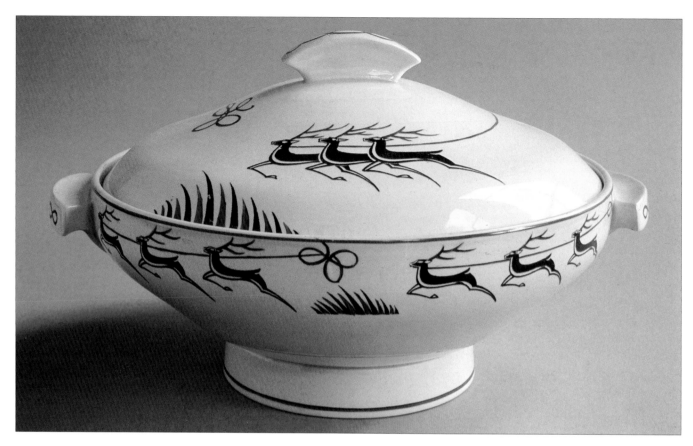

Plate 7.9. *An earthenware tureen decorated with the printed Reindeer pattern designed by Harold Holdway, Spode Copeland assistant designer.*

Country Souvenir (Plate 7.12), described in the promotional leaflet as:

This clear cut design carried out on warm cream Jasmine glaze and coloured in brown and black shading into grey, shows the skill of the artist and craftsmen to perfection. The decoration has a balance and character of its own, and is striking in its simplicity of line and colour.[1]

In 1926 Mr Ronald and his wife embarked on a promotional tour of America and Canada that proved a marketing success.[2] Mr Ronald spoke of the days of Josiah Spode, of how the name Spode stood for quality, innovation and good design, that the Copeland family had been proud to maintain the same high standard and that all the ware was still produced and decorated at the Spode Works in Stoke-on-Trent, Staffordshire.

The American market now demanded the name Spode Copeland on the backstamp whilst the company's German agent, August Warnecke, was marketing the ware in Europe as Copeland Spode.

Copeland's were at this time experimenting with new coloured glazes. Velamour (Plate 7.13) was an ivory body with a vellum textured glaze, Jasmine gave pieces a fine cream tinge, Royal Jade (Plate 7.14) added a totally new green colour to the range and a new earthenware body, a subtle grey called Onyx, was introduced, ideal for shapes designed by Erling B. Olsen. Olsen was born in 1903 and trained at the Oslo School of Art in Norway and the St Martin's School of Art in London. He first joined Josiah Wedgwood and Sons Ltd, designing ornamental goods that were exhibited at the Exhibition of British Goods in Copenhagen, Denmark, in 1931. He left Wedgwood in 1935 to join Copeland where he was given his own studio. (The only other artist at Copeland to have had that privilege was Charles Ferdinand Hurten, the floral artist.) Olsen was one of the leading modellers of the day and his ideas and artistic talent brought a new look to Copeland's range of fancy ware. The simple vases, ashtrays, and candlesticks, decorated with fine sweeping lines, were an immediate success (Plate 7.15), as were the Velamour Kicking Horse

Plate 7.10. A period image of a group of traditionally styled wares decorated in the Lauristan pattern designed by Harold Holdway, mid-1930s.

Plate 7.11. The Little Fisherman designed by Harold Holdway in the late 1930s, inspired by a Chinese design. From the Yorkshire Observer Modern Homes supplement, March 1935.

Plate 7.12. *A group of earthenware items including a plate, tureen and cover, Country Souvenir designed by Agnes Pinder Davis.*

bookends. But it is the Olsen animals that were unique and have become collectors' items. He designed two elephants, a polar bear, a cat, a rabbit and a greyhound that were promoted in the reports of Spode Copeland in the leading magazines of the time (Plates 7.16-17).

The 1936 British Industries Fair opened in London in February. The ceramic section was housed in the Empire Hall at Olympia and Spode Copeland designed a superb exhibition stand. Reports tell of their new designs mixing with old favourites and providing an impressive range of goods (Plate 7.18). At the British Industries Fair of 1937 a sample plate of *Lowestoft* shape decorated with a bird inspired from Dutch tiles, designed by Harold Holdway, appealed to Queen Elizabeth (the late Queen Mother), who ordered a service. It was still the Spode Copeland tradition to design each piece of a service with a different motif on the same theme and Holdway had

Plate 7.13. *A period article illustrating the Velamour crocus vase.*

Plate 7.15. Bridge cigarette box containing four matching ashtrays in grey Onyx glaze, a pottery with a delightful soft sheen and texture. Price 10s.5d. The elephant ornament is of the same pottery and cost 8s.3d. The grey Kicking Horse bookends are 10s. a pair. From Ideal Home, 1936.

Plate 7.14. Dressing table accessories in Spode Royal Jade from Britannia & Eve, March 1936. Candlestick 2s.6d., scent spray 5s.5d., powder bowl 2s.6d.

Plate 7.16. The dog measures 4in. (10.16cm) long and the little vase 4in. (10.16cm) high. They are in the new lavender grey Copeland Spode Onyx range, price 1s.9d. each (carriage paid in the London area) from Maples of Tottenham Court Road, London W. From 'Loveliness in your Home' in My Home, June 1936.

quickly to design the rest of the service that met with royal approval and was called *Queen's Bird* (Plate 7.19). In 1938 Holdway designed another modernistic pattern, *Christmas Tree*. The triangular Christmas tree on a circular plate was an imaginative idea and found instant appeal with the buying public. It is colourful, symbolic of the festive season and remains one of the most popular designs still produced today. By 1939 Spode Copeland had developed a range of patterns and fancy goods in traditional art deco and modernistic patterns, but with the advent of the Second World War the picture changed for ever.

Plate 7.17. Popular polar bear designed by E.B. Olsen produced in Onyx and Velamour.

1. A twenty-one piece tea service was marketed at 40s.
2. *The Boston Science Monitor* on 6 October 1926 reported their visit.

Plate 7.18. W.T. Copeland & Sons' showroom of the 1930s.

Plate 7.19. Queen's Bird pattern designed by Harold Holdway. From Woman's Journal, *1936.*

8.

Minton

Paul Atterbury

BY THE 1920S MINTON, the greatest name in British pottery and porcelain in the Victorian era, was a shadow of its former self. The decline had started in the late 1880s with the death of Colin Minton Campbell, the company's most adventurous and dynamic owner and manager. Inadequately controlled by the next generation of the Minton family, and challenged by the new rising stars of the ceramic firmament, such as Doulton, Minton's spirit of innovation slowly faded away. By 1900 the company was virtually bankrupt. Two years later Secessionist Ware, that artistic and colourful slip-trailed art nouveau range, was launched, a last attempt at matching the taste of the marketplace.

The designers were Leon Solon, Minton's Art Director and son of the famous creator of pâte-sur-pâte, and John William Wadsworth, who had recently graduated from the Royal College of Art. Wadsworth, who joined Minton in about 1902, was born in Macclesfield in 1879. After studying locally and working as a designer in the local silk industry, a scholarship took him to London. Immediately he made his mark with the Secessionist range and in 1905 he was made Art Director. Over the next few years he worked to bring Minton's tableware patterns up to date, developing at the same time a lasting enthusiasm for French art and design. However, it was an uphill struggle in a company that was financially insecure and unable as a result to invest in its future. Instead, there was increasingly reliance upon the safe styles of the past. In 1915, having done his best, Wadsworth left to become Art Director at Royal Worcester.

He was to stay at Worcester for the next seventeen years, working primarily with tablewares but involved with famous decorators and modellers. He introduced new tableware ranges that reflected contemporary French art deco styles. Eventually frustrated by the overridingly traditional attitudes at Worcester, however,

Plate 8.1. A period advertisement illustrating the Solarno Ware range from the late 1930s.

he went freelance in 1932 and spent the next two years designing for a number of Staffordshire potteries. By now the spirit of art deco was flourishing in Stoke-on-Trent, thanks largely to the success enjoyed by the jazzy patterns and geometric shapes of Clarice Cliff and her followers. From the early 1930s the style had entered a new phase of modernism, all rounded forms, soft glazes and matt finishes. Wedgwood were the trendsetters and all their rivals wanted to follow them. At this point, in April 1935, Wadsworth returned to Minton, again as Art Director. Now financially secure, Minton were ready to ride the tide of modernism and so the managers gave Wadsworth his head. He quickly produced his Solarno tableware range (Plate 8.1), whose rounded forms and

Plate 8.2. An earthenware plate decorated with the stylised hand-painted pattern Sailing Ships *designed by Reginald Haggar, c.1930. Diameter 7⅞in. (20cm).*

soft colours gave Minton a contemporary look. Other designs followed, for tablewares and ornaments, reflecting both modernism and French art deco.

After the war Wadsworth continued to drive Minton forward, concentrating now wholly on tableware. In 1949 he designed *Haddon Hall*, one of the best-selling tableware patterns ever and one that was to be synonymous with Minton for the next fifty years. It was also the first Minton pattern to be produced by lithography. He went on to design ranges for the Festival of Britain and the Coronation, and his crowning achievement was the Queen's Vase with its accompaniment of Royal Beasts, presented to Her Majesty by the Federation of Pottery Manufacturers in 1953. Wadsworth, little known today but at the time one of the few ceramic designers in Britain who fully understood French art deco, died in 1955, still working for Minton.

When Wadsworth returned to Minton as Art Director in 1935, he replaced Reginald George Haggar. Born in Ipswich in 1905, Haggar never lost his Suffolk roots, which gave him a lifelong love of landscape and an enduring background to his work as an artist. After studying at the Royal College of Art, he came to Minton in 1929 as assistant to Walter Stanley Woodman, the rather pedestrian Art Director who had guided Minton through the 1920s by concentrating largely on reviving past styles. Woodman left in 1930 and Haggar took on the Art Director's mantle.

A dedicated modernist, Haggar developed new tableware and children's ranges with contemporary shapes and patterns that echoed both French art deco and the modern enthusiasm for woodcuts and graphic art (Plate 8.2). In this area, he had much in common with Victor Skellern at Wedgwood. His art deco designs often brought him into conflict with Minton's rather conservative management, who at this stage tended to prefer the past to the present. For example, when he prepared displays for exhibitions and trade fairs, he concentrated on the modern wares (Plate 8.3), only to find that when his back was turned they had been replaced by Sèvres revival porcelains and other traditional wares. As a result many of his designs did not go into production and survive only as drawings in the Minton archives. Notable is a tableware design featuring the Potteries skyline with smoking bottle ovens (Plate 8.4). Today this looks dynamic and avant-garde, but at the time it cannot have aroused much enthusiasm from the management. Haggar and his work are notably

Plate 8.3. An earthenware plate decorated with a stylised printed and hand-painted pattern known as Modern Art and designed by Reginald Haggar, c.1930. Diameter 9in. (22.8cm).

(Below) Plate 8.4. A proposed pattern depicting smoking bottle ovens designed by Reginald Haggar.

absent from a Minton promotional booklet issued in 1933. For all these difficulties, Haggar was an adventurous and much under-rated designer, with a clear contemporary vision. He left Minton in 1935 when he became Master in Charge at Stoke School of Art, but continued to work as a freelance designer for a number of Staffordshire companies.

A charismatic teacher, Haggar was at the art school until 1945, when he left to become a freelance lecturer, writer and artist. One of the first to appreciate the particular qualities of the Stoke landscape, he started a long series of watercolours depicting the buildings and bottle ovens of the pottery industry, elements that were beginning to disappear at an alarming rate. These paintings place him firmly in the British watercolour tradition. He also had a great appreciation of ceramics old and new throughout his life, and lectured and wrote widely on subjects as diverse as contemporary ceramic sculpture, Continental porcelain and Mason pottery and porcelain. A collector of extraordinary diversity and a founder member of the Northern Ceramic Society, he was a key figure in the development of a modern approach to the study of ceramic history. Haggar died in 1988.

9.

Doulton Art Deco:
A Talent for Reinvention

Julie McKeown

MUCH OF WHAT CONTINUES to be written about Royal Doulton today draws on research by company historian, Desmond Eyles,[1] whose book *Royal Doulton 1815-1965* was published some forty years ago to celebrate the 150th anniversary of the firm's founding. His was the first attempt to write about Doulton's complex manufacturing history, placing the increasingly collectable Lambeth and Burslem decorative wares in the context of an equally diverse range of sanitary, industrial and architectural ceramics. Writing of the company's critical success at the 1893 Chicago World Fair, Eyles quotes the ceramic historian J.F. Blacker:

> Essentially [Doulton's] genius was modern with no records or triumphs dating from the eighteenth century and, fortunately, no hide-bound traditions to be followed.[2]

By the 1920s and '30s, the decades more usually associated with art deco, Royal Doulton had collected awards at all the major international exhibitions of Victorian and Edwardian times. How difficult was it for this now old established company to reinvent its 'genius' for a style whose essential aim was to be 'moderne'? That Eyles devotes comparatively little space in his book to answer this question should not be surprising. At the time he was writing, the term 'art deco' was not yet coined[3] nor defined by those now well-documented characteristics: the bright, bold and bizarre; the stylised shapes and iconography; the zigzag geometry; and the exotic mish-mash of motifs stolen from other times and cultures. Eyles' failure to independently recognise or comment on these significant stylistic features may also be due to their relatively short-lived application throughout the company's wide range of mass-produced wares. The instinctive conservatism of the British consumer, with which Royal Doulton has always maintained an empathy, also demanded the filtering of the more *outré* elements of the style prevalent elsewhere in Europe, resulting in designs often more reassuring than overtly radical.

This apparent dilution and commercialisation of art deco may explain why Royal Doulton is today less associated with the style than many other British ceramic manufacturers, but a closer look at its inter-war manufacture reveals many outstanding examples of art deco. Designs which drew on standard iconography of the 'high style' are most evident in tableware and sculptural figures. However, other influences of art deco consolidated and originated products which are not now recognised as representative of the style. Orientalism was exploited in the company's inter-war production of art studio pottery, for instance, whilst popular commercial interpretations – some might say transgressions – of the art deco style prompted series of 'novelties' and nurserywares, such as character jugs and *Bunnykins*. That these now familiar Doulton collectable giftwares are still in production today, but not especially identified with the art deco period, says much for Royal Doulton's capacity for reinventing its own past designs, imbuing them with longevity and marketing them for a modern consumer.

At the time of the 1925 Paris Exposition, a more significant reinvention was under way, as Royal Doulton continued its transformation from a Victorian family firm into a modern, technologically advanced, public owned company. Financial buoyancy resulted from sanitary and industrial ceramics manufacture which then accounted for some 75 per cent of company sales.[4] With changes in taste and style, the muted ornamental stonewares the company had made at Lambeth since 1866 were seen as anachronistic in the bright and simple interiors of British suburbia. Whilst question marks over its profitability remained, the Lambeth Studio was allowed to continue with just twenty-five or so artists reporting to Art Director Joseph Mott.[5]

As production of decorative ceramics concentrated in Burslem, the old Nile Street factory was modernised and new continuous gas and electric kilns were installed. This was especially welcomed by Art Director Charles Noke. Trained as a modeller at Worcester, Noke had been lured to Doulton's Burslem factory in 1889 for 'the freedom and the promise'.[6] The inter-war years came at the end of his long career and many of his team of designers and modellers had also been apprenticed at the close of the nineteenth century. Amongst the few significant new arrivals during the 1920s were Noke's architect-trained son (Cecil) Jack Noke (who succeeded his father as Art Director in 1936) and Burslem School of Art alumnus Fred Moore.

In the production of experimental glazed wares between the wars, Charles Noke was pleased to draw on the past experience of long-time employees Harry Nixon and Arthur Eaton. Doulton's *Flambé*, developed with assistance from Bernard Moore, had been launched to great acclaim at St Louis in 1904 and between then and c.1919 the company went on to produce lustre and further transmutation glazes: *Crystalline, Titanian, Peach Blow, Haricot* and *Lapis Lazuli*. The Orientalism that had inspired *Flambé* was a key characteristic of the art deco style and was especially evident in European, particularly French, studio pottery. Doulton's marketing of its inter-war ranges of transmutation glazed ceramics, *Sung, Chinese Jade* and *Chang*, capitalised on their eastern source which was often reflected in their consciously exotic, though not necessarily accurate, Chinese names.

The British Industries Fair of 1920 provided the showcase for *Sung*, most effective of the glazed wares, which was characterised by bright yellows, greens and blues 'mottled', 'veined' or 'feathered' beneath a flambé glaze. Stunning images of birds of paradise, fantastic dragons and swirling tropical fish were hand-painted by Nixon, Eaton and later Fred Moore (Plate 9.1). Its showing at the 1925 Paris Exposition led Gordon Forsyth,[7] otherwise critical of the British ceramics displayed, to comment: 'No firm deserves greater praise than Messrs Doulton's for their constant endeavour to produce pottery of a high artistic order'. The 1920 British Industries Fair also saw the re-launch of Royal Doulton Figures,[8] a number of which depicted the Oriental or North African characters favoured by exponents of the art deco style. Some of these, such as Noke's *The Carpet Vendor* and *The Moor* and Harry Tittensor's series *One of the Forty*, were painted with *flambé* and other experimental glazes.

Also issued in around 1920 was *Chinese Jade*, as its name implies a whitish green-veined glaze decorating Oriental style vases, figures and animals. The discovery two years later of Tutankhamun's tomb saw the introduction of a range of wares featuring printed Egyptian motifs, much favoured during the art deco period, beneath a smoky blue *Titanian* glaze. In about 1925 *Chang*, an entirely original thick and 'suety' opalescent glaze, streaked with brilliant colours, was created for use on chunky shaped pots or huge twisting dragons, more usually modelled in coarse refractory marl.

The Lambeth Studio's director, Joseph Mott, also a highly regarded glaze chemist, developed various glazes for use on a stoneware body. They included lustre, matt and semi-matt glazes, *sang de boeuf*, peach blow and crystalline. His brighter colours were used by long term artists William Rowe and Harry Simeon and newcomers Vera Huggins and Doris Johnson on pots more usually tube-lined or incised with stylised foliate designs. Although more in the spirit of French art deco, their pseudo-primitive style received only limited praise when shown at the 1925 Paris Exposition. Rowe and Simeon had earlier in the 1920s developed a *Persian Ware* range of pots, plaques and tiles. This revival of the Iznik-inspired wares produced at Lambeth in the 1880s was also replicated at Burslem in 'print and tint' Series Ware patterns *Blue Persian* and *Bird of Paradise*.

Whilst historical authenticity was paramount in the development of some Royal Doulton wares, other designs took an element of past ceramic manufacture and subverted it into something different. During the economic recession of the 1920s and '30s, this was a common resort of struggling pottery firms, desperate to originate ever more 'modern' inexpensive designs for novelty-hungry consumers. To the despairing Design and Industries Association, their products were often closer to the definition of kitsch than good design: camouflaging form or function; misconstruing past styles; and assuming a false exclusivity or novelty value.[9] Royal Doulton was not averse to competing in this trend, which

Plate 9.1. *Jardinière decorated with fighting eagles under Sung glazes, designed by Charles Noke, c.1925. 15in. (38.1cm).*

critics saw as a vulgar transgression of the art deco style, though the company consistently maintained high levels of skills in manufacture. Many of its current range of 'collectables', with their emphasis on craftsmanship and hand painting, may be traced back to the 'novelties' it produced then.

Especially successful have been Royal Doulton character jugs, the first of which, *John Barleycorn*, was issued in 1934. Inspired by eighteenth century Staffordshire Toby wares and London stoneware 'face' jugs, the pre-war character jugs were designed and relief-modelled in earthenware by Noke and his

assistant Harry Fenton. Most depicted a traditional or legendary figure, whilst others featured characters from literature, usually Dickens (whose works also inspired designs for Royal Doulton Figures and Series Wares).[10] A range of character jug 'derivatives' followed: teapots and tea wares; ash bowls; and even musical jugs which played an appropriate tune on being raised!

A notion of exclusivity was added to Royal Doulton's marketing of a series of brightly painted, relief-modelled 'Limited Edition' jugs and loving cups. Issued from 1930 in numbered editions, these were sold with elaborately printed certificates, a ploy used since in the sale of many of the company's giftware ranges. Their design by Harry Fenton recalled the eighteenth century Staffordshire tradition of relief-moulded jugs.[11] Also drawing on earlier English ceramic manufacture were cottage-shaped wares and such items as brightly coloured fruit-shaped jam pots which the company produced in small quantities.

Eighteenth and nineteenth century manufacture of animal figures was revived in the 1931 series 'Championship Dogs'. Realistically modelled by freelance designer Frederick Daws, the range was expanded to feature model dogs on brooches, alabaster ash trays, mahogany bookends and 'wood ovals'. In a more idiosyncratic – and less commercially successful – style was the series of animal models commissioned by Jack Noke from freelance sculptor Raoh Schorr in the mid-1930s. At the same time, a relief-decorated coffee set, *Reynard the Fox*, was produced, its triangular whip-shaped handles lending it a characteristic art deco styling.

Doulton had a long tradition of producing animal figures, first at Lambeth and from the early 1900s at Burslem where Noke's small models were decorated with experimental glazes. A lop-eared rabbit from that time was the inspiration for the first six *Bunnykins* figures and a range of tea wares produced briefly during the late 1930s. These bright relief-modelled earthenwares bear little similarity to today's series which has mushroomed more than their originator, Barbara Vernon Bailey (the daughter of Cuthbert Bailey), could ever have imagined. *Bunnykins* tablewares had been launched in 1934 and for several years afterwards Barbara Vernon submitted sketches from the convent she entered as a young woman. Her designs were subsequently translated into prints, initially for Royal Doulton's art deco tableware shape, *Casino* (Plate 9.2).

Barbara Vernon also participated, through her father, in tableware design, suggesting, Fred Moore recalled,[12] that the company:

should make something which was ethereal in quality as opposed to the hard outlines of the standard litho or transfer process...

Plate 9.2. 'Bunnykins' nurseryware from the late 1930s: Casino shape teapot with Greetings lithographic design by Barbara Vernon and a hand-painted rabbit shaped teapot modelled by Charles Noke. Teapot right 5in. (12.7cm).

Plate 9.3. *Bright young things, all designed by Leslie Harradine and produced in bone china with hand-painted decoration. Left to right: Scotties HN1281, 1928-36; The Swimmer HN1270 1928-38; Negligée HN1228, 1927-36; Lido Lady HN1220, 1927-36; and Sunshine Girl HN1344, 1929-38. Tallest 7¼in. (18.4cm).*

This resulted in five earthenware 'print and tint' patterns, *Oakland, Melody, Fantasy, Castleford,* and *Moonlight,* on the traditional fluted *Delta* shape. The floral designs were sketchily outlined with predominantly hazy blue and green colours under a distinctive mottled glaze. Backstamped 'Barbara Vernon Production', it seems likely that Doulton had intended to follow the '30s fashion for marketing a female designer but production was cut short by the Second World War.

Many earlier nurserywares had been issued as Series Ware; *Gnomes*[13] was one example, a pattern which, like Royal Doulton figurative and sculptural ranges, capitalised on the 1920s vogue for fairies, florals and whimsy. Whilst some concessions to art deco style may be seen in Series Ware shapes, such as popular rectilinear sandwich sets and octagonal fruit sets, most patterns continued to feature prints of traditional subjects from literature, history and Olde Worlde imagery. Exceptions from the 1930s were rack plates with brightly coloured block-printed abstract patterns or hand-painted designs of stylised flowers, such as *Tulips* or *Sweet Peas*. Rarer were those with contemporary figurative subjects, such as

Surfing with its sporty beach-side belles.

Sea bathing was ostensibly the subject for the Royal Doulton figure, *The Bather*. First issued in 1924, this risqué female nude was painted with a more modest swimsuit from 1938. Royal Doulton's 'Pretty Ladies' are now identified as essentially nostalgic, with their crinolines and bonnets, but a number of figures from the '20s and '30s, such as *Scotties*, depicted bright young things sporting bobbed hair and fashionable dresses (Plate 9.3). Designed and modelled by freelance artist Leslie Harradine, who had previously worked at the Lambeth Studio, these figures were perfect vehicles for art deco's fascination with high fashion. Also characteristic of the style are those figures inspired by contemporary theatre, ballet or the circus, such as *Pierrette, Marietta, Columbine* and *Butterfly,* or by Hollywood glamour, like *Gloria, Clothilde* and *Marlene Dietrich* who was portrayed on a wall mask. But perhaps in deference to their market, Royal Doulton tended towards the sensible rather than the seductive, as in the pastel-painted head-and-shoulder portraits of girls-next-door *Vera* and *Gladys*. Likewise, *Sunshine Girl, Negligée*

Plate 9.4. Figures designed by Richard Garbe, Professor of Sculpture at the Royal College of Art, and produced by Royal Doulton from c.1937: The Cloud (HN1831), Spring (HN1827) and Dryad of the Pines (HN1869). Tallest 23in. (58.4cm).

and *Lido Lady* may be posing in swimsuit, negligée and pyjamas, but there is a domestic wholesomeness to them with their coy expressions and puppy dogs. There were some more daring nude studies, such as *Susanna* and *Circe*, but these too lacked the streamlined style, the smart sophistication and heady decadence of European bronze and ivory figurative sculpture.

More in the French sculptural art deco style were the late '30s figures *The Cloud, Spring* and *Dryad of the Pines* (Plate 9.4) by Richard Garbe (1896-1957), Professor of Sculpture at the Royal College of Art. These were amongst a number of his designs produced in

limited editions at both Burslem and Lambeth in response to the Council for Art and Industry's initiative to forge links between contemporary artists and commercial manufacturers. Doulton already had a successful record in these partnerships, having produced wares by such people as Reco Capey (1895-1961), Professor of Design at the Royal College of Art, whose designs were produced at both factory sites, and Frank Brangwyn (1867-1956), whose ornamental ranges and tablewares, such as *Harvest,* were manufactured as *Brangwyn Ware* at Burslem between 1930 and 1939. This example of 'Manufactured Art Ware', with its chunky uneven shapes,

"Brangwyn" Dinner Set for 6 persons—116/-   "Brangwyn" design

Plate 9.5. Table and ornamental wares designed by Frank Brangwyn RA, illustrated in a 1930s catalogue.

earthy colours and limpid glazes, deliberately emulated rustic, hand-crafted pottery (Plate 9.5).

Doulton's Lambeth Studio mounted an impressive display of its pottery at the Royal Academy Exhibition of British Art in Industry in 1935. Joan Cowper's arrival the following year consolidated a move towards more contemporary design; hand-thrown pots in coarse clay, decorated with plain bands of colour, splashes of glaze and spare brush strokes drew comparisons with the Japanese-inspired wares of Bernard Leach and other studio potters. Although the Lambeth Studio pottery emphasised simplicity of form and economy of design (Plate 9.6), it was in fact Doulton's utilitarian industrial wares which conformed more to the ideals of Modernism. Its functional factory-made wares – stoneware pots, industrial acid jars and plain garden wares and flower pots – were especially singled out for praise by art critics such as Pevsner.[14] Items of Doulton laboratory porcelain were even selected by Frank Pick as examples of good mass-produced design for the Council for Art and Industry's exhibition 'English Pottery Old and New' held at the Victoria and Albert Museum in 1935. Doubtless this amused Cuthbert Bailey whose contribution to a debate on modern art at a meeting of

the North Staffordshire branch of the Society of Industrial Artists had been entitled 'From the Point of View of the Average Person'.[15]

Royal Doulton tableware of the 1920s and '30s was characterised not by simplicity but by diversity of design. Conservative customers were well served by long-term traditional favourites such as Watteau, Old Leeds Sprays and Countess as well as new conventionally-styled designs such as the earthenware pattern Minden and china-bodied Clovelly. Under Jack Noke's influence, a variety of more original and adventurous art deco tableware (and sometimes complementary giftware) was marketed. During the early '30s designs ranged from inexpensive earthenware patterns such as the Islamic-inspired Syren and Mecca, available with optional matching tablecloths (Plate 9.7), to De Luxe, a smart and stylish geometric pattern promoted through advertisements for Lipton's Tea. De Luxe was produced on Fairy, a delicate china shape with open triangular handles, which contrasted with the more streamlined, rounded and practical shape of Casino. Its patterns included, on china, Tango, a stylised semi-circular sunburst design whose restrained and elegant pattern also decorated jazz age conical cocktail glasses; and, on

Plate 9.6. Vera Huggins incising a stoneware pot. The artist was employed at Royal Doulton's Lambeth Studio in London from 1923 until 1950.

Plate 9.7. Traditional and 'modern' tableware patterns were also available with matching tablecloths, as advertised in Pottery Gazette, August 1932.

earthenware, *Marquis* and *Radiance* whose simple black lines and bold bands of colour anticipate the utility style of the 1940s and '50s. At the time of their introduction in 1933 the *Pottery Gazette* was reporting that Doulton's designs:

indicated that the old established houses in the manufacturing circles of the pottery trade are not necessarily hide-bound by conservatism.[16]

Of course, design compromises, mixing conventional patterns with modern shapes and *vice versa,* were commonly made, with varying degrees of success. *Eden,* a stylised asymmetrical arboreal pattern, was teamed with the traditional shape *Lincoln* (Plate 9.8) whilst *The Coppice,* a naturalistic representation of a pheasant in flight, was used on the amalgam of geometric forms which made up the *Embassy* shape. *Gaylee* on *Dandy* provided a perfect marriage of exuberant colour and curvaceous form (Plate 9.9). As the decade progressed, the more extreme features of the Jazz Moderne style were abandoned: stepped shapes became simpler and more rounded, colours grew more muted and patterns plainer, comprising bands, lines and dots, for example

Plate 9.8. *Successful design compromise evident in two ivory bone china tableware patterns:* Eden (V1112) *on the traditional* Lincoln *shape (left) and* Daffodil (V2050) *on the triangular-handled* Fairy *shape (right).*

Radio on *Saville* and *Scala* on *St James*. Similar restraint was shown in designs for shipping companies and London hotels, the Savoy, Claridge's and the Waldorf.

The Savoy was just one building of many since the early nineteenth century to have employed Doulton architectural and sanitary wares.[17] During the inter-war years the company provided sculptors and architects with architectural materials for a variety of buildings in the art deco style. Doulton Carraraware, adaptable, brightly coloured and easily cleaned, became popular for facing modernist designs such as cinemas whilst polychrome stoneware became a favourite medium of Gilbert Bayes[18] whose long association with the company produced garden wares and other sculptures. His largely figurative architectural ceramics were used extensively for the decoration of the Sidney Street housing estate in north London, developed by the St Pancras House Improvement Society between 1930 and 1938. Most innovative of the sculptors to work with the company was Frank Dobson, later Professor of Sculpture at the Royal College of Art, whose symbolic sculptural relief was made in Doulton polychrome stoneware in 1932 to decorate the spectacular – and at the time controversial – Hay's Wharf building in London.

Whilst this superb example of art deco architecture remains, other buildings have not been so fortunate. Amongst them was Doulton House (Plate 9.10), built in 1939 as the company's own headquarters on London's Albert Embankment. This distinctive modernist block, faced with black and ivory Carraraware, was one of the last building schemes to use Doulton & Co architectural ceramics. When demolished in 1978, Gilbert Bayes' polychrome stoneware frieze, 'Pottery Through the Ages', which decorated its façade, was saved,[19] restored, and may now be seen in the ceramics department of the Victoria and Albert Museum. Sadly, in 2005, bulldozers were again at work, this time on the site of Royal Doulton's Victorian Nile Street factory in Burslem. Wisely safeguarding the company's remaining museum pieces, including some marvellous examples of art deco, Waterford, Royal Doulton, now in the ownership of Wedgwood, must continue its talent for reinvention.

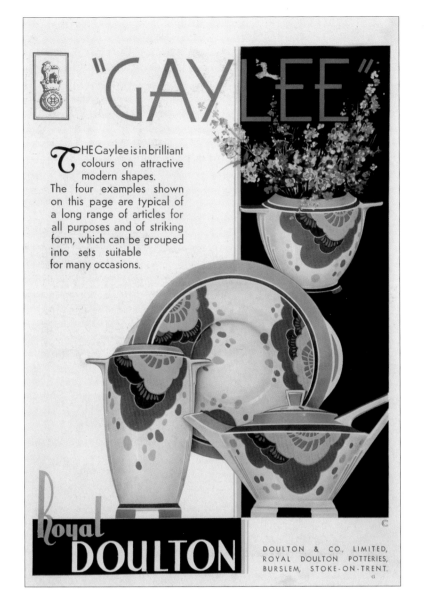

Plate 9.10. An architect's drawing of Doulton House, the company's modernist headquarters on the Albert Embankment which was demolished in 1978.

(Left) Plate 9.9. Royal Doulton's Gaylee, a tableware and ornamental pattern shown advertised on the Dandy earthenware shape, c.1933.

1. Desmond Eyles worked for Royal Doulton from the 1940s. He was responsible for all the classic reference books, some written following his retirement from the company in 1971. He died in 1987.
2. Desmond Eyles, *Royal Doulton 1815-1965*, pp.105-6, Hutchinson & Co, 1965.
3. Hilary Gelson's 1966 article 'Art Deco' for *The Times* was described in Bevis Hillier's 1969 book of the same name.
4. Desmond Eyles, *Royal Doulton 1815-1965*, p.140, Hutchinson & Co, 1965.
5. A total of 370 artists were employed by the Lambeth Art Pottery in 1897. Desmond Eyles, *Royal Doulton 1815-1965*, p.148, Hutchinson & Co, 1965.
6. Desmond Eyles, *The Doulton Burslem Wares*, p.28, Barrie & Jenkins/Royal Doulton, 1980.
7. Forsyth was then Superintendent for Art Instruction in Stoke-on-Trent and Art Adviser to the British Pottery Manufacturers' Federation.
8. Doulton had produced figurative studies first at Lambeth and from the 1890s at Burslem but its current HN-range was issued in 1913. It was so numbered after the initials of supervisory artist Harry Nixon.
9. Judy Spours, Chapter Six, 'Novelty and Kitsch' in *Art Deco Tableware*, Ward Lock Ltd, 1988.
10. Series Ware, introduced in the early 1900s, was the name given to a collection of different items, most usually rack plates, decorated with 'print and tint' scenes following a similar theme.
11. Burgess & Leigh, for example, was another company producing jugs based on earlier relief-decorated designs.
12. An interview with Fred Moore by Louise Irvine and Marguerita Trevelyon Clark, which appeared in the Royal Doulton International Collectors' Club magazine of Summer 1983, was referenced in two articles entitled 'Tableware 1930s and '40s' by Julie McKeown appearing in the Winter 1995 and Spring 1996 issues of the RDICC magazine, *Gallery*.
13. Similar in style, though not decoration, to Wedgwood's *Fairyland Lustre*.
14. N. Pevsner, *An Inquiry into Industrial Art in England*, Cambridge, 1937.
15. Reported in the *Pottery Gazette*, November 1932.
16. Judy Spours, *Art Deco Tableware*, p.128, Ward Lock Ltd, 1988.
17. For descriptions of Doulton's architectural and sculptural work, see Paul Atterbury and Louise Irvine, *The Doulton Story*, Royal Doulton, 1979.
18. Louise Irvine, Paul Atterbury, with Peyton Skipwith and contributors, *Gilbert Bayes, Sculptor 1872-1953*, Richard Dennis, 1998.
19. Paul Atterbury received a National Art Collection Award in 1989 for the rescue of the Gilbert Bayes frieze. It was restored by the Ironbridge Gorge Museum before being presented to the V & A in 1988.

10

Moorcroft

Paul Atterbury

FOR MOORCROFT, the 1920s and the early 1930s represent an era of achievement and consolidation. William Moorcroft had started his own pottery in 1913, with the backing of Liberty's, and had enjoyed immediate success. The First World War intervened but by 1919 the business was making healthy profits, a pattern to be continued through the 1920s. The pottery was enlarged and new staff were employed. Financial security allowed Moorcroft to relax and concentrate on design and many new patterns emerged as a result, along with developments of established ones, such as *Pomegranate, Toadstool, Pansy* and the *Landscape* series. The strong colours and the dramatically drawn flower and fruit patterns matched well the taste of this early phase of art deco. On the home market retailers clamoured for the wares and the export business was thriving, in the colonial market, in Scandinavia and in South America. Many pieces were metal mounted, especially for Liberty's Tudric range, and there was still demand for the lustre-finished monochrome wares. However, the pottery's best selling ware, and its staple product, was the ever-expanding range of speckled blue tableware, known generically as powder blue or Moorcroft blue.

The greatest achievement of the 1920s was the introduction of high temperature reduction-fired flambé. Moorcroft built a special flambé kiln in 1919 and over the next few years perfected the complicated process. Moorcroft flambé glazes occur in two forms, one used as a spectacular and random effect over the conventional slip-trailed patterns and the other as a pure glaze effect inspired by Chinese *sang de boeuf* or peach blow transmutation flambés. These wares were highly regarded, both by Moorcroft himself and by his clients at home and overseas. In Britain his most famous client was the Royal Family, and particularly Queen Mary, an

Plate 10.1. An earthenware vase decorated with the Moonlit Blue pattern, 1925.

avid Moorcroft enthusiast. A reflection of this was Moorcroft's award in 1928 of a Royal Warrant, with the unusual benefit of being allowed to call himself 'Potter to

Plate 10.2. Moorcroft pottery decorated with later versions of the Peacock Feather *pattern, 1934. Note the banding characteristic of the 1930s.*

Her Majesty the Queen'. From about 1930 the phrase was used as part of the factory mark. A great self-publicist, Moorcroft made sure his products were widely shown at exhibitions, in Britain and abroad. At the British Empire Exhibition at Wembley in 1924 the Moorcroft stand was the focal point of the ceramics display, overshadowing famous names such as Wedgwood. He also enjoyed success at the Paris Exhibition of 1925, won a Grand Prix at Antwerp in 1930 and a Diploma of Honour at Milan in 1933.

For Moorcroft, as for many other Staffordshire potters, the plateau of success and stability was gravely shaken by the Wall Street crash in 1929. Major clients vanished overnight and suddenly richly decorative and luxurious patterns seemed out of place. Throughout the industry there was a move away from bright colours to softer, pastel tones and matt glazes, and Moorcroft, always market alert, was quick to respond to this change in taste. Designs were simplified, patterns became more abstract, and grounds became pale and glazes matt. There was also an increasing emphasis on finishes that underlined handcraft techniques, drawing inspiration from the popularity of studio pottery. In its most extreme form Moorcroft referred to this as 'natural pottery'.

Survival was the name of the game, and survival depended upon adaptability in design and manufacture and the full exploitation of export markets. In the mid-1930s Moorcroft was selling his wares predominantly to Canada, Australia and New Zealand, but also to the United States, Bermuda, Mexico, Argentina, Norway, Sweden, Italy, Spain, Holland, South Africa, Rhodesia, Kenya, Egypt and Japan. In 1937 his display at the Paris exhibition was well received, the French press referring to 'la valeur exceptionnelle des créations'. For the home market, it was much harder. New shapes and designs were rapidly introduced, and rapidly withdrawn, to suit the whims of the buyers. Children's wares and commemorative pieces were introduced and a huge diversity of patterns and colours were made, often in small quantities and to satisfy the needs of clients. At this point, anything could and would be made. At the British Industries Fair in 1939 Moorcroft displayed nineteen different patterns, some in several colourways, along with flambé wares. These ranged from old favourites such as *Pomegranate* to brand new designs such as *Spring Flowers* and *Flaming June*.

Plate 10.3. An earthenware vase decorated with a tube-lined design known as the Honesty pattern, c.1930. Height 7in. (18cm).

Plate 10.4. An earthenware ginger jar and cover decorated with a tube-lined painted pattern Dawn, 1928. Height of item 7½in. (19cm).

As a maker of decorative, and thus luxury, wares, Moorcroft was in the same position as other potters. However, as an adaptable designer and the owner of a small factory, he was able to be more flexible than some of his rivals, particularly as he had a good relationship with his workforce and greatly respected their skills. He acknowledged that his primary duty was to keep his staff employed, and thus design had to match market requirements. The result of this is that collectors today are faced by a bewildering range of patterns, styles and colours from this period, many of which were made in very small quantities. Some may even be unique. Despite the consistency of his style and production techniques, Moorcroft responded to a wide variety of sources during his lifetime, and none more so than during the art deco era. China, Japan, the Middle East and the natural world were always favourites, but in this period he was also influenced by French art deco, studio pottery and

Plate 10.5. An earthenware vase decorated with the tube-lined Yacht *pattern, c.1934-1938. Height 9⅞in. (22.5cm).*

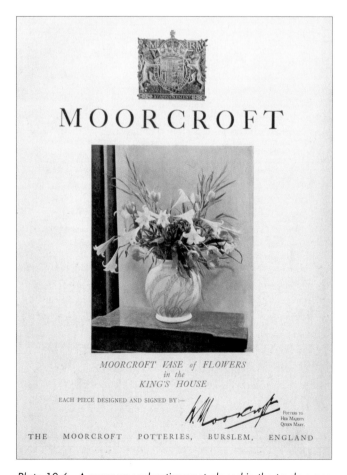

Plate 10.6. A company advertisement placed in the trade press in 1938, featuring the Waving Corn *design.*

the kind of stylised modernism represented by his *Yacht* and late *Peacock* designs. Moorcroft flourished in the 1920s and survived the 1930s, thanks to flexibility and diversity. However, the Second World War was a different kind of challenge and nearly brought Moorcroft to his knees. In the event, he struggled through, largely by sheer will power, and died in 1945 just after his son Walter had been released from the army. Another chapter started.

11.

Shelley Pottery

John Barter and Linda Ellis

THE LATE 1920s and 1930s is one of the most important periods of production of the whole history of the Shelley factory. Throughout that period the factory employed innovative and forward thinking Art Directors, designers and marketing men and reaped huge success, even at a time of uncertainty and depression generally in the country and especially in the pottery industry.

The factory was founded in 1853 evolving out of early pottery manufacturing partnerships. By 1856 Henry Wileman had full control of the business and he was succeeded by his sons James and Charles. In 1862 Joseph Ball Shelley joined the business as a traveller and was taken into partnership by James Wileman ten years later. James Wileman, on his retirement in 1884,

dissolved the partnership in the china works leaving Joseph Ball Shelley as sole proprietor. Percy Shelley had joined his father in 1881 and took over management of the business in 1896 on Joseph's death, continuing to trade under the name Wileman & Co.

Despite the evident depression in the pottery trade at that time, by the late nineteenth century Wileman's

---

Plate 11.1. A selection of Shelley tea ware. Left to right: a Vincent shape cup, saucer and plate, pattern 11722, a Vincent shape cup, saucer and plate, pattern 11683, a tall Queen Anne shape cup, saucer and plate, pattern 11875 and a Queen Anne shape coffee cup and saucer decorated in 'Cottage 1', pattern 11604/8.

Plate 11.2. Queen Anne shape cup, saucer and tea plate, milk jug and bread and butter plate in Balloon Tree, pattern 11624, with matching Irish linen tablecloth and napkins.

Plate 11.3. Shelley tea ware. Left to right: a Queen Anne shape cup, saucer and plate decorated with pattern 11837, a Queen Anne shape jug with a flower handle, pattern 2164, a lamp base decorated with the Archway of Roses pattern 11606, a Vogue shape cup, saucer and plate, pattern 11754/4. Height of tallest item 5in. (12.5cm).

business was expanding and the factory was extended to meet the increased demand. By 1896 Percy Shelley had realised that the quality of the factory's bone china was key to the business's future success. Over the next twenty to thirty years the composition of the bone china body was developed until the company was producing what Shelley claimed was the very best fine bone china any factory could produce.

Following the loss of a court case in 1910 with E. Brain & Co over the use of the 'Foley China' backstamp and trademark, Wileman & Co started to use the 'Shelley China' backstamp including the legend 'Late Foley'. The backstamp was changed to just 'Shelley' in 1916 though the firm still marketed itself as Wileman & Co. Eventually on 1 January 1925 the company's name was changed to Shelley's.

Percy Shelley had a reputation for producing high quality contemporary wares. Alongside domestic and kitchen items, he introduced brilliant art pottery for the specialist market outlets such as Liberty's of London. Frederick A. Rhead, as Art Director from 1895 to 1905, had an enormous influence on the design of shapes, patterns and decoration of both earthenware and china tableware, as did Rowland Morris, a famous sculptor, with his new tableware shape called *Dainty* in 1896.

In 1905 Walter Slater became Art Director and stayed with the company until his retirement in the 1930s. His son, Eric W. Slater, had joined the company as a design apprentice in 1919, working with his father. During his seven years of training he had attended the Burslem School of Art under the directorship of Gordon M. Forsyth and had won the award for best student in 1923. He was always interested in the engineering problems of design, having originally wished to make engineering

Plate 11.4. Illustration from the Shelley 'Silver Book' featuring several patterns including the Archway of Roses pattern 11606 applied to Queen Anne shape, tea and coffee ware, a Vincent shape cup and saucer decorated with the Garden Urn pattern 11618, two Queen Anne shape teacups and saucers, decorated with patterns 11621 and 11607.

his career. By 1926 he had designed a new tableware shape, *Queen Anne*, which was based on a more classical shape called *Antique*, designed some years earlier (Plate 11.1).

In the field of tea and dinner ware, Shelley had great success with its *Queen Anne* shape with more than 170 patterns being applied to it (Plate 11.2). The traditional labour intensive print and enamel designs used were predominately floral and stylised scenes. Some of the more familiar patterns, such as *Blue Iris, Sunrise and Tall Trees, Cottage* and *Black Leafy Tree,* all show this floral bent. Some geometric patterns, however, were designed to enhance the panelled shape, a good marriage between the traditional and the modern (Plate 11.3). Eric Slater created several of his popular patterns for the *Queen Anne* shape after seeing the window displays of a large London department store that had been inspired by a Buckingham Palace Garden Party. These included

Archway of Roses and *My Garden* and the *Cottage* patterns (Plate 11.4).

With an understanding of the need for new ideas in ceramic production Shelley looked towards current trends in European design, although they continued to produce the more traditional tablewares for their established markets. In 1930 Shelley introduced the *Vogue* and *Mode* shapes, a dramatic departure in design (Plate 11.5). These shapes were conical in body with triangular solid handles, decorated with striking geometric patterns using strong colours and some incorporated gold and platinum. The *Vogue* shape had a shallow cup tapering steeply to the base with a flared foot, whereas *Mode* was of a less pronounced angle and had a smaller foot. These new shapes, designed by Eric Slater, demonstrated his innovative design ability.

Although other pottery manufacturers were producing similar examples, it appears that Shelley were among

Plate 11.5. Shelley tea wares. Left to right: a Mode shape coffee cup and saucer decorated with one of the cottage patterns, pattern 2115, a Vogue shape teacup and saucer, pattern 11750 and a Mode shape coffee cup and saucer decorated with Horn of Plenty, pattern 11771/4.

Plate 11.6. A Vogue shape teaset decorated with the Sunray pattern 11742.

Plate 11.7. Examples of Mode and Vogue shape tea ware. Left to right: a Mode shape teacup, saucer and plate decorated with pattern 11871, a Vogue shape teacup, saucer and plate decorated with Fruit pattern 11880 and a Mode shape teacup, saucer and plate, pattern 11757 Note the handle is decorated with a butterfly wing.

the first to register their conical shape range with the UK patent office. However, none of its competitors could match the impact of the Shelley wares, which were produced to the highest standard in bone china, decorated with striking patterns to complement the design of the shapes. At first patterns were updated, geometric versions of the band and flower motifs. In the first batch of patterns there was one design that came to represent all that was characteristic of the times, *Sunray* introduced in 1930, with wide bands of yellow and orange radiating from a black centre at the edge of the cup (Plate 11.6). Later, patterns became more geometric with squares, rectangles, chevrons and lines in various combinations, sometimes overlapping, in bright colours with contrasting silver or black, all motifs now associated with the art deco style (Plates 11.7 and 11.8). Alongside bone china tea and coffee ware, dinnerware was manu-

factured in earthenware, as was the usual policy. New vegetable dishes and a sauceboat were designed with Cubist handles and the fashion for square plates in three sizes was continued.

There was a mixed reaction to these new designs but an extract from the *Pottery Gazette* in 1930 described Shelley Pottery as being '...daring in spirit...' and:

They may or may not carry the public by storm, but one thing they certainly will do, they will cause people to stop and think and if one can do that there is something to be hoped for. There are those who for a long time past have been agitating for a more adventurous spirit in the manufacturing circles of the pottery trade. Well, here it is.[1]

Unfortunately, these conical shapes were not a lasting success – it was believed that the wide bowl of the cup

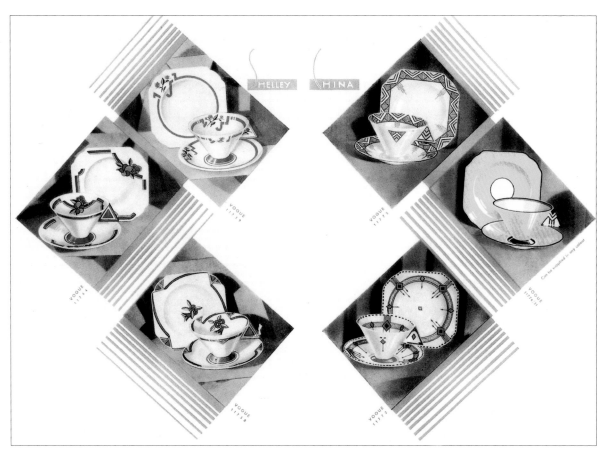

Plate 11.8. Illustration from the 'Silver Book' showing Vogue tea ware. Top to bottom: patterns: page 4, 11739, 11744, 11738; opposite page, patterns 11775, 11776/31, 11772.

Plate 11.9. A page from an advertising leaflet, c.1932, illustrating the Eve shape coffee and dinnerware patterns: coffee set in Yellow Motif, 12572; tea set in Green Motif, 12560 and dinnerware in Pink and Blue Motif, 12559. Also shown is a Mabel Lucie Attwell lamp in 'Our Pets', L.A.19 with a Velinoid shade, approximate height 8in. (20cm).

Plate 11.10. Shelley tea ware. Left to right: a Regent shape coffee cup and saucer, pattern 12289, an Oxford shape teacup and saucer, pattern 12328, an Eve shape coffee cup and saucer, specials pattern 298. This last design would have been specially commissioned and was likely to have been sold as a boxed set of six with matching spoons.

allowed the tea to cool too quickly and the solid handles were difficult to hold; furthermore, some customers had complained that the cups could not be hung up on their usual hooks – and so production ceased in about 1933. It was reported that Shelley's reply was '...we fear we shall have to somehow manage to bore holes through this very attractive handle'.[2] In 1932, however, a new shape range was introduced called *Eve*, based on the *Mode* shape, but with an open triangular handle. Several geometric designs were created for this shape, whilst some of the block patterns originally designed for *Mode* were continued, but the patterns were predominately floral in softer colourways (Plate 11.9).

During the same year another tableware shape range,

Regent designed by Eric Slater, was introduced (Plates 11.10 and 11.11). This tea ware, with its trumpet-shaped cup and a ring handle, was considered to be practical, well balanced and easy to drink from. Again geometric designs were used alongside floral patterns, some of which had been first applied to *Vogue, Mode* and *Eve* shapes. This was another very successful range, being produced right through to the 1950s, with over 220 patterns applied to it. This cup shape was eventually selected by Gordon Forsyth to illustrate good design in his book *20th Century Ceramics* published in 1936.

One of the last Art Deco styled tea ware ranges was *Oxford*. Introduced in 1934 and continuing in production until the late 1940s, it was, like *Regent,* used

Plate 11.11. *Shelley tea ware. Left to right: an Oxford shape cup, saucer and plate, pattern 12381, a Regent shape cup, saucer and plate, decorated with Cape Gooseberry, pattern 12299 and an Oxford shape cup, saucer and plate, pattern 12363.*

for a mixture of geometric and floral designs, with more than 170 patterns and colour variations used for decoration (Plates 11.12 and 11.13).

The number of designs and patterns in production was phenomenal; the shape ranges mentioned here were not the only ones being made and decorated. Looking through the pattern books of the company shows that hundreds of patterns were designed and introduced each year on tableware. In the early 1920s the overall organisation of the works had been redesigned for greater efficiency and many labour saving practices were introduced. Shelley also developed their export markets by maintaining showrooms with major agents throughout the world, especially in the important

colonial markets of Australasia and South Africa. They also appointed agents in Toronto, Canada and New York, U.S.A. and by the end of the 1930s at least sixty percent of production was exported.

Alongside the china production Shelley continued to manufacture earthenware vases, bowls and jugs. In 1931 a new range of matt glazed pottery was introduced decorated with geometric style flowers in bright colours on a pale yellow background banded in brown and blues. These patterns were called *Moresque*, *Flora* and *Persian* and were applied to angular shaped vases and bowls as well as traditional shapes. *Moresque* was not a new pattern but an adaptation of an earlier design by Walter Slater in about 1919 with a lustre glaze

Plate 11.12. A page from an advertising leaflet, c.1932. Posie Spray pattern no 12576 in Oxford tea and dinner ware table settings.

called *Roumanian*. There was also an up-to-date treatment of the black pottery with floral motifs that had proved popular from around 1910 to the early 1920s, using bright colours and a better finish to the black. Patterns such as *Tulips, Jazz Circles* and *Balloons and Splashes* brought a more modern look to the pottery (Plate 11.14).

In 1932 Shelley introduced their range of pottery, *Harmony Ware*, with the initial aim of providing decorated wares in a variety of colours to complement any domestic colour scheme. From the simple banded decoration in graduated shades of one colour, the design developed into bands of different colours running in free flow down the pot, creating a unique design each time (Plate 11.15). The colours used were vibrant oranges, greens and blues with softer pinks mixed with grey and purple. The range was extended to include ginger jars, candlesticks, powder bowls, and items for the table such as teapots, coffee pots, muffin dishes, along with lemon and grapefruit squeezers. The list reads like the earlier production of White Ware china and, indeed, they were probably items originally intended to be sold undecorated but now given the modern treatment.

Plate 11.13. A Shelley lamp base with a rare surviving matching china shade, diameter 8in. (20cm), and Oxford tea cup, saucer and plate decorated with Posie Spray, pattern 12576.

Plate 11.14. A selection of earthenware Shelley Pottery decorated with hand-painted patterns. Left to right: a Cone vase, shape 945, decorated with the Flora pattern 8719, a Volcano vase, shape 926, decorated with the Persian pattern 8724, a space capsule vase, shape 935 decorated with the Moresque pattern 8718, a black vase, shape 776 decorated with the Jazz Circles pattern 8462 and a Cone vase, shape 945 decorated with the Tulips pattern 8727. Height of tallest item 6½in. (16.5 cm).

At the same time there was a range of wares in plain colours with a stippled sponge effect that seemed to progress naturally into the *Handcraft* series (Plate 11.16). The decoration consisted of six patterns of dots, dashes and lines but instead of the bright strident colours of the early 1930s the decoration was muted, which reflected the fashions of the late 1930s.

The greatest change to the entire Shelley marketing strategy probably began in 1925 when Smedley's advertising agency was appointed by the company. This coincided with the change in the design of the backstamp trademark. The company took a full-page advertisement each month in the *Pottery Gazette* and the selection of wares shown changed too, including lines such as jelly moulds, nursery ware by Hilda Cowham and Mabel Lucie Attwell, and decorated earthenware (Plate 11.17). W.H. Smedley, who was from Stoke-on-Trent, came to prominence as a fresh thinker in the pottery advertising business. His reputation had become so large in the industry that he was invited to speak to the Ceramic Society. Smedley's message was simple and his motto was: 'There is no secret in advertising...it is simply a matter of communication and truth'.[3] He believed it was far better to sell the commodity than the

Plate 11.15. A group of Harmony Wares produced from 1932 in many varied combinations of colours. Left to right: a pink and purple 'Apple' preserve jar in Old Hall stand, a space capsule vase in purple through to blue with green interior, an earthenware charger decorated in blue and yellow, diameter 14⅜in. (36.5cm), a small vase in orange, green and grey over pale yellow, a Tulip shape teapot and cup and saucer from a tea for two set in purples over grey, with yellow handles to match the inside of the cups, sugar and milk.

manufacturer's name. As a result the Shelley name took secondary position to the products in these advertisements.

From as early as 1916 Shelley had produced full colour illustrated leaflets for each product line, and even individual patterns, that were distributed to retailers and to the public in response to postal enquiries. National advertising in newspapers such as in *Punch, Good Housekeeping, Radio Times* and the *Daily Telegraph* reached a readership of seven and a half million people. Other publications included *Nursery World, Women's Journal, Home Magazine, Tatler, The Times,* the *Observer*

and the *Daily Mail*. Retailers were reassured that advertising would appear regularly and there would be '...no gap during which the public can forget Shelley China'.

From 1927 to 1931 Shelley produced a magazine called the *Shelley Standard*, published every two months, which was sent out to retailers. The magazine stated, 'Having spent a considerable number of years perfecting Shelley China... the policy we are pursuing is to tell the public – possible purchasers more about its qualities'.[4] It quickly became the vehicle for informing retailers about salesmanship and advertising as well as giving ideas on

Plate 11.16. A selection of hand-painted items from the Shelley Handcraft Series. Left to right, a preserve jar, pattern 8816, a bowl (pattern number unknown), a biscuit barrel and candlestick in pattern 8794, an unusual hand painted vase, shape 977, pattern 383.B and a preserve jar, pattern 8819. Height of biscuit barrel 6in. (15cm) and diameter of candlestick 5⅛in. (13cm).

how to market the *Queen Anne* shape and the new *Vogue* and *Mode* tea ware. The appropriation for advertising had been increased considerably and new literature in the modern style was produced for retailers in the form of better-designed leaflets to be mailed to their customers. The style of the presentation of the ticketing, store cards and leaflets was tied into the national advertising campaigns.

Importantly, the *Shelley Standard* demonstrated that Shelley ware needed special modern displays and suggested window treatments such as friezes of *Mode* cup shapes made with cheap crepe paper[5] and new, well laid out stands which could be supplied by John Sayer, Shelley's representative in Holborn, London to give a

modern effect instead of the normal cluttered look of a china shop window. By July 1930 Shelley were promoting yet another idea. Large backdrop screens measuring 3ft. (0.9m) high and 4ft. (1.2m) wide were available decorated with one of the six major Shelley patterns on them: *Garden Urn, Archway of Roses, Chelsea, Blue Iris, Crabtree* and *Idaleum.*[6]

From 1931 the public could also ask for the new Silver Book of patterns to be sent directly to their home. This catalogue was the ultimate in design (Plate 11.18). Incorporating modern stylish printing and borders with an embossed silver effect cover, it included twenty or more pages showing the most overtly Art Deco styled patterns, especially on the *Vogue* and *Mode* shapes. This

Plate 11.17. A leaflet, c.1930, illustrating Mabel Lucie Attwell designed tea ware, featuring the Animal Series tea set with Duck teapot, Rabbit milk jug and Chicken sugar bowl.

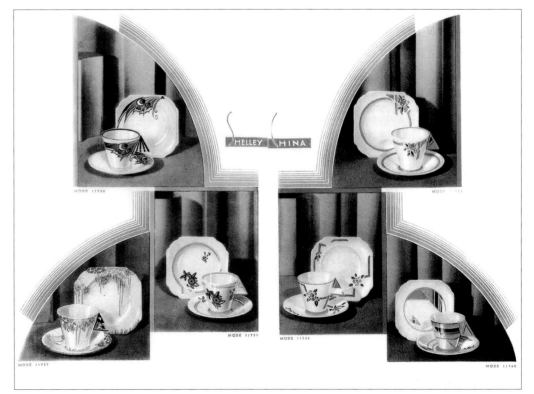

Plate 11.18. Illustrations from the Silver Book showing Mode tea ware. Top to bottom, patterns: page 8, 11758, 11759, 11757; opposite, page 9, 11755, 11756, 11760.

Plate 11.19. An example of the hand-painted bone china Shelley Girl figure used to advertise Shelley Pottery in window displays, c.1925-26. Height of figure 12in. (30.5cm).

catalogue was so popular the firm received over a thousand requests a month for it.

The cost of these co-ordinated advertising campaigns was very expensive with the company spending about £10,000 per year, a huge amount when considering a paintress' weekly wage was less than £3. In order to finance this campaign Percy Shelley had to sell a large number of houses to accumulate the capital that was needed instead of financing his retirement. The advertising was successful, however, and retailers inundated Shelley with orders. Unfortunately Shelley had underestimated the huge demand and had not increased productivity to match the likely orders. The retailers found it hard to get their orders met and cancelled orders were common. This overstretching of production, coupled with Percy Shelley's retirement in 1932, meant that suddenly Shelley reduced their advertising in volume but not quality, which remained high.

One important promotional device was The Shelley Girl created by Smedley Services, in 1927 (Plate 11.19). This stylish figure became a major theme of the advertising to the trade and public, including the famous picture by Elsie Harding of a woman drinking from pure white *Dainty* tea ware (Plate 11.20). She also graced the covers of the *Shelley Standard* magazines where she is hoisting the 'Union Jack of Quality'. As a promotional gimmick paintresses from the factory, dressed in paisley with bobbed hairstyles, were sent out to major department stores to demonstrate the art of painting bone china. They often sat in the shop window so that passers by could be drawn in to watch and then buy some 'finished' Shelley china to take home.

In 1937 Smedley and Shelley parted company due to a dispute over the use of the advertising budget and this resulted in a court case.[7] The quality of presentation of advertising and retail leaflets deteriorated. From February 1938 a new firm, Warwick Savage, Colour Printers of Burslem, Stoke-on-Trent was used to design and print what were now more modest brochures.

During the late 1920s, alongside their national advertising campaign, Shelley ware was shown at several important exhibitions and trade fairs that promoted the Shelley China name and the innovative products that were currently so fashionable. The most important exhibitions of the period that displayed Shelley pottery included:

1. The British China and Glass Exhibition held in

Plate 11.20. *An advertising leaflet for* Dainty White *featuring the Shelley Girl illustration by Elsie Harding (1894-1967). Elsie Harding was a well-known freelance commercial artist and illustrator whose work appeared on the covers of major magazines such as* The Tatler *and* The Illustrated London News.

November 1929 at Chesham House in Regent Street. There the Shelley stand was modern in treatment, being black and white with a background of silver.

2. At the British Industries Fair in 1933 Shelley exhibited *Queen Anne* (decorated with the popular *Sunset and Tall Trees* pattern), *Eve*, *Regent* and

Floral Dainty as well as *Harmony Ware* pottery. The trade press commented that the '... *designs were characteristically free in their conception and the colours fresh and appealing*'.

3. Another important and prestigious exhibition was the Exhibition of British Industrial Art in Relation to the Home at Dorland Hall in London in 1933. Here Shelley showed examples of the new geometrical designs on the *Regent* shape. Gordon Forsyth, the Chairman of the Selection Committee, particularly praised the *Regent* shape.

4. Lastly, at the exhibition 'Everyday Things' at the Royal Institute of British Architects in 1936, a *Regent* shape tea set in the graduated banded pattern called *Swirls* was selected to be shown.

In 1932 Percy Shelley retired to Bournemouth and, following ill health, died in 1937. By the end of the First World War all his sons, Percy Norman and the twins, Kenneth Jack and Vincent Bob, had joined the company and played significant roles in the management of the company. Norman was involved in production, Bob looked after the warehouses and stock control and Jack took charge of the finances. In 1933 Jack Shelley, who had been instrumental in initiating the successful advertising campaign, died in hospital just when his contribution to the firm had begun to bear fruit. It must have been his vision and manipulation of the financial resources that ensured Shelley had the grounding to survive throughout the 1930s.

Finally, it is apparent that, during what is now regarded as the Art Deco period, not only was Shelley at the forefront of the pottery industry at that time with the products of their factory, they were well advanced in their philosophy of advertising. We would think nothing today of a co-ordinated advertising campaign but in the 1930s to gear up their retailers with the slogan 'Our National Advertising is Your Selling Machine'[8] must have been a new and innovative thing.

The Shelley Pottery was known for the improvements they made in the quality of their production and output and the attention they paid to other parts of their business, but it is the china that has stood the test of time. Percy Shelley and his sons after him were, with the help of their Art Directors, determined to produce the finest product they could. On all the literature issued by the factory were the legends 'The trade mark "Shelley" stands for highest quality in pottery of all kinds'[9] and 'As Fine as Fine China can be'.[10] Today collectors of Shelley out hunting for that special item see the Shelley mark on the bottom and, in the words of the catalogues of the time, 'WE ARE SATISFIED – IT'S SHELLEY'.[11]

1. *Pottery Gazette*, 1930, quoted by Watkins, Harvey & Senft, p.101.
2. *The Shelley Standard*, No. XIV, April 1931.
3. Watkins, Harvey & Senft, p.114.
4. *The Shelley Standard*, No. I, January 1927.
5. *The Shelley Standard*, No. XV, October 1931.
6. *The Shelley Standard*, No. X, July 1930.
7. Watkins, Harvey & Senft, p.122.
8. *Pottery Gazette Directory & Diary*, 1937, p.19.
9. Leaflet, *Satisfied It's Shelley*, Whiteware catalogue, c.1925.
10. Leaflet, *Shelley Dainty China*, 1929.
11. Leaflet, *Satisfied It's Shelley*, Whiteware catalogue, c.1925.

12.

Carter, Stabler & Adams

Michael Jeffery

ALTHOUGH CONCENTRATED IN Stoke-on-Trent, the pottery industry in England also had regional satellites, such as Carter, Stabler & Adams in Poole, Dorset, that were set away from the local rivalries enabling them to develop their own unique and individual style.

Although there are records of pottery being made in the region of Poole since pre-history, it was the Industrial Revolution of the nineteenth century, and in particular the growth in use of ceramic tiles, that acted as a catalyst for a concerted development. The perfect geographical location, a coastal port, and fine Dorset clay provided the raw materials and in 1873 Jesse Carter purchased a derelict pottery site on the harbour side. Carter's, as it would become known, produced tiles and architectural pottery which was exhibited as 'Handcraft Pottery' at the British Industries Fairs between 1917 and 1921. It was at

the 1921 exhibition that Charles Carter, Jesse's son, met and formed a relationship with Harold and Phoebe Stabler and with their friend John Adams, leading to the formation of Carter, Stabler & Adams Ltd the same year.

Harold and Phoebe Stabler were a truly dynamic couple. Inspired by and involved in the Arts and Crafts movement, they were also aware of the possibilities of modern manufacturing techniques and materials. Their association with the Carters dates back to before 1921, designing a range of figures, including The Bull, originally made in 1914. Harold was both a designer

Plate 12.1. A selection of figures by Royal Worcester, Carter, Stabler & Adams and by Phoebe Stabler at Hammersmith including The Bull designed by Phoebe and Harold Stabler. These were produced between 1910 and the 1930s.

Plate 12.2. A period display of pottery at the Gieves Gallery c.1923 including Phoebe Stabler's Piping Boy figure, about 1923.

Plate 12.3. A stoneware sculpture of The Galleon designed by Harold Stabler and produced about 1925. Height 10½in. (52cm).

and maker of objects, apprenticing as a cabinet maker and stonemason, rising to director at the Keswick School of Industrial Arts, teaching at the Royal College of Art and a co-founder of the Design and Industries Association. As well as understanding all of the processes of design, he gave to Carter, Stabler & Adams a broad network of important and influential clients; he also brought his wife whom he had met in 1907.

Phoebe Stabler (neé McLeish) developed a range of stoneware figures from 1911, often firing examples in a kiln in her Hammersmith garden. These figure designs were then produced under licence by Carter, Stabler & Adams and also the Ashtead Pottery, Royal Worcester and Royal Doulton. Some of the large scale architectural pieces, including The Galleon, Piping Boy and The Bull, were often used to decorate Carter, Stabler & Adams' exhibitions including their stand at the 1925 Paris exhibition, where they were awarded a Diploma of Honour (Plates 12.1-12.3).

John Adams and his future wife, Truda Sharp, studied at the Royal College of Art and Adams learnt his craft in Stoke-on-Trent. They married in 1914 and went to teach in South Africa, returning in 1919. Following the creation of Carter, Stabler & Adams in 1921, Adams took on the role of managing director (which he held until 1949) whilst still overseeing specific design and glaze experiments. Under Adams' leadership Carter, Stabler & Adams produced a range of simple, often stark, designs (probably designed by him) that reflected the fashion of modernity. Everest and Plane ware were two ranges introduced in the early 1930s that show an understanding of form and design taking it to almost architectural levels. These angular vases, lamps and bowls decorated with angular flange handles, conical feet and simple grooves moulded or cut into the body show inspiration from Continental metalwork and glass designed by companies such as Desny, Tétard Frères, Jean Luce and also the Wiener Werkstätte. These items were often illustrated in black and white in *The Studio* magazine and other trade publications throughout this period and thus were visible to young British designers. Where colour is used it is muted, almost pastel in tone, spray glazed on to the pot using the latest technology and machines. These designs must have sat uncomfortably, for some, with the more traditional hand-painted designs. Although short lived, they are the precursors of Keith Murray's radical designs for Josiah Wedgwood and Sons and provided the experience for further more successful ranges. The company received critical approval and current ranges were illustrated in the *Pottery Gazette* in 1933.

These glaze experiments were further developed with ranges called *Picotee* and *Twintone*, spray glaze novelties including wall-pockets, sculptures and dishes that were more commercially successful. John Adams created a range of graduated wall decorations between 1936 and 1939 including the now traditional bluebird, mallard ducks and seagulls and a complementary range of graduated sailing yachts for the table.

As well as novelties, John Adams also developed the tea ware ranges adding designs to Harold Stabler's classic *Studland* shape. As managing director he saw the business opportunities of the expanding market and with designs including *Purbeck* and *Streamline* he provided the consumer with modernist ceramic domestic ware that was decorated with simple spray glazed colour combinations.

His wife, Truda Adams,[1] was in charge of developing patterns to fit the rapidly growing range of shapes

Plate 12.4. An earthenware vase decorated with the rare pattern 916/AW designed by Truda Carter, about 1928-34. Height 14⅛in. (36cm).

Plate 12.5. A French pochoir print showing the direct inspiration for Truda Carter's AW pattern.

Plate 12.7. An earthenware dish decorated with the Leaping Gazelle pattern (EF), designed by Truda Carter and painted by Anne Hatchard, c.1930. Diameter 9½in. (24.5cm).

Plate 12.6. A lesser known design by Truda Carter 693/AB, from about 1926-31. Height 12½in. (32. cm).

Plate 12.8. A wall charger decorated with the SL pattern, probably designed by Truda Carter, about 1935. Diameter 14½in. (37cm).

Plate 12.9. Three vases designed by Truda Carter: twin-handled JX pattern vase painted by Eileen Prangnell, tall BR pattern painted by Anne Hatchard and BX painted by Eileen Prangnell, c.1935.

produced. She designed over a twenty-year period. Carter's had developed a range of simple foliate designs to decorate their early wares and Truda Carter developed these into complex polychrome patterns filling more of the surface area. These designs, like those of her contemporaries (most famously Clarice Cliff),

relied on the skilled brushwork and interpretation by her paintresses including Anne Hatchard, employed from 1918, and Ruth Pavely from 1922. The floral patterns became both more complex and also more geometrically abstract as she took inspiration from the Continental designs for textiles and paper. This can clearly be seen in

Poole Pottery

Painting the Design

Plate 12.10. An archive photograph showing paintresses decorating pottery.

synonymous with Carter, Stabler & Adams (Plate 12.7). This design, attributed to both John Adams and Truda Carter and probably a collaboration, was used as a painted design on plates and vases and also modelled as a freestanding book-end. This image has strong connections with their African homeland but was also used by Robert Bonfils on both a poster and the cover for the catalogue for the Exposition Internationale des Arts Décoratifs et Industriels Modernes.

Although Truda Carter produced the majority of the designs for the company during this period, other artists and designers were invited by both Harold Stabler and John Adams to create patterns. Often these artists were London friends or had developed links from the Royal College of Art. A notable example was the work of Olive Bourne who created a small but distinctive range in the late 1920s. These designs included a rare use of a painted human form in designs *Leipzig Girl* and *Sugar for the Birds* exhibited at the international Exhibition of Industrial Art, Leipzig 1927. Other artists, including the sculptor Harold Brownsword FRBS (1885-1964), designed figural candlesticks, animal book-ends and a knight on horseback book-end.

Edward Bawden was another Royal College of Art student who designed for the company. In 1932 he produced a series of tile designs, including a portrait of the Poole factory, that were used to decorate the Tea Room at the pottery. The tiles depicted fashionably dressed young people driving past the factory with smoke billowing from its bottle kiln. As well as producing designs for tiles the fashionable vignettes were also used for publicity brochures for the factory (Plate 12.12).

Carter, Stabler & Adams, free from the oppressive nature of the Potteries as a location and led by a group of forward-thinking modern designers, was able to produce a range of unique designs that were at the height of fashion. Taking inspiration from the Continent, the exotic Orient and Africa, whilst not forgetting the long history of hand-painted decorative ware produced in Britain, its ability to cater for a variety of different markets led to a large expansion of the company during the period from 1914 to the outbreak of World War II. Over this period the company expanded from eleven employees to eighty-five in 1938 and plans were drawn up for building a new factory.

some of the boldest designs such as AW with its striking wavy black columns lifted directly by Truda Carter (Plate 12.4) from the art deco designs from pochoir prints by artists including Edouard Bénédictus and Atelier Martine who themselves sought inspiration from the exotic designs of ancient Egypt and classical civilisation (Plate 12.5). Truda Carter also drew from African tribal art, another source of inspiration for avant-garde art deco designers, although she and her husband would have seen this exotic in its homeland when they lived in South Africa (Plate 12.6).

One other inspiration can be seen in the classic leaping gazelle or stag that, in England, has become

1. She was better known as Truda Carter. She divorced John Adams in 1925 and married Cyril Carter in 1929.

Plate 12.11. A large drum vase decorated with pattern LG, designed by Truda Carter, about 1928. Height 13⅜in. (34cm).

Plate 12.12. A selection of tiles from the Tea Room at the Poole factory designed by Edward Bawden, c.1932.

13.

Burleigh Art Deco:
A New Dawn

Julie McKeown

FOR SOME BURLEIGH MEANS ONLY ONE THING: blue and white. But for others the brand name used by Burgess & Leigh[1] will always be associated with art deco. In fact, both types of pottery represent consecutive high points of success in the history of the Potteries family firm, export of underglaze blue printed domestic wares establishing the company's global reputation in the nineteenth century and mass production of hand-painted 'fancies' and tablewares consolidating it in the twentieth.

It is interesting to question how a company like Burgess & Leigh, whose mainstay of manufacture since 1862 had been traditional, utilitarian patterns like *Willow*, *Rhine* and *Asiatic Pheasant*, came to adopt the art deco style so emphatically during the 1920s and '30s. What led to the introduction of its innovative, high-fashion, hand-decorated pottery: tube-lined designs by Charlotte Rhead; yellow glazed flower jugs modelled by Charles Wilkes and Ernest Bailey; and stylish tablewares by Harold Bennett? The answer predictably lies in economics. In the 1920s Burgess & Leigh Ltd[2] faced increased competition for both its shrinking colonial export market and recession-hit home trade. Changes in lifestyle also caused a drop in sales of many of its staple items: large ornamental items such as jardinières and stands; toilet sets; and the multiplicity of domestic-ware items used in large pre-war households. All were now surplus to requirement in the 'homes fit for heroes' of Britain's suburbs.

The search to identify new profitable areas of production became part of a wider debate on popular taste and design, which in the Potteries was led by art educationalist and ceramics industry adviser Gordon Forsyth.[3] Doubtless, Burgess & Leigh was initially more concerned with financial survival than art school

Plate 13.1. *An advertisement for Dawn, Burgess & Leigh's most successful art deco tableware pattern, from Pottery Gazette, 1 April, 1932.*

theorising on good design. However, under its pragmatic leadership,[4] the company was prepared to follow the example of similar sized earthenware manu-facturers, Myott & Sons, Meakin and A.J. Wilkinson,[5]

104

Plate 13.2. The Decorating Shop at the Middleport Pottery in the 1930s, with paintresses freehand painting Dawn tableware and flower jugs.

who, in response to Forsyth's recommendations, had placed original design and craftsmanship at the heart of their manufacture. Importantly, their new, commercially successful art deco wares did not require expensive investment in the sub-standard lithographic sheets then available; they were hand painted by easily trained (and lowly paid) females (Plate 13.2) and could be quickly changed or adapted for a fashion-conscious public.

The company's first steps towards new innovative products were tentative. The Design Studio established at the Middleport Pottery[6] in 1889 could not boast an influential and individualistic art designer, just two little known, long-term employees, 'Designer' Edwin Leigh[7] (d.1936) and modeller Charles Wilkes (1864-1957).[8] Securing the loyalty of conservative customers,

'Designer' Leigh introduced new conventional patterns, such as Ye Olde 'Dillwyn' Willow which utilised the pottery's traditional and versatile method of underglaze printing, and the heavily promoted (but ultimately unsuccessful) series 'Merrie England' (Plate 13.3) which was decorated with brighter lithographic-printed designs by the illustrator Cecil Aldin.[9]

Rising to the challenge of attracting a new consumer with a jazz age aesthetic, 'Designer' Leigh also oversaw more contemporary designs which were well received at the British Industries Fairs. Decorative ranges such as the 1920 lustre glazed Urbino 'bid fair appeal to the modern taste'[10] whilst a 1921 collection of large Arts and Crafts style wall plaques by freelance designer Louis Thomas Swettenham[11] were 'splendidly drawn,

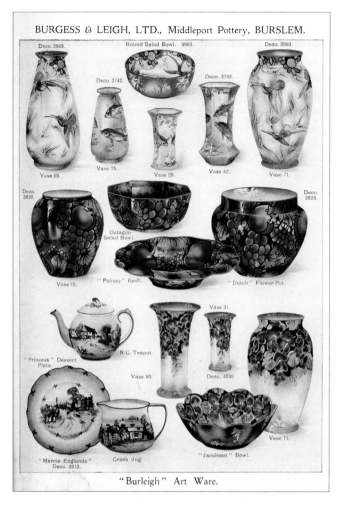

Plate 13.3. *Page from a Burleigh catalogue of c.1927 showing wares including Merrie England, bottom left, and more modern design, shapes and decoration, such as, in the centre, a lustre pattern decorated by William or George Adams.*

Plate 13.4. *Burleigh Art Ware patterns from a catalogue of c.1927. Those illustrated include Charlotte Rhead's tube-lined designs: with anemone border (3973); Gouda (4001); with peonies (4002) and with fruits (4016).*

wonderfully free in their conception and execution, and worthy of finding a place of honour amongst the ceramic relics of the present age.'[12] 'Designer' Leigh selected popular '20s motifs – Oriental birds, exotic fish and fruit, mermaids and dolphins, butterflies, insects and dragons – for printing on to Wilkes' versatile and fashionable shapes: square spill jars, trinket-sets, powder-bowls and floating-bowls and registered 'suite ware'[13] items, such as the *Windsor, Richmond* and *Crescent* sandwich sets and the *Avon, Rex* and *Regina* fruit sets.

These so-called *Burleigh Art Wares*, together with printed suite ware ranges such as *Satsuma* and *Paisley*, capitalised on the art deco vogue for bright colours and

glazes. Vivid reds, oranges, yellows, blues and mauves were favoured, often with a contrasting black. Such colours might be painted underglaze or hand enamelled. Backgrounds were mottled, aerographed or lustred by decorators William Adams and his son George on patterns such as *Pomegranate, Lilium* and *Sunflower*. The distinctive decoration of *Riverside*, issued in 1925, prompted the *Pottery Gazette* to report that Burgess & Leigh were 'not afraid of producing treatments which are quite different in type from anything which has previously been offered'.

Such encouragement in the year of the Paris Exposition may have prompted the company to recruit new blood to the Design Studio the following year. The choice of

Plate 13.5. Underglaze painted plaque (4111), tube-lined by Charlotte Rhead, c.1928. Its design was inspired by a 1921 plaque by Louis Thomas Swettenham. Diameter 14in. (35cm).

Charlotte Rhead (1885-1947) may also have been influenced by the attention then being received by female designers. Rhead's family could boast a distinguished background in ceramic education and design and her artistic credentials were emphasised in Burgess & Leigh's announcement in the *Pottery Gazette*[14] that they had 'secured the services of the accomplished lady artist Charlotte Rhead who has produced for us a number of original decorations, all pure Handcraft.' The claim for originality was not entirely true as the decoration of some of Rhead's earliest Burleigh patterns drew heavily on designs she had previously produced for Wood & Sons[15] where her father was Art Director. However, the shapes used by Rhead, although shared with a

Plate 13.6. Burleigh deco tea ware, shape by Ernest Bailey and patterns by Harold Bennett, left to right: Seville (5021) on Zenith shape teapot and jug; Riviera (5088) on Imperial shape teapot and jug; and unnamed pattern (4823) on Zenith shape teapot. Height approximately 7in. (18cm.)

variety of other Burleigh wares, were unique to Burgess & Leigh. They included both ornamental and tableware items, modelled by Wilkes and from 1927 his young assistant Ernest Bailey (1911-1987),[16] and occasionally shapes embossed with a vine or strawberry pattern taken from nineteenth century Davenport sprig moulds.[17]

Whilst the tube-lining technique used by Rhead and her small team of artists[18] dated from the 1890s, her stylistic influences owed more to contemporary art deco: exuberant colour; Orientalism; geometric motifs; and stylised patterns based on natural forms of fruit, flowers, and females. *Gouda*, a stylised rose design inspired by Dutch art pottery, was one of four of Rhead's earliest patterns illustrated in Burgess & Leigh's catalogue of c.1927 (Plate 13.4). Around that time she tube-lined a number of large, complex wall plaques: a Japanese woman; a pheasant amongst pomegranates; a Persian floral pattern; and an exotic female with grapes (Plate 13.5).[19] Cost seems to have deterred production and she afterwards concentrated on simpler, economical patterns with a reduced palette, like *Garland*, a leaf and apple border, and *Sylvan*, with stylised trees.

Rhead's early underglaze colours, a feature of Burleigh Wares, were later replaced by bright on-glaze enamels and lustres. Occasionally her designs were also translated into prints, such as *Rutland* (also called *Trellis*), a rectilinear fruit pattern produced on tea wares and sandwich sets. One of the simplest and most effective of Rhead's designs was *Sunshine*. Composed of short dashes tubed in black against an aerographed yellow border, this pattern was applied not only to a fifty-four piece dinner service but a huge variety of suite ware items including egg sets, cruets and five-bar toast racks. Clarice Cliff's *Bizarre* ware may have prompted more dramatic colours, evident in such patterns as *Carnival* which was enamelled in bold black, red, coral and yellow. However, Rhead's colouring subsequently became more subdued and her designs pared down, as seen in *Florentine*,[20] a geometric design, lustred in muted greens and browns on a mottled brown ground, whose chunky shapes suggest an influence of studio or medieval Italian pottery. *Florentine* was introduced shortly before the designer left the Middleport Pottery in 1931. A reticent personality, Rhead was not especially well known in her lifetime and even today her reputation as an art deco designer is overshadowed, not least by that of her brother, Frederick H. Rhead, designer of Homer Laughlin's influential modernist tableware pattern, *Fiesta*.[21] None the less, for five years Rhead's popular, inexpensive designs pronounced the arrival of Burgess & Leigh as a modern, competitive presence within the industry.

From 1929 this endeavour was shared by Harold Bennett RI, NRD (1893-1976) who replaced 'Designer' Leigh as Art Director in 1931.[22] As a watercolour artist of local and national recognition, Bennett also brought an artistic sensibility to Burleigh art deco wares, but, whereas Rhead's decorative style was, paradoxically, more flamboyant and exotic, the lightly printed, hand-enamelled tableware designs of the extrovert Bennett demonstrated a relatively quiet restraint. Most depicted trees, such as the extraordinarily successful and innovative *Dawn* (Plate 1) which the trade press described in 1932 as:

> so un-like anything they had previously attempted, and yet so obviously sympathetic towards the changing outlook of ordinary folk contemplating the purchase of a new suite of tableware... [It] revealed an intelligent appreciation of what the public was demanding, or was likely to demand...

portraying a very effective modern style of treatment, striking a note of real distinction, yet setting, as it were, a new fashion.

Favourite flowers of the '30s were chosen for patterns such as *Lupins*, *Bluebell*, *Pansy* and *Daffodil* whilst a more whimsical note was sounded in *Dawn*'s rival, *Pan*.[23] The simply drawn outlines of Bennett's designs and the economy of clear, bright colour created subtle nuances of place, mood or time which were quint-essentially English. Even those patterns with more cosmopolitan aspirations, such as *Biarritz* or *Riviera* (Plate 13.6), evoked the safety and security of the south of England rather than the sophisticated pleasures of France.

The success of Bennett's patterns was partly attributable to the compatible art deco tableware shapes designed by Ernest Bailey, particularly the conical-shaped *Zenith* of 1931 and the more ovoid *Imperial* of 1934. Their naturalistically moulded details, a stylised leaf decoration in the case of *Zenith* and a geometric 'cottage' of *Imperial*, had the effect of softening, even Anglicising, their design. Described in the trade press as 'completely modern without reaching extremes',[24] *Zenith*'s design had immediate appeal to the fashionable rather than *outré* home market whilst the

Plate 13.7. Kitsch 'fancies': a wall plaque, wall pocket and variously coloured posy troughs, modelled by Ernest Bailey in the form of a Native American Indian, c.1935. Largest diameter approximately 13in. (33cm).

Plate 13.8. Burleigh yellow glazed flower jugs, modelled by Ernest Bailey. Left to right: Squirrel with printed leaf pattern (5059); Squirrel with freehand tree and blue leaves (5247); Harvest with cornflowers (5076); Fox and Flowers (pattern number unknown); and Fox in the Cornfield (5151). Tallest 10in. (25.4cm).

more conventional *Imperial* also found acceptance, as its name implies, with Burgess & Leigh's conservative colonial market. The mid-1930s saw the introduction of *Belvedere,* with an embossed ribbed effect, and *Balmoral*, whose streamlined curvilinear shape with the *Moiré* pattern brought enduring commercial success. The option of more traditional patterns, such as *Indian Tree*, was made available through the 1937 acquisition of Keeling & Co's *Losol Ware* brand.

In complete contrast were Burleigh Ware 'fancies' (Plate 13.7). Modelled by Bailey, these novelties – including posy troughs with seagull, sailing ship or polar bear motifs; gladioli or budgerigar-shaped wall pockets; hat-shaped flower baskets; Native American Indian wall masks; and *Cauliflower Ware* – all veer close to the commercial kitsch produced by many pottery manufacturers during the art deco period. (That Bailey had other aspirations is evident from his prototype modernist sculptures for a series putatively called *The Age of Speed*.) *Verona,* a later 1930s relief-decorated series by Wilkes, displayed more subtlety, with muted green matt or oatmeal glazes. This range included a plaque with the omnipresent art deco motif, the deer, moulded in sharp relief against a striated background.

Bailey, together with Wilkes, was also responsible for the modelling of Burleigh Ware flower jugs (Plate 13.8). Selling some 250,000 from the 1930s to after the war, they were, together with *Dawn* tableware, the most successful of Burleigh art deco wares. The inspiration for these 'modern' jugs was prompted by the discovery of the company's nineteenth century Samuel Alcock & Co moulds[25] and drew on earlier Staffordshire relief-decorated jugs. Production was again economical, utilising factory space and sometimes moulds previously employed in the manufacture of large toilet jugs. Individually quite distinctive in subject matter and design, the collection of some twenty-five jugs[26] shared certain decorative characteristics: low relief modelling; a 'feature' handle usually modelled as an animal, a bird or a person; a distinctive primrose yellow glaze to the exterior; a vivid contrasting colour aerographed to the interior; and bright hand-painted decoration, sometimes including a rim of black painted dashes (Burleigh's so-called 'sunshine' edge also used on tableware patterns). In common with most '30s Burleigh wares, the jugs were available in several colour and glaze versions, with some designs also inspiring ranges of embossed tea wares.

Although more often painted in on-glaze enamels by

Plate 13.9. *Stylised flower jugs and vases, modelled by Ernest Bailey with decoration devised by Harold Bennett. Left to right: Ovoid (5214); Troy (5170); Meridian (5176) painted by William Adams; Luxor (5166) with Leaping Gazelles pattern; and Ovoid (5205), c.1933-1934. Tallest approximately 8in. (20cm).*

Plate 13.10. *Items of named Burleigh nurseryware patterns, all printed on-glaze in black, with enamelled and aerographed colours, and black 'sunshine' edges, 1930s. Largest plate diameter 8¾in. (22cm).*

piece-work paintresses, some jugs were given subtle underglaze shading by male decorators such as Adams and Fred Ridgway.[27] The men also occasionally worked on other contrasting series, including a range of stylised jugs, *Zenith, Ovoid, Meridian, Argosy, Luxor* and *Troy* (Plate 13.9), whose geometric forms and vivid abstract or naturalistic patterns represent the high style of art deco, and a collection of relief-decorated figurative *Reproduction Period Jugs* featuring reissues of Alcock jugs and several new designs modelled by Bailey in a similar traditional style.[28]

Burleigh flower jugs earned royal approval with their purchase by Queen Mary in 1932. The following year she also ordered items of *Chick-Chick*, one of a number of quirky art deco nurserywares designed by Rhead and

Bennett.[29] Decorated with playful 'print and tint' patterns over aerographed colours, a black 'sunshine edge' and a printed pattern name such as *Bunny, Quack Quack* or *Bow-Wow*, these tea wares for fashion-conscious under-fives demonstrated a clear departure from the self-improving nature of the company's Victorian printed children's ware (Plate 13.10).

Art deco brought a bright, transient release from the monochromatic sobriety of much of Burgess & Leigh's earlier manufacture, with *Dawn* heralding a dazzling decade of creative, commercial – and economical – pottery manufacture. Whilst blue and white has remained in permanent production, Burleigh art deco enjoys episodic revivals, its passing from innovation to tradition signifying its enduring and appealing style.

1. Burgess & Leigh's brand name, Burleigh Ware, was registered in 1903. In 1999 the five-generation firm was saved from receivership by Rosemary and William Dorling and now trades as Burgess, Dorling & Leigh from the Grade II listed Middleport Pottery. Initially reproducing a selection of 1930s designs, it has now returned to its roots manufacturing Victorian-style printed earthenwares, of which the best known is blue *Calico*.
2. Burgess & Leigh became a limited company in 1919.
3. Forsyth was Superintendent of Art Instruction for Stoke-on-Trent City Art Schools and Art Adviser to the British Pottery Manufacturers' Federation.
4. The company was then in the sole ownership of the Leigh family. Edmund Leigh JP (1854-1924), son of the founder, was Company Chairman. Perhaps the key figure in Burgess & Leigh's early success, he was a progressive, paternalistic employer and also played a significant role in municipal life and local politics as a Liberal. Following his death in 1924, he was succeeded by his sons Kingsley and Dennis.
5. Edmund Leigh became co-owner of A.J. Wilkinson in 1894.
6. Burgess & Leigh occupied the Central Pottery (1862-68) and the Hill Pottery (1868-88), both in Burslem, before moving to its modern architect-designed canal-side works, the Middleport Pottery.
7. 'Designer' Edwin Leigh was not related to the Leigh family, owners of the pottery. Little is known of his background before his appointment by Burgess & Leigh in 1889.
8. Burslem School of Art educated, Wilkes was apprenticed at Josiah Wedgwood & Sons before his appointment as modeller at the Middleport Design Studio in 1889. He retired in 1943.
9. Bumpus, Bernard, 'Cecil Aldin's Pottery Designs', *The Antique Collector,* August 1988.
10. *Pottery Gazette,* 1920.
11. Records in the Burgess, Dorling & Leigh archives

indicate that the Minton-trained artist Swettenham had provided freelance designs for the company since the late nineteenth century. He also worked for Royal Doulton.
12. *Pottery Gazette,* 1 April 1921.
13. 'Suite ware' was a range of complementary tableware items, such as fruit and dessert services, single-, double- and triple- sweet trays, 'tennis-sets', toast racks, egg-baskets and sardine boxes, which Wilkes designed for the company from the 1890s.
14. *Pottery Gazette,* 1 March 1927.
15. Rhead also worked for Wood & Sons' allied companies, Bursley Ltd and the Ellgreave Pottery Co.
16. Bailey was a prize-winning student at both Newcastle-under-Lyme and Burslem Art Schools before joining Burgess & Leigh. He retired c.1981.
17. In 1928, the year Cliff launched her 'Bizarre' range which utilised old stocks of inferior ware, Burgess & Leigh reproduced a collection of suited tea wares, *Old Davenport,* embossed with a vine or strawberry pattern, from sprig moulds they had acquired on the closure of Davenport c.1887. They were usually decorated by William and George Adams, in a variety of different finishes including lustring, gilding and bright enamel colouring.
18. It is thought that Rhead trained about three or four artists to tube-line her patterns.
19. This latter was based on Louis Thomas Swettenham's 1921 design.
20. *Florentine* was also the name of an earlier Rhead pattern with fruits and leaves on a dark blue ground.
21. F.H. Rhead was Art Director of the Homer Laughlin China Company in West Virginia, USA, from 1927-1942.
22. Bernard Bumpus suggests that Rhead had a clash of personalities with Bennett. Her departure coincided with Bennett's appointment as Art Director, a post she may have wished for herself.
23. The design of *Pan* is remarkably similar to a

1928 Royal Doulton Series Ware pattern, *Pipes of Pan* (D4784).
24. *Pottery Gazette,* 1 April 1932, p.457.
25. On moving in 1868 to the Hill Pottery, previously home to S. Alcock & Co, Burgess & Leigh had acquired a number of jug moulds and copper engravings at auction.
26. The jugs are known as: *Squirrel, Parrot, Kangaroo, Dragon, Kingfisher, Flamingo, Harvest, Dick Turpin* or *Highwayman, Guardsman, Fox in the Cornfield, Stork and Fox, Monkey and Cat, Rock Garden, Galleon, Palm, Honeycomb, Pheasant, Butterflies, Budgerigar, Vine* and *Pixie.* A set of *Sporting Jugs* comprised: *Cricketer, Golfer* and *Tennis Player.*
27. Ridgway had trained Clarice Cliff at the Newport Pottery before coming to Burgess & Leigh c.1931. Casey, Andrew, *20th Century Ceramic Designers in Britain,* Chapter 3, *The Original Bizarre Girl, Clarice Cliff,* p.72, Antique Collectors' Club 2001.
28. The jugs produced in the '30s were Alcock's *Old Feeding Time* and Bailey's original *Sally in our Alley, The Stocks, The Runaway Marriage* (or *Gretna Green*) and *The Village Blacksmith.* The designs were also used for a series of relief-decorated underglaze painted plaques.
29. It is not clear whether it was Rhead or Bennett who designed the earliest Burleigh nurserywares of the 1930s: *Bunny, Quack Quack, Bow-Wow, Baa-Baa* and *Chick-Chick.* Their pattern numbers were amongst those allocated to Rhead but the nurserywares were issued following her departure in 1931. Factory records show Rhead's name written against the following: *Chickens, Cats, Dogs* and *Jack and Jill Went Up the Hill, Mary Mary Quite Contrary* and *Cinderella,* these last nursery rhyme patterns being stylistically identical to those she produced for the Crown Ducal brand.

14.

A.J. Wilkinson

Greg Slater

STARTING IN THE LATE 1920s, the products from a myriad of British potteries offered at low cost the less affluent a little or a lot of eye-catching pottery whose bright cheerful colours and intriguing shapes captured a small part of an exotic 'modern' world. Significant amongst the many potteries in Stoke-on-Trent, A.J. Wilkinson became one of the most successful producers of British art deco ceramics. Drawing inspiration from Continental sources, its own in-house designers produced an interesting and diverse range of designs and shapes that developed this particular British art deco style, extending it well into the 1930s. In an ironic echo of the Wiener Werkstätte movement, this mass-produced ware was frequently offered as 'art for the table'.[1] With less irony, it was actually affordable to the public and profitable to the firm.

A.J. Wilkinson pottery was established in 1885 by Arthur J. Wilkinson, whose daughter was to marry Arthur Shorter, the owner of the pottery, Shorter and Co. Following the untimely death of Arthur Wilkinson, Arthur Shorter acquired the company in 1894. In 1898 Colley Shorter joined his father at A.J. Wilkinson's and became a director of the company in 1916, the same year that Clarice Cliff was employed at the pottery. From its beginning, A.J. Wilkinson was a successful pottery whose porcelain and earthenware found a ready market in conventional decorative and hotel ware. With the employment in 1904 of John Butler as Art Director, the range of ware offered expanded to include quality studio art pottery that would attract high praise and industry awards.

During the 1920s, A.J. Wilkinson regularly received supportive publicity from such periodicals as *The Pottery and Glass Record*. Although most of the designs used at A.J. Wilkinson for both shapes and patterns were Edwardian and traditional in style, articles in this publication frequently gave high praise to the quality and imaginativeness of the ware and its decoration. The periodical often admired the factory's constant search for new ideas in pattern and shape design together with its inventive on-glaze and under-glaze treatments. Noted for particular praise in an early review, Clarice Cliff was described as 'a clever lady modeller'.[2] This is a description that would become true throughout her working lifetime of over three decades. The reporter commented favourably on the quality of Cliff's figurines including *London Cries* and a *Milady* powder puff-box. Although much of A.J. Wilkinson's later art deco inspired designs are inextricably linked to Clarice Cliff's name, it would appear from the shapes that were produced by this pottery in the mid-1920s that this outstanding female designer was yet to be influenced by Continental fashions. Despite the predominantly traditional factory output, there is some evidence in the remaining factory pattern books that John Butler was at least aware of and interested in experimenting with the leading European design concepts.

Early A.J. Wilkinson art deco

In 1924 John Butler designed a number of tableware patterns whose combinations of geometric and stylised floral elements both separate them from the other still Edwardian patterns and suggest Continental influences.[3] The combinations of geometric and stylised floral elements in these designs predict many of Clarice Cliff's early 1930 patterns. For his 1925 *Egyptian Lotus*[4] design, John Butler drew on ancient Egyptian depictions of lotus flowers to develop this simple but distinctive design (Plate 14.1). Most likely inspired by the heightened interest in ancient Egyptian themes, occasioned by the discovery of Tutankhamun's tomb in 1922, this hand-enamelled lithograph was decorated in

Plate 14.1. A pattern book entry showing pattern number 6997, Egyptian Lotus, designed by John Butler in 1925.

a startling array of colours and glaze treatments. Whether sparingly or intricately hand enamelled, *Egyptian Lotus* was easily produced in many colourways.[5]

The *Lotus* and *Isis* shapes, for which this pattern was designed, attracted much praise in 1922 for their clean lines and hand-thrown appearance.[6] 'Art for the table' had met an Egyptian pastiche – art deco had arrived at A.J. Wilkinson. Arguably, these became the first art deco designs to be produced by A.J. Wilkinson representing a pre-echo of Clarice Cliff's later *Le Bon Dieu* and *Lynton* shape ranges that were specifically slip cast to look hand thrown. John Butler's *Isis* and *Lotus* vases were handsome pieces that remained in production at A.J. Wilkinson until well into the 1930s. They were a sympathetic shape on to which some of the most striking art deco patterns were later to be decorated. Despite this

promising start, John Butler did not pursue the development of further patterns that reflected contemporary European design styles. From inspection of the A.J. Wilkinson pattern books, most designs over the next two years (1925-27) were to be traditional Edwardian patterns with a slant towards adapted Oriental decoration.

In 1924 there appears to have been a tentative attempt by A.J. Wilkinson to produce its own version of European peasant pottery with a pattern called *Keltique* and bearing a facsimile of Colley Shorter's signature. This design shows stylised flowers and leaves outlined in blue and painted underglaze. To fill the undecorated space, contour lines have been added. Although there is no information in the Wilkinson pattern books to identify the author of this pattern, the subject matter and its style of execution is indicative of that which Clarice Cliff was later to use with great success. The use of a signature as part of the backstamp shows A.J. Wilkinson's active searching for additional advertising 'angles' that would give the ware extra 'cachet'.

By the beginning of 1928, probably motivated by the unexpected success of Clarice Cliff's experiment (now known as *Original Bizarre*), art deco inspired patterns started to appear in the Wilkinson pattern books. Rather than relying on a single designer's approach to this 'new', colourful ware, it is noticeable that A.J. Wilkinson encouraged three distinct but related design streams, each by a particular designer pursuing his or her own style. The already established designers, John Butler and Dolly Cliff, began experimenting with colourful designs whilst Clarice Cliff moved into her expanded role of pattern and shape designer to advance the evolution of her *Original Bizarre* patterns into more sophisticated designs. Together, all three designers contributed to the success of the factory and a market prominence that was to remain strong well into the 1930s. Driven by market demands, the suddenness and extent of the inclusion of new, hand-painted patterns alongside traditional lithographed and hand-enamelled designs was remarkably swift.

John Butler

Apart from exercising artistic direction across the entire A.J. Wilkinson range, John Butler supervised his own studio where exquisite, high quality, studio ware was produced. His three principal studio ranges were *Oriflamme*, *Rubáíyát* and *Tibetan*[7] ware, all three of

Plate 14.2. An earthenware dish decorated with the Tahiti Camellia *pattern number 8645 designed by John Butler, 1929.*

which represented a high point in A.J. Wilkinson art pottery that the factory was afterwards never to match in terms of technique and complexity of decorating techniques. In 1928, John Butler moved away from *Oriflamme, Rubaíyát* and *Tibetan* ware to produce patterns that captured the feeling of the new design movement. This was not a particularly radical move as these already established studio ranges did, in fact, mix various styles with complex designs drawn from various sources and re-worked in novel ways. However, the newer designs in 1928, when compared with the

contemporary A.J. Wilkinson mainstream, are at once striking and fresh, indicative of his flexible and adaptive design genius.

Probably the first of John Butler's 'new style' designs was his August 1928 reworking of *Storm*.[8] This was to be the first of many similar patterns in which he fused art nouveau flowers with abstract motifs. Perhaps his most successful range, from the late '20s, was the *Tahiti* series. The range name extends from *Rubaíyát* and *Tibetan* to reflect Butler's awareness of the commercial value of exotic place names. Escapism and the exotic are

Plate 14.3. An earthenware Isis vase decorated with the hand-painted Tahiti Foam *pattern number 8643, designed by John Butler 1929.*

recurrent themes within Wilkinson's pattern and shape names. Although quite distinct from other A.J. Wilkinson designs, *Tahiti* ware has been generally thought to utilise Clarice Cliff's *Inspiration* ware techniques for its decoration. Reference to pattern book instructions indicate that the *Tahiti* range was decorated using conventional on- and under-glaze painting methods together with an imaginative use of matt glazes and lustres. All of these techniques were already well established at A.J. Wilkinson.

Commencing in November 1928 with pattern number 8573,[9] this series of at least twenty-two designs was to include the last patterns that John Butler would design for A.J. Wilkinson. Produced in February 1929, the exquisite *Tahiti Regatta, Foam, Papaver* and *Camellia* (Plates 14.2 and 14.3) exemplify this range's urbane patterns that were in sharp contrast to the striking contemporary abstracts and landscapes that Clarice Cliff was producing. Aimed at a section of the market different from *Bizarre* ware, *Tahiti* included designs of fish, butterflies and flowers mostly decorated on a soft, matt blue glaze. This range continued John Butler's factory contribution, at a lower price level, from his by then dated, high quality and expensive studio ware.

Tahiti patterns were complex hand-painted designs. Requiring high-level painting skills together with multiple firings, this range did not lend itself to high volume production or low input costs. As in most of John Butler's late 1920s patterns, long and detailed pattern book instructions attest to the complexity of production. Frequently, these designs bear either a signature of John Butler or L. Allen and it is thought that this latter person was a paintress, '…Mrs Allen, who sat at the back of the Bizarre decorating shop, painting special patterns'.[10]

Promoted until 1930 as middle market, studio ware,[11] *Tahiti* enjoyed considerable popularity despite its comparatively high retail prices. Of the many *Tahiti* designs identified in the A.J. Wilkinson pattern books, only one pattern in this range, *Leaf Tree,*[12] was to be re-issued by Clarice Cliff in 1932 as part of her *Café au Lait* series.

Contemporary with the *Tahiti* range, John Butler produced some surprising designs for tea ware whose patterns were inspired by the style of abstract painters[13] of the period (Plate 14.4). As with *Tahiti* and similar designs, these remarkable patterns were complex and time consuming to decorate.

It is perhaps a measure of John Butler's artistic integrity that he had difficulty in moving away from studio designs that needed skilled operatives and many production steps. Although he demonstrated the ability to design contemporary patterns, they could not be easily decorated on a production line, making them uneconomic in comparison to *Bizarre* ware. Not only were John Butler's patterns complex, but they required a different level of painting expertise from that required to decorate Clarice Cliff's designs. Close inspection of hand-painted designs in the *Rubáiyát* or *Oriflamme* ranges reveals a painting skill far above that which was essential in the *Bizarre* shop and this requirement was to be the same for the *Tahiti* range. To decorate his studio patterns, John Butler needed technically outstanding

Plate 14.4. An earthenware side plate decorated with the hand-painted Picasso *pattern designed by John Butler, 1928.*

decorators, whereas Clarice Cliff required young paintresses with native intelligence, a steady hand and the capability to work quickly. This is not to say that the *Bizarre* paintresses were unskilled but rather that the *Bizarre* shop patterns were neither 'high art' nor a technical tour de force. In comparison with Butler's highly skilled operatives, *Bizarre* girls could be paid less, thus further reducing factory outlays.

Displaced by the potent success of Miss Cliff, John Butler completed his employment at A.J. Wilkinson by outlining some of Clarice Cliff's *Appliqué* designs and left the Wilkinson works in 1930, a much underrated design genius. In his legacy, he left a variety of decorating techniques, aerographed and enamelled lithographic patterns together with design ideas that would continue to be influential at the pottery.

Dolly Cliff

Although overshadowed by her better-known sister Clarice, another significant designer for A.J. Wilkinson was Dolly Cliff. A few years younger than Clarice, Dolly supervised her own decoration shop at A.J. Wilkinson as early as 1926 and whilst Clarice was still engaged as a modeller and shape designer. Dolly Cliff's name is to be found in the A.J. Wilkinson pattern books and was attached to a variety of patterns in 1926. This, together with her own decorating shop, is an indication of the significant place that she occupied in the A.J. Wilkinson factory.

Dolly Cliff's small staff of freehand paintresses was responsible for the decoration of much of the hand-painted work produced by A.J. Wilkinson. Rarely exceeding sixteen in number, the paintresses in this specialised decorating shop enjoyed wide and varied training. Whereas in other parts of the factory operatives may have been exclusively freehand paintresses, enamellers, banders or gilders, in Dolly Cliff's decorating shop, operatives were trained in all decorating techniques.[14]

Starting in late 1927, the compulsory re-allocation from this specialised area of many trained paintresses, including Marjory Higginson, Mary Brown and Gladys Scarlett, to the *Bizarre* decorating shop was to be a source of friction between Clarice and Dolly Cliff.[15] Gladys Scarlett was to make her mark as a designer in her own right after her move in 1932 to Royal Venton Pottery.

Dolly Cliff's freehand patterns prior to 1928 were rather conventional, if bright, depictions of fruit or flowers. Her graceful 1927 design *Wheat* (pattern number 5176)[16] is of particular note in that it was to be reissued under Clarice Cliff's name in 1936. Clarice Cliff's borrowing of Dolly Cliff's early patterns[17] was not infrequent and was the source of yet another tension between the two sisters.[18]

Starting in 1928, Dolly Cliff produced the first of her many hand-painted bright, stylised floral and fruit patterns. Pattern numbers 8462, 8463 and 8464 were entered in the pattern books on 1 May 1928.[19] This suggests that they were in production at least a few weeks earlier and close on the heels of the February 1928 release of Clarice Cliff's *Original Bizarre*.

For most of these new patterns, Dolly Cliff drew inspiration from Middle European peasant pottery[20] and likewise most of her floral and fruit designs in that naïve style were simple in execution. Landscapes did figure sometimes in her design range and were generally Oriental in composition. The most notable of these was *San Toy*[21] (June 1928), a hand-painted version of the *Willow* pattern. In August 1928 Dolly Cliff produced at least two designs for flatware that resembled Clarice Cliff's early *Bizarre* ware. These geometric designs, pattern numbers 8492 and 8514, are simple border decoration using only one or two colours. It was not until 1930 that Dolly Cliff patterns incorporated conventional art deco ideas. For example, the 1930 pattern *Leonora*[22] fused stylised flowers with 'step-down' design elements to create an interesting, but somewhat awkward pattern.

The main characteristics of Dolly Cliff's freehand designs are the lack of an outline and fully freehand decoration. As she used the same colour palette as her sister, but lacked her own distinctive backstamp, Dolly Cliff's designs are frequently mistaken for 'unsigned' *Bizarre* ware. Because Clarice Cliff's distinctive shapes were also used for decoration at A.J. Wilkinson and in Dolly Cliff's decorating shop, the potential for confusion is even greater (Plate 14.5).

Despite her small staff, Dolly Cliff managed a remarkably large volume of ware including both tableware and fancies. Rather than adopting European art deco design elements, Dolly Cliff's cheerful patterns contributed to the particular style that is identified as British art deco. This remarkable, but largely unknown Cliff sister supervised her decorating shop up until her untimely death in 1936 when its direction passed to Aubrey Dunn.[23]

Clarice Cliff

Without doubt, Clarice Cliff was the most significant, the best known and most influential art deco designer to work for A.J. Wilkinson. In 1927, having been given studio space in the Newport pottery[24] and a small staff, some of whom were re-allocated from her sister Dolly's decorating shop, Clarice Cliff embarked on the decoration of surplus, often unsaleable Newport glost ware[25] with bold and colourful geometric designs that are now known as 'Original Bizarre'. Market tested in February 1928, the brash and deliberately casual application of colour caught the imagination of the public and was an immediate commercial success (Plate 14.6).[26]

Bizarre ware made no pretence to be comparable in quality to the studio ware produced under the direction of John Butler or even the standard A.J. Wilkinson ware. It was the very avoidance of careful decoration and the emphasis on visible brushstrokes that was a deliberate

Plate 14.5. Earthenware pottery with patterns designed by Dolly Cliff. Back row: pattern number 9285 (1932). Middle row: pattern number 9291 (1932); Nasturtium, pattern number 8518 (1928); pattern number 9470 (1934); pattern number 9167 (1931); pattern number 8716 (1929). Front row: Morning, pattern number 8677 (1928); pattern number 8678 (1928); Orange Blossom, pattern number 8998.

marketing point. The consumer was to be left in no doubt that the ware had been painted by hand. The unsympathetic combination of traditional shapes, including outmoded items such as candlesticks, with startling colour mixes widely separated it from most of Clarice Cliff's market rivals and ensured *Bizarre* ware's commercial visibility (Plate 14.7).

The early *Bizarre* ware was fast and inexpensive to produce, finding a ready market as gifts for the less affluent part of the market. The price, set well below John Butler's more sophisticated and technically superior output, further assisted its market acceptability.

Whilst the original *Bizarre* ware patterns were not particularly reflective of European art deco, one design aspect that it did capture was that of bright colours. The dramatic use of colour in fabric designs of Sonia Delaunay, the bold blocks of colour used in posters for the London Underground[27] and Cubist painting are amongst those sources, cited by many writers, to have been influential to Clarice Cliff's style.[28] Of particular interest, Dr Philip J. Woodward, in his excellent catalogue notes,[29] convincingly analyses Clarice Cliff's use of colour in relation to Eugène Chevreul's rule of Simultaneous Contrast. In short, Dr Woodward notes that, as Clarice Cliff used a non-primary colour outline to separate primary colours, she avoided the disharmony that Chevreul said would occur if primary colours were adjacent to each other.

Plate 14.6. An Original Bizarre pattern applied to a *Tankard* shaped earthenware coffee set, 1929.

Plate 14.7. Period advertisement for Bizarre ware 1928, Clarice Cliff.

Plate 14.8. An earthenware cup, saucer and sandwich plate decorated with the hand-painted pattern Trees and House (red) pattern designed by Clarice Cliff, from the Octagonal shape range, 1929.

Plate 14.9. The Trees and House (pastel) pattern decorated on a display plate from the Octagonal shape range, 1929.

The economic factors driving the early *Bizarre* ware production frequently led to low production values, principally in firing. This meant that some colours were not fired to their own correct temperatures. The result was poor fusing of colour to the glaze, most noticeable with blue. Despite the shortcomings in quality, the success of Clarice Cliff's project, together with a well-directed and intense publicity campaign, launched her career. A significant message in the publicity campaign was that here was a working class woman who 'made good', designing ware for the middle and working classes. Another influential marketing tool was the determined publicity campaign to promote a woman designer producing ware for women. Although women designers were not unknown in the potteries,[30] to ensure that the buying public received the message Clarice Cliff was given her own distinctive backstamp with occasional advertising copy, disingenuously suggesting that Miss Cliff signed each piece.[31]

With her own studio, the *'Bizarre shop'*, a staff of *'Bizarre girls'*[32] and the backing of the factory owner, Clarice Cliff was in a unique position to give free rein to her creative genius. The staffing numbers of the *Bizarre* shop continued to grow throughout 1929 and 1930 in order to meet the demand for *Bizarre* and *Fantasque* branded ware. The multitude of shapes and patterns that followed established her as one of the most innovative ceramic designers of the twentieth century. As a measure of success, by the early 1930s around 18,000 pieces of *Bizarre* ware were produced per week earning the pottery around £100,000 per year. The income from *Bizarre* ware represented almost 30% of factory sales.[33]

To maintain the momentum following the success of 'Original' *Bizarre*, Clarice Cliff's original geometric designs would soon evolve into much more sophisticated geometric or organic designs. These highly recognisable patterns included *Sunray*, *Sliced Circle* and *Mondrian*. Soon to become her particular 'trademark', stylised landscapes, showing partly concealed cottages, for example *Trees and House* (1929), complemented a cascade of distinctive floral and fruit patterns (Plates 14.8 and 14.9).

The Production Line

In keeping with machine age principles of mass-production and the division of labour, Clarice Cliff's *Bizarre* decorating shop depended on a small number of talented outliners who would apply an outline of a pattern on glost ware using either enamels or India ink. Lesser skilled operatives would then take up the outlined ware and apply enamel colours.[34] If appropriate, the ware would be passed to a bander for the application of coloured bands. This division of labour lent itself to the production of large volumes whilst maintaining the appearance of hand-painted studio ware. To avoid a uniform depiction of the design and to add interest, the outliners would exercise some artistic freedom in the composition of the pattern. This freedom was expressed by leaving out a particular pattern element or subtly changing the element's relationships to the whole. Whilst most of the designs were produced on this 'outlining production line', a smaller number was produced fully freehand, i.e. without outlines.

ART DECO DESIGNS
Tableware

Often overlooked in favour of more striking designs for decorative ware, some of Miss Cliff's tableware patterns from 1929 to 1934 are amongst her strongest art deco designs. Of all her tableware patterns, designs such as *Ravel*,[35] *Brunella* and *Bignou* are amongst the best (Plate 14.10). Matched with her *Conical*, *Stamford* and later *Biarritz* shapes, such designs as *Ravel* were to continue in production until after 1936.

In 1929, and amongst the rapidly growing stream of her new patterns, Clarice Cliff produced a range of hand-enamelled lithographs under the range name *Moderne*. Each lithograph depicted a vignette showing stylised flowers, trees or landscapes. This short-lived tableware range, as its name implies, was Modernistic in style, giving an uncluttered appearance and accentuating the *Conical* shapes on which the designs were mostly applied.

As early as 1929, Clarice Cliff recognised the commercial value of fusing table and decorative ware making her designs 'art for the table'. Appealing particularly to women, Miss Cliff ensured that an owner could have a distinctive tableware setting whose design was repeated on vases, wall plaques, lampshades and even table linen.[36] This approach was very much in keeping with the unifying style that characterised art deco as probably the last combined style that encompassed architecture, ceramics, textiles, furniture, motorcars and even locomotives.

In the mid-1930s the characteristic art deco 'step-down' design elements would be re-introduced in other tableware patterns such as *Victoria* and *Savoy* (Plate 14.11).[37]

Plate 14.10. A group of wares from the Conical shape range decorated with Ravel (green), pattern number 5799, 1929; back row, Brunella, pattern number 5800 from 1929, and front Bignou, pattern number 5824, from 1929.

Plate 14.11. A collection of wares with the Biarritz plate decorated with the Savoy pattern (left) and a Trieste trio decorated with the Victoria pattern (right), 1936.

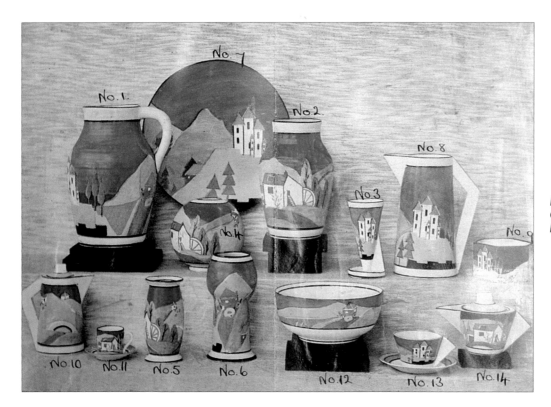

Plate 14.12. Appliqué. Clarice Cliff salesman's brochure.

DECORATIVE WARE
Archaic

Extending John Butler's tentative experiments with Egyptian themes, Clarice Cliff's *Archaic* range of 1929 copied shapes and patterns of the Ancient Egyptian column capitals that were published in *The Grammar of Ornament* by Owen Jones. These architectural shapes were reproduced in earthenware as vases making them both 'kitsch' and truly art deco. Although the brilliant and colourful *Archaic* patterns captured the exotic feel of ancient Egypt while boasting an individual backstamp that connected the pottery with the original architecture, this range was not popular. The shapes, however, were more successful and continued to be produced well into 1931.

Studio ware

Some attempts were made at producing studio ware such as *Inspiration*, *Latona* and *Appliqué* but, by 1932, these were discontinued, probably more out of economic considerations than changes in taste.

Appliqué

Appliqué (1929-1932), priced only slightly higher than standard *Bizarre* ware, presented a series of landscapes, flowers or trees (Plate 14.12). A few of the designs in this range, such as *Appliqué Lucerne*, were influenced by the prints of the Pochoir designer, Edouard Bénédictus.[38] However, most of the fourteen known patterns in this range appear to be original Clarice Cliff ideas with one design, *Appliqué Eden*,[39] re-issued as a hand painted version of the A.J. Wilkinson *Indian Summer* lithograph (1928).

Latona

At the same time Clarice Cliff pursued her interest in coloured glazes[40] and significant amongst her broadening range was *Latona* (Plate 14.13). This high priced range was not restricted to a milky white, matt glaze from which its name was drawn, but also included glazes in dark blue and pink and pale brown, all released under the *Latona* name.

The *Latona* range contained a remarkable variety of modern designs. Compared with the yellow glaze or the paler honey glaze on which most *Bizarre* and *Fantasque* ware was produced, the white *Latona* glaze, by its starkness and absence of glaze reflections, intensified the colours in the designs. Most patterns in the *Latona* range were strongly art deco in concept and mainly depicted stylised flowers or strict geometric designs (Plate 14.14). Only a few of these designs, most notably *Flowerheads*,

"LATONA" gives the full glory of modern colouring on beautiful satiny matt glazes of varying tones.

Plate 14.13. Latona. Clarice Cliff salesman's brochure.

Plate 14.14. An earthenware plate decorated with the Latona Bouquet pattern on a white glaze, about 1929-1930.

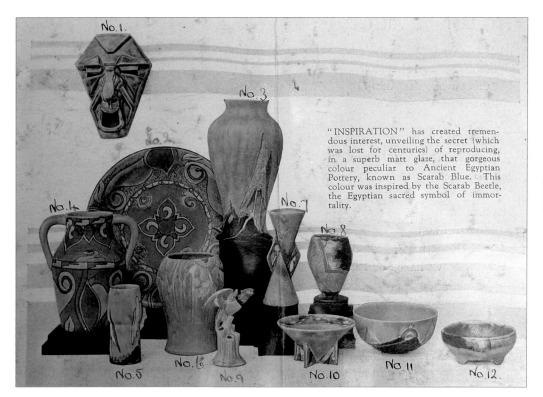

"INSPIRATION" has created tremendous interest, unveiling the secret (which was lost for centuries) of reproducing, in a superb matt glaze, that gorgeous colour peculiar to Ancient Egyptian Pottery, known as Scarab Blue. This colour was inspired by the Scarab Beetle, the Egyptian sacred symbol of immortality.

Plate 14.15. Inspiration. Clarice Cliff salesman's brochure.

Eden and *Blossom*,[41] were to be re-issued on other glazes.[42] Clarice Cliff never ceased to experiment with novel glazes and even coloured earthenware bodies such as *Damask Rose* and *Goldstone*.

Inspiration

The *Inspiration* range was Clarice Cliff's most expensive studio ware (Plate 14.15). Although difficult to produce, it was made from 1929 to 1932 and falsely marketed as 'unveiling the secret (which was lost for centuries) of reproducing in a superb matt glaze, that gorgeous colour peculiar to ancient Egyptian pottery...'.

Choosing from various art deco design elements, Miss Cliff decorated this ware with variations on the *Caprice* landscape, abstracts, floral motifs and even copies of Persian patterns. A number of these 'new' patterns would reappear in conventional colours as part of the *Bizarre* range.

Art Deco Shapes

Although much more attention is paid towards her patterns, it is evident that Clarice Cliff was principally a designer of shapes, some of which were copied as far afield as Japan and Australia. Miss Cliff trained as a modeller at the Hanley School between 1922 and 1925,

continuing for a short time in 1928 at the Royal College of Art.

Whilst her modelling work in the mid-1920s was traditional in approach, it was in 1929 that she successfully translated the art deco metalware shapes of European designers into earthenware to match her emerging range of patterns. In 1929 and 1930 Clarice Cliff drew inspiration from such eminent European designers[43] as Josef Hoffmann, Jean Tétard, Jean Luce, Lalland and Desny to produce her most identifiable shape ranges including *Stamford, Bonjour* and *Biarritz*.

Separate to the shapes inspired by European designers, Clarice Cliff's *Conical* range appears to have been an entirely original design. Although Miss Cliff acknowledges user difficulties in relation to the handles of the cups,[44] the *Conical* range was perhaps her best art deco shape design (Plate 14.16). It was Clarice Cliff's genius at developing or adapting difficult art deco shapes for production in earthenware and fusing them with bright, showy designs that made her unique amongst her fellow pottery designers.

The period during which A.J. Wilkinson produced strong art deco shapes and patterns was quite short – it covered only about eight years from 1928 to 1936. The high point of the pottery's art deco period was reached about 1931

Plate 14.16. An earthenware teapot from the Conical range decorated with Delecia, 1929-1930.

Plate 14.17. Advertisement proof for Bizarre/Fantasque ware, Clarice Cliff, 1932.

Plate 14.18. A beer set decorated with the Capri (orange) pattern hand painted on yellow size, about 1935.

when Clarice Cliff's *Bizarre/Fantasque* (Plate 14.17), *Appliqué, Latona* and *Inspiration* ranges were inundating the market with a bewildering cascade of shapes and colours. At the same time, the design output of Dolly Cliff remained strong and offered the market alternative, brightly coloured ware at a lower price.

After 1935, most noticeably in her tableware, Clarice Cliff's designs began to reflect the quieter tastes of the market (Plate 14.18). Whilst some remarkable new patterns (Plate 14.19) appeared, most new shapes or patterns tended to be more restrained with only passing references to art deco influences. The adoption of matt glazes in yellow (Raffia glaze) or mushroom further restrained the patterns. Occasional patterns that were released after this time may show one or two art deco design elements, but for the most part the patterns were becoming conventional in approach (Plate 14.20).

It is difficult to say when A.J. Wilkinson last produced art deco. Some shapes such as *Windsor* (1937), with its art deco finials on the tea or coffee pot, were produced into the 1950s, but brightly coloured ware and abstracts ceased by World War II. This is conventionally taken to be the end of the art deco period. To A.J. Wilkinson goes the credit for supplying inexpensive, earthenware, art deco shapes and bright patterns that contributed a 'modern touch' to the homes of ordinary people on at least five continents.

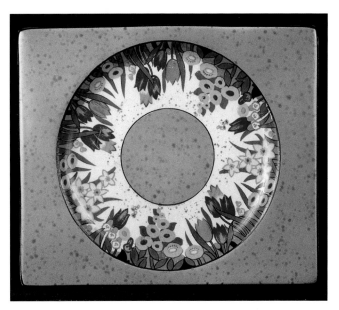

Plate 14.19. An earthenware vase (shape 363) decorated with the Flowerheads *pattern on a Raffia glaze, 1936.*

Plate 14.20. A Biarritz plate decorated with the Chloris pattern, printed with green speckled decoration, 1937. This was produced for Wilkinson's.

1. Karen McCredy, *Art Deco and Modernist Ceramics,*Thames and Hudson, 1995, pp.19-21.
2. *The Pottery and Glass Record,* 1 September 1924, p.155.
3. *PA W-N 81 A.J. Wilkinson Pattern Book plus Illustrations of Clarice Cliff and factory. 192- to 195-.*
4. Modern working name.
5. *PA W-N 81, A.J. Wilkinson Pattern Book plus Illustrations of Clarice Cliff and factory. 192- to 195-.*
6. *The Pottery and Glass Record,* 1 April 1922, p.537.
7. Clarice Cliff was to re-use this name in 1931 to describe her banded *Inspiration* ware.
8. Pattern number 8470 *Storm PA W-N 34* requires a page of decorating instructions.
9. *PA W-N 34 Decoration Description Book,* May 1925 to December 1928.
10. Private correspondence between the author and Marjory Higginson, *Bizarre* shop paintress.
11. *The Home,* 1 November 1929.
12. Modern working name.
13. Pattern number 8497, June 1928. Modern working name *Picasso.*
14. Private correspondence between author and Marjory Higginson, *Bizarre* paintress.
15. Ibid.
16. *PA W-N 34 Decoration Description Book,* May 1925 to December 1928.
17. Dolly Cliff's 1928 pattern, number 8646, was also released under Clarice Cliff's *Fantasque* mark in 1929.
18. Private correspondence between author and

Marjory Higginson, *Bizarre* paintress.
19. *PA W-N 34 Decoration Description Book,* May 1925 to December 1928.
20. *Titian* ware (1920-1940), a peasant style pottery produced by William Adams and Sons pottery, may also have influenced Dolly Cliff and her sister, Clarice.
21. Pattern number 9030.
22. Pattern number 8499 *PA W-N 34 Decoration Description Book,* May 1925 to December 1928.
23. Private correspondence between author and Eric Grindley, Newport Pottery administration.
24. An adjacent pottery acquired by A.J. Wilkinson in 1920.
25. Glazed, but undecorated ware.
26. *Pottery Gazette,* 1 March 1928, p.445 and 1 February 1929, p.251.
27. Dr P. Woodward, *Clarice Cliff – An Exhibition of Ugly Ware,* Vardy Gallery September 1999 catalogue, p.4.
28. 'I utilised every opportunity to study the products of other people who were more advanced than I', ibid.
29. Ibid., p.6.
30. The industry already had such women designers as Daisy Makeig-Jones, Charlotte Rhead, Susie Cooper, Truda Carter and Millicent Taplin.
31. *The Home,* June 1929.
32. First reference in factory literature to 'Bizarre girls' PA W-N 35 Pattern Description Book Samples and Early Bizarre pattern numbers.

33. Dr P. Woodward, *Clarice Cliff – An Exhibition of Ugly Ware,* Vardy Gallery September 1999 catalogue, p.9.
34. L. Wentworth-Shields & K. Johnson, *Clarice Cliff,* L'Odéon, 1979, p.16.
35. *Pottery Gazette,* 2 June 1930, p.943.
36. L. Wentworth-Shields & K. Johnson, *Clarice Cliff,* L'Odéon, 1979 p.21.
37. 'Savoy' – modern working name.
38. Dr P. Woodward, *Clarice Cliff – An Exhibition of Ugly Ware,* Vardy Gallery September 1999 catalogue, p.5.
39. Modern working name.
40. 'We were always experimenting with slips and glazes', Clarice Cliff, The Brighton Museum and Art Gallery catalogue February 1972.
41. 'Flowerheads', 'Eden' and 'Blossom' are all modern working names.
42. 'Flowerheads' was re-issued in late 1936 on the matt yellow, 'Raffia' glaze. 'Blossom', a hand-painted and simplified version of Davies 'Yellow Chintz' lithograph, also appeared as a pattern in the Appliqué range. 'Eden', a hand-painted and simplified version of Clarice Cliff's lithograph pattern 'Indian Summer', was also released as an Appliqué pattern.
43. Dr P. Woodward, *Clarice Cliff – An Exhibition of Ugly Ware,* Vardy Gallery September 1999 catalogue, p.5.
44. Clarice Cliff, The Brighton Museum and Art Gallery catalogue February 1972, p.9.

15.

E. Brain & Co

Andrew Casey

THERE WERE NOT MANY POTTERY COMPANIES IN Stoke-on-Trent that were ahead of their time. Only a handful could claim to be at the leading edge of new contemporary pottery production which combined consideration for both pattern and shape. Many of these pioneering designers and art directors are well known today with several books playing homage to their achievements. The firm of E. Brain & Co, however, is probably not as well known now, but through the best part of the twentieth century it was associated with good taste and modernity.

Based at the Foley Works in Fenton, Stoke-on-Trent, on a site previously used by Robinson & Son Ltd, the company was formed in 1855. When the founder died

in 1910 his son William Henry Brain took over the firm. To seek new trade he built up contacts and clients and travelled extensively through Australia and New Zealand. His son came into the business just before the First World War.

During the early part of the century, and before many of its competitors, the firm, known as Foley China, had begun to develop modern practical domestic tablewares. As early as about 1913 E. Brain & Co took on board the design principles as expounded by the

---

Plate 15.1. An earthenware Cube shaped tea set decorated with a print and enamelled pattern, probably 1920s.

Design and Industries Association (DIA). They decided to focus on utilitarian productions rather than decorative wares and set about reducing the range of shapes they produced, creating a simpler more practical range that was easy to use and clean.[1] In addition, the patterns were simpler and used more sparingly on the ware; typical examples were *Checker Border* and *Tudor (Green Edge)* launched in about 1922. These new designs set new standards of modernity and were launched at a time when most pottery manufacturers were still selling ornately shaped wares decorated with a combination of poor quality stock lithographic prints and over-gilding. These were clearly from a much earlier period and, as tastes had changed, so had customer demand. The customer was waiting for something new and E. Brain were ready to supply them.

This move to create pottery that applied the modern principles of design not only gained them an excellent reputation for good taste, for the middle and upper classes, but also influenced many other manufacturers some years later. Pottery that was both durable and attractive, as well as being restrained, would prove popular in the '30s. One of the earliest of this new range, *Swansea* introduced in 1922, was a good example of this. The trade press commented that the pottery was:

> accepted nowadays by the majority of the discriminating dealers as typifying a class of china of a durable and attractive body, finely surfaced and brilliantly glazed, whose decorations are characterised by their simplicity and restraint, combined with really good taste.[2]

The growing trend for the often garish, hand-painted patterns in the pottery industry presented a problem for E. Brain as these fashionable new ideas did not concur with their design ethos for practical shapes and restrained patterning. With the well-documented success of these art deco styled wares enjoyed by many other pottery manufacturers it was clear that eventually E. Brain would have to respond, if not only for commercial reasons. The first results of this new avenue of production were two new patterns that nodded to the art deco movement, *Cubist Sunflower* and *Cubist Landscape*, launched in 1928.[3] The latter featured a stylised border rather than an overall decoration and was applied to *Cube* tea wares (Plate 15.1) and a

Plate 15.2. A bone china trio decorated with a hand-painted stylised floral pattern, designed by Freda Beardmore about 1933.

traditionally styled shape. Whilst these patterns were the first to make an impression, the trade press warned:

> the pendulum has swung back, E. Brain and Co. are now having to compromise. The public want colour, and they will see that they get it.[4]

In response to the demands of the market, E. Brain started to develop new patterns which, whilst being colourful, were simple ones that would not be too outrageous to offend their established market. These new patterns, both decorated on an earlier shape from

about 1922, featured pictorial images: one of a stylised cottage surrounded by trees and the other depicting stylised trees. On this new departure into art deco patterning the trade press stated that:

> such designs are true to the instincts of the age for which they seek to cater – a little advanced it may be, but someone is bound to give the public a lead.[5]

Within a few years E. Brain started to develop a limited range of modernist patterns that began with the introduction of several new shapes including *Devon* and

Plate 15.3. A bone china dinner service decorated with a stylised flower pattern designed by Freda Beardmore, early 1930s.

Plate 15.4. A bone china teapot decorated with the printed and painted Gladiola pattern (V189), possibly designed by Freda Beardmore, about 1933. Height of teapot 6¾in. (17cm).

New Regent shape in 1931. New patterns included the art deco inspired *Windmill* (709), though applied to an older shape called *Perth*. The most important shape, however, was *Pallas*, a striking form that expressed a European modernity rather than the Staffordshire interpretation, and was quite unlike anything the company had introduced before. New shapes such as *Essex* and *Regent* were added to the range in 1932 alongside new printed and hand-painted patterns such as one depicting a bird with a floral decoration in blue and orange (848),[6] At about the same time William Brain formed a close association with the designer Freda Beardmore, who worked as the company designer of both patterns and shapes. Her *Savoy* shape from 1932 was typical and decorated with modern stylised patterns and she also created a wide range of stylish hand-painted floral patterns (Plates 15.2 and 15.3). Another new shape, *Langham*, was used for several new patterns that bore more than a passing resemblance to shapes made by Shelley, and in particular their *Regent* shape (Plate 15.4). Also in 1932 Thomas Acland Fennemore was appointed Managing Director, having previously worked at Paragon.

The company showed five new patterns at the prestigious Exhibition of Industrial Art in Relation to the Home at Dorland Hall in London in 1933. The most important range on display was the new modern *Mayfair* (Plate 15.5), consisting of straight black lines complemented with squares and circles of bold colourings that created a:

careful balance and admirable restraint to invest in design with a character and smartness peculiarly its own.[7]

Plate 15.5. A company advertisement for the Mayfair range, 1933.

Distinguished British Artists Exhibit their designs at Harrods

A New Fashion in Pottery

Harrods are indeed happy to introduce the work of these distinguished British Artists and they cordially invite all those who are interested in the progress of Art in Industry to visit this unique Exhibition.

Here you will see beautifully made China, Pottery and Glass designed by famous Artists. The work reveals a definitely English type of contemporary and modern design and it possesses a freshness of outlook and originality of treatment which is altogether delightful.

For the first time in the history of the Pottery Industry there will be a limited first-edition of each design for the Dinner, Tea, Coffee and Breakfast Services and no additional charge will be made for these. Each piece of China and Pottery bears the Artist's signature and the copyright is strictly reserved.

All the China and Pottery in this Exhibition was made by two Staffordshire pottery firms :— E. Brain & Co. Ltd., makers of Foley China, and A. J. Wilkinson, Royal Staffordshire Pottery. The Glass by Stuart & Sons, Stourbridge.

The Exhibition will be held in the China Salon on the Second Floor October 22nd to November 10th

'Circus' Dinner Set by Dame Laura Knight, D.B.E., A.R.A. 52 Pieces £35 0 0

'Marine' Dinner Set by Dod Procter, A.R.A. 26 Pieces £4 4 0

'Fairing's' Tea Service by Ernest Procter, A.R.A. 21 Pieces £3 10 6

'Lustre' Tea Service by Duncan Grant. 21 Pieces £3 10 6

'Chaldean' Dinner Set by John Armstrong, 26 Pieces £3 5 0

'Cupid' Tea Set by Dame Laura Knight, D.B.E., A.R.A. 21 Pieces £2 10 6

Plate 15.6. Period publicity material illustrating examples of different designers' work including Vanessa Bell and Duncan Grant.

The range, decorated on bone china rather than earthenware, consisted of twelve different patterns that proved a success in the middle class market.[8] Also on display were several modern hand-painted floral designs including the *Clovelly* pattern, probably designed by Beardmore, which was, according to the trade press, approved by Her Majesty the Queen to be used in the Queen Mary Home for Army Nurses at Fleet.[9]

Apart from developing new patterns and shapes, Fennemore gained a reputation for inviting a number of designers, including Milner Gray, to design for the company. One of Gray's patterns for E. Brain, *Convolvulus,* was shown at Dorland Hall, though not included in the catalogue.[10] This came at a time when there were serious debates about uniting art and industry, crystallising in a special ceramics project that brought together a number of British fine artists. The resultant exhibition, entitled 'Modern Art for the Table', was staged at Harrods in London in 1934 and is discussed in depth in Chapter 5.

Three companies were involved with this venture: E. Brain (bone china), A.J. Wilkinson Ltd (earthenware) and Stuart and Sons (glass) In total twenty-eight artists and designers contributed to this project creating patterns for both earthenware and bone china tablewares. In retrospect, however, the patterns for A.J. Wilkinson Ltd are better known today than those by E. Brain, perhaps because of the close association with Clarice Cliff and the fact the designers used her *Bonjour* shape. Notable patterns for Foley included *Cupid and Dove* by Dame Laura Knight, *Pink Rose* by Graham Sutherland, *Forest* by Paul Nash and *Swirls* by Ernest Procter (Plate 15.6).[11]

Despite these innovative manoeuvres to promote a new modernity for ceramic design with new practical shapes and restrained patterns, by the late '30s the company was using the more traditionally styled *Ascot* and *Savoy* shapes, which may have been older shapes, for a series of more conventional floral designs.[12]

1. These new shapes were illustrated in the trade press: 'Buyers Notes', *Pottery Gazette,* 1 June 1922, p.869.
2. Ibid.
3. Ibid., 1 October 1928, p.1601.
4. Ibid., 2 September 1929, p.1407.
5. Ibid., 1 October 1928, p.1601.
6. Ibid., 2 May 1933, p.613.
7. *Pottery Gazette,* 1 July 1933, pp.840-841.
8. The *Mayfair* range was illustrated in *Pottery Gazette,* 1 December 1932, p.1487.
9. This pattern was illustrated in *Pottery Gazette,* 1 July 1933, p.840.
10. Ibid., 1 July 1933. p.841.
11. These patterns are illustrated in the Clarice Cliff auction catalogue, Christie's South Kensington, 2 November 2001, pp.27-30.
12. These shapes were illustrated in *Pottery Gazette,* 1 October 1936, p.1355.

16.

C.T. Maling & Sons

Steven Moore

THE 1920s AND '30s WERE for all British potteries a period of change. C.T. Maling & Sons, established in Sunderland in 1762 and moving to Newcastle in 1815, had been in family ownership from the start, but by the end of this era it was to find itself in highly changed circumstances that would lead to the family selling the firm just after the Second World War.

In 1859 Maling moved from its small Ouseburn Bridge works to the large, purpose-built Ford A pottery. Early deployment of mechanisation saw the business prosper and in 1878 they built the massive Ford B pottery on a nearby green field site. The B pottery was said to be the largest pottery in the world and was built on a free flow principle to maximise efficiency, with large workrooms

and modern facilities for staff, such as kitchens and laundries. A few years later Maling became the first potter, and probably the first factory in the world, to install electric lighting.

Maling entered the new century in good form and, despite the death of C.T. Maling, the firm's driving force since 1853, they prospered. They enjoyed large commercial contracts to supply jelly and jam jars, pudding basins, electrical cells and other commercial pottery to many firms in both the home and world markets. Particularly strong links were enjoyed with the Empire and Maling had many representatives across the globe. The good profits from this commercial ware had allowed Maling to diversify into decorative pottery from

Plate 16.1. An aerial view of the Maling Ford B factory, 1952.

C. T. MALING & SONS, FORD POTTERIES, NEWCASTLE-ON-TYNE.

LONDON SHOWROOMS: MORLEY HOUSE, 26, HOLBORN VIADUCT, E.C.1.

Plate 16.2. A period advertisement showing the range of art deco patterns and shapes introduced in 1930.

the late nineteenth century with lithographed decoration produced in their own 'chromolithographic plant.' Later on Maling introduced 'Cetem Ware', a range of decorative fancies designed in house by (Harry) Clifford Toft from 1908.

Rarely at the cutting edge of design, Maling none the less produced well-made products that followed, rather than led, fashions. They had employed their own designers from the 1880s and produced practically everything in house. They were well known for the range of lamp bases with either electric or oil fittings as well as floating bowls, often on a black ground. The *Pottery Gazette* credits Maling with the introduction of black ground wares and floating bowls and these wares were strong sellers until the outbreak of World War II.

December 1921 saw the death of Harry Clifford Toft

(1861-1921) who was replaced as designer by Charles Newboult Wright in early 1922. Wright's career had seen him work at Royal Crown Derby, Josiah Wedgwood and Sons Ltd and Royal Doulton Ltd. Maling's designers after Toft seem to fit a distinct pattern, which suggests that it was the firm's management who had the final, cautious, say in what went into production. New designers seemed to move slowly introducing new patterns, whilst updating or reworking existing or older designs often adapted from the vast back catalogue of designs of both Maling and other local potteries that Maling had bought up on their closure.

Typical of Wright's new designs was *Blyth*, featuring black swags and arabesques set upon a coloured ground with enamelled 'jewels.' This simplicity is characteristic of his designs for Maling. Wright produced many stylish border designs that were highly adaptable to Maling's vast shape range with typical examples including *Wylam, Tyne, Dublin Bead, Benton, Grafton* and *Milan*. Another introduction made by Wright was lustreware, referred to by the firm as 'New lustre art wares' and introduced in 1923. Lustre finishes had been used at the Ford Pottery before but the extent to which Wright used it was completely new. Many of the early 'new' designs were in fact a reworking of previous designers' work, such as *Orchard*, originally designed by Toft but recoloured by Wright typically on a gloss black ground with a gold printed pebble design or on a plain blue ground. Toft's *Aquatic* pattern also reappeared in a new lustred guise, as did many other designs from the back catalogue.

Wright was also responsible for a technique called 'stencilled' decoration. This, especially when combined with gold printing, produced highly decorative wares at a fraction of the cost of hand-painted lines. Shapes were aerographed in a gloss colour, usually black, and then printed in a design in outline only; this was blocked in with a type of slip developed by Fred Maling. The

Plate 16.3. Examples of the Anzac pattern applied to art deco styled earthenware Jazz shape, 1930. Height of teapot 5¾in. (14.5cm).

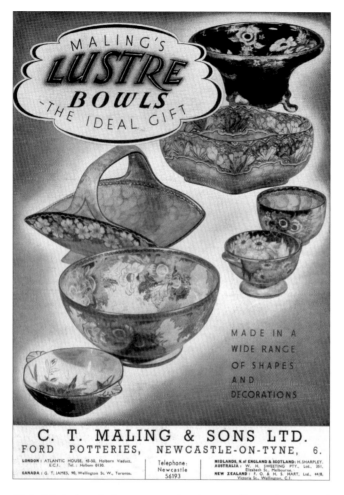

Plate 16.4. A period company advertisement illustrating several lustre decorated bowls, 1938.

Early pieces from the change-over period can often be found with both a Cetem and a Maling Ware mark.

Wright left Maling in 1926 and was replaced by Lucien Emile Boullemier (1877-1949). Boullemier had worked at both Minton in Stoke and Lennox in the United States of America where he decorated high quality porcelain, often in the Sèvres style. Much was made in the trade press of Boullemier's appointment, where he is inevitably described as 'having recently left Messer [sic] Minton's' when this was in fact almost ten years earlier! Boullemier continued Maling's tradition of the reworking of earlier designs, but he quickly introduced new styles and much needed glamour and confidence into the firm's products. *Windmill* is typical of his early designs; dating from 1927, it is a gold printed design of a moonlit windmill amongst foliage, mostly seen on a cobalt blue ground, but produced on more exotic colours like gloss black, yellow, lilac, pink and turquoise. Also typical of Boullemier's working practice, the same design is encountered where the windmill has been replaced by a gold moon and two flying ducks.

1929 saw Maling presented with a massive showcase in the form of the North East Coast Industries Exhibition held between May and October that year. This was organised by Sir Arthur Lambert, Lord Mayor of Newcastle and personal friend of the Maling family, and

blocked out pot would then be aerographed in a second colour, typically a matt shade such as red or yellow, and the pot fired. The blocking slip would be brushed off revealing the gloss decoration. The pattern's details were added with the use of gold printing. The combination of newly introduced lustrewares, stencilled and hand-painted designs gave Maling enough confidence to launch their 'Maling Ware' brand in 1924.

Maling's products in both domestic and decorative lines were referred to as 'Cetem Ware' by the firm from 1906. The original reason was to distinguish Maling's commercial lines such as jam and jelly jars from its other products. A further distinction was made with 'Maling Ware', which referred only to decorative fancies. Confusingly for collectors, the Cetem Ware mark was used until 1931 and can appear on any type of ware.

Plate 16.5. An earthenware gravy boat decorated with the hand-painted Ruche *band, 1933.*

was designed to provide a boost to local industries. Maling shared a stand with Lambert's company, china and glass retailers Townsend and Co Ltd. Visitors to the stand could see Maling workers producing and decorating wares as well as try their luck at a Maling coconut shy, where coconuts were replaced by sturdy pieces of Maling pottery. One bedpan apparently survived the duration unscathed! For the exhibition Boullemier introduced many new designs as well as special commemorative items. *Huntsman, Fruit Border* and *Peona* were all popular designs introduced at the exhibition. *Peona* was to become Boullemier's signature design, the *Peona* motif appearing in many guises up to the factory's closure in 1963.

Amongst the souvenirs Boullemier produced special *Exhibition Chintz*, a blue printed sheet design incorporating views of the new Tyne Bridge or exhibition buildings. This was a massive seller and can be found on all manner of Maling shapes, often old stock found in the depths of the warehouse! Better quality souvenirs were the plaque showing the Tyne Bridge and local industries, interspersed by the *Lucerne* border and the coloured views of the exhibition, matched with the *Benton* border. He also produced the model of the *Old Keep* of Newcastle, from which the city took its name.

Following the success of the exhibition and to reflect changes in taste, Boullemier introduced new designs much more in tune with the period. *Tango, Anzac, Luxor, Harebell and Cobble, Tulip and Cobble* and *Crocus and Cobble* (Plate 16.2) were introduced in 1930 and were a departure for the firm. These modern designs were painted in bright enamel colours such as yellow, green, red, orange, blue or white and mostly made for export to Australia or New Zealand. These patterns were the firm's only foray into the sphere of 'art deco' but they sit awkwardly in the cannon of Maling patterns. The bold, bright designs seem to have been produced almost grudgingly and Lucien Boullemier did not seem happy with them.

Harebell, Crocus and *Tulip and Cobble* were in fact the same basic design, the only difference being the type of flower inserted into the pattern. One of the problems was the lack of suitably modern new shapes. Boullemier was a skilled modeller himself but he simply did not have the time to design both shapes and patterns and much of his work was spent rescuing finished lustreware by enamelling over small pinholes and other minor kiln faults.[1] He did produce the *Jazz* shape, a range of tea

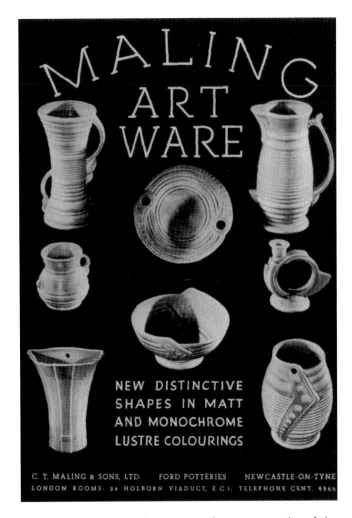

Plate 16.6. A period advertisement showing examples of the new Maling Art Ware, 1936.

wares, and, when combined with the equally angular *Anzac* design, it looks well (Plate 16.3).

Several patterns in this range were also produced in underglaze colours with lustre and gold printed finishes. For Maling collectors the foray into deco is a fascinating one, but Maling's customers, or possibly the management of the firm, were clearly not as keen and the range was in production for just over a year.

A greater success, and as modern in its own way, was *Cobblestone*, a new innovative range of kitchenware introduced in 1931 that took the trade by storm. An all-over sheet design printed in brown, but soon followed by blue or green, it was applied to all manner of kitchenwares and proved a strong seller until 1941.

Another designer had begun at the pottery in 1926 in

Plate 16.7. A twin-handled vase from the Ripple range designed by Norman Carling, 1936.

the shape of Theo Maling, Fred Maling's daughter. Theo started working two days a week whilst she was studying art and design at university. Soon after she established her own studio and began to decorate her own wares. Theo rarely drew her designs on paper, but would simply decorate directly on to pots. With close friend Peggy Bullock, the two girls spread time between painting samples and trial designs along with creating their own work. Each year the two friends held a studio sale and had numerous exhibitions, including one at Harrods, the well-known London store, in 1931. Several designs made production, such as *Salmon Fly, Anemone, Apple Tree* and *Flower Garden*. Studio pieces are usually signed with initials 'TM', 'MB' or 'T Maling', 'M Bullock' occasionally with 'Hand painted' and a date added. Peggy Bullock died after a brief illness in 1931, but Theo continued until 1936 when she married and went to live in London.

Lucien Boullemier was joined at the Ford Pottery by his son, Lucien George, in 1933. Initially the two designers worked together, often correcting small firing faults with enamel decoration on lustrewares, but Lucien junior quickly established himself in his own right by designing both new shapes and patterns for the pottery. He brought with him knowledge of glaze and colour production and this helped the firm to introduce many new matt effects in line with current trends. His first design was *Pastel,* soon followed by *Ruche band* (Plate 16.5) and *Gloria.* These new designs are much lighter and fresher than his father's work and are often seen on his new range of shapes – *Regent,* an up-to-date streamlined design, or *Empress,* a more traditional range with small embossed bouquets of flowers around the edge.

During his youth Boullemier knew Frederick Rhead as well as his daughter Charlotte, who were close family friends. The Rheads popularised tube-lined decoration and Boullemier introduced embossed designs that mimicked this style. Made in a mould, they were much more economical to produce. The first embossed design was *Embossed Pansy* from 1933, soon followed by the ubiquitous *Embossed Peona.* Other designs such as *Tulip* and *Delphinium* also became part of a range of embossed plaques that would become some of Boullemier junior's most popular designs, many of which were in production until the pottery's closure. Embossed plaques fit into two main categories: floral plaques such as *Iris, Gladioli* and *Narcissus* and pictorial plaques such as *Galleon, Windmill* and *Japanese lantern.* Other rare designs such as *Cockatoo, Peach Tree, Crocus, Fish* and *Dragon* exist but are rarely seen. The vast majority of plaques known today are post war; pre-war designs are usually better made and have a gold lined edge.

In 1935 Maling employed a new modeller, Norman Carling (1902-1971). Carling had previously worked at A.J. Wilkinson Ltd for Clarice Cliff and brought with him new ideas that took the pottery into new areas. Apart from designing shapes, Carling introduced his own designs, his first being *Blossom Time* in 1935, followed by *Bambola* the following year. Both designs relied on heavy moulded floral patterns set on strong backgrounds. Produced in various on-glaze enamels and matt grounds, both were reintroduced post-war on mother-of-pearl grounds not produced pre-war. 1936 also saw the introduction of Carling's *Ripple Ware* (Plate 16.7), a modern range of shapes with ribbed, angular

Plate 16.8. An earthenware vase, Flight, decorated with low relief flying birds, designed by Norman Carling.

produced several samples. Surviving Maling mould lists suggest that many figures were designed, but in reality they must have been made in such tiny quantities that they are highly prized by collectors today. Only one figure, *Lady Nicotine*, a novelty smoker's companion in the form of a crinoline lady concealing a cigarette holder and ashtrays, seems to have been produced in any large numbers, mostly for export. *Lady Nicotine* was designed by Carling, but produced in 1948 two years after he left the firm.

Lucien Boullemier senior left the Ford Pottery in 1936, leaving his son in charge of the design department. His last work was to be a poignant one. For the coronation of Edward VIII Boullemier designed an elaborate plaque and matching jug featuring a cameo of the king which he had modelled. This was surrounded by heraldic lions, flags and surmounted by a crown set on a rich blue ground. With added gilding and hand-painted inscriptions these rich items would have been a fitting legacy to Boullemier's time at the pottery. Fate, of course, stepped in and with the abdication these expensive souvenirs became useless.[2] Ironically part of the design was 'rescued' by Boullemier senior as the lithograph for the much simpler 'Royal Souvenir casket' produced for Ringtons Tea Ltd in 1937. This was the very last example of Maling pottery designed by L.E. Boullemier.

The closing years of the decade were to prove difficult for Maling. Following Fred Maling's death in 1937 the firm was being run by managers and directors other than the family for the first time in its long history. Caution was the watchword and risks were not taken on design forcing Boullemier junior to play a steady hand. Simple borders teamed with waved grounds reigned along with the ever-present tradition of 'new' designs from the back catalogue, often only lifted by new shapes by Norman Carling. When asked, in the 1980s, if a 'new' design of 1939 called *Briar Rose* was in fact an old pattern called *Eglantine* of the 1890s, Lucien George Boullemier answered: 'that was just an old design that they put on lavatories. I made it into something!'

or geometric elements. These shapes were teamed with *Lustreen*, a decoration of pink, yellow and buff patched lustre, which also came in a blue, green and purple colour scheme. One of Carling's most stylish designs was *Flight* of 1938 (Plate 16.8). Typical of the period, it showed three stylised ducks in low relief flying over reeds and a lake, with ribbing adding a stylish finish. *Flight* was advertised as being available in 'Two matt colour schemes on new artistic shapes'.

With Carling's work firmly established at the pottery the introduction of figures was considered and Carling

---

1. It is for this reason Lucien Boullemier was joined by his son in 1933.

2. Such was the feeling about the abdication that Theo Maling recalled seeing employees smash coronation items. Interestingly Lucien Boullemier

kept all the jugs and plaques safe in his studio where many remained until the factory's closure in 1963.

17.

Gray's Pottery

Clive Hillier

A.E. GRAY LTD WAS FOUNDED in Stoke-on-Trent by Albert Edward Gray (1871-1959) in 1907 as a ceramics decorating business. Initially selling toilet wares, decorated with patterns topical of the day, they developed a range of stylish patterns under the direction of Art Director John Guildford. The first known Gray's advertisement boasted that they produced, 'tea, dinner and toilet services, vases and general sundries in choice decorations'.[1] Royalty patronised Gray's Pottery, most notably Queen Mary; she was a keen admirer and collector of pottery and purchased some Gray's Pottery in 1915.

Importantly, Gray's specialised in hand-painted decoration that proved popular during the '20s and '30s fitting perfectly with the art deco style with its vibrant colours and freehand designs. Edward Gray once said 'Colour is Courage' and this describes well the wares produced at the factory.[2] Interestingly, Gray's did not produce pottery themselves and bought in white wares from several local companies, most notably Johnson Brothers, Lancaster & Sons, Kirkland & Co and Alfred Meakin. These blanks came to their factory situated at the Glebe Works in Mayor Street, Hanley, where their decorators hand painted each piece. The workforce throughout the '20s and '30s was in the region of eighty employees with the majority being female.

Throughout the many years of production the company used a series of backstamps depicting galleons that were large enough to cover the mark of the original manufacturer. The decorators often signed the ware with an initial, sometimes accompanied by a pattern number. Unfortunately the company's pattern books have never been discovered which makes the study of Gray's pottery even more fascinating; for example, often there is no definite proof of a piece being designed by the renowned Susie Cooper, or of a lustre piece by Gordon

Forsyth. What is certain is that from the early '30s, at the time of the factory moving to the new site in Stoke, they introduced an A prefix to the pattern number which dates any pattern in this range after about 1933.

Edward Gray was a highly respectable man within the pottery industry, founder of the Stoke-on-Trent Rotary Club, and was looked upon in high esteem by many local pottery businessmen. He believed in supporting the local area and tended to select young people straight from school, giving them six months' training at the factory and training at one of the local art schools.

The types of decoration that Gray's produced during the '20s and '30s can be separated into five main categories: lustre designs, floral hand-painted wares, banded designs, nursery wares and the limited range of geometric patterns. The company also produced commemorative wares, a range of animal studies and a small range of wall masks. The *Gloria Lustre* range commenced in 1923 under the direction of Gordon Forsyth (see below) alongside Susie Cooper (Plate 17.1). The range of patterns incorporated stylised dragons, rampant lions, rams, goats, birds, fruit and flowers in a range of lustres including silver, bronze, copper, purple, pink, blue and orange chiefly applied to plaques, ginger jars and large bowls (Plate 17.2).[3] A number of *Gloria Lustre* patterns were designed by Susie Cooper including one of cherubs under a fruit tree from 1924. Examples of her work from this range were often marked with her monogram S.V.C. The *Gloria Lustre* range, which was given a special backstamp, was exhibited at both the British Empire exhibition in 1924 and the Exposition des Arts Décoratifs et Industriels Modernes in Paris a year later where Gray's won a silver medal (Plate 17.3.). In 1923 the *Pottery Gazette* noted that the Gray's stand had:

some neat and effective treatments also in hand painted

Plate 17.1. An earthenware plaque hand-painted with a stylised Phoenix design (4141), c.1923-1924. Possibly designed by Gordon Forsyth. Diameter 14¼in. (36.2cm).

lustres designed by Mr. Gordon Forsyth who was congratulated by the King on some of these.[4]

The fashion for brightly coloured floral ware is thought to have begun with the import of Czechoslovakian ceramics and Edward Gray wanted to compete with these 1920s imports. He asked Susie Cooper to develop a range of similar patterns boldly painted in bright colours. During the early '30s Gray's produced a wide selection of hand-painted floral patterns on large plaques, plates, dessert sets, coffee and tea sets alongside lemonade sets and 'Paris' shaped jugs, all decorated with a multitude of different flowers. Paintresses sometimes signed their names on these pieces. Some well-known patterns include *Trellis, Hampton, Summertime* and *Roumanian*. Some of Susie Cooper's earliest patterns, such as *Almond Blossom* and *Golden Catkin*, utilised the print and enamelled technique for decoration which required more detailed hand work, thus making them more expensive than hand-painted or printed patterns.

The popular range of banded designs introduced in the mid-'20s were probably created by Susie Cooper, and relied on string bands of colour for full visual impact

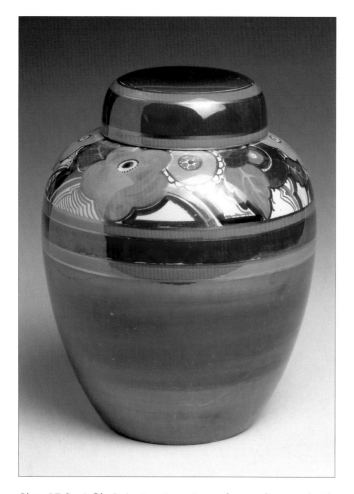

Plate 17.2. A Gloria Lustre *ginger jar and cover decorated with a floral leaf design, c.1924. Height 9½in. (24.1cm). Designed by Susie Cooper.*

Plate 17.3. A Gloria Lustre *ginger jar decorated with stylised flowers and stem work, c.1925. Height 8½in. (21.6cm). This pattern (5399), decorated on a similar vase, was exhibited at the Paris exhibition in 1925.*

(Plates 17.4 and 17.5). Notable examples include *Layebands* and *Harmony*, the latter used on an extensive range of storage jars and other kitchenware. Occasionally some patterns, such as the *Aquamer*, from 1929, used vertical banding. The method yielded dramatic results and was not particularly time consuming or expensive.

Gray's produced a range of nursery wares from about 1922 with one of the first probably *Quadrupeds*. The pattern, printed in blue with hand-painted decoration, depicted animals such as cows, sheep, pigs, giraffes and polar bears interspersed with apple trees. Another well-known pattern was *The House that Jack Built*. Children's sets were sold by Peter Jones Ltd and John Lewis & Co Ltd.

The most important pattern ranges from this period were the art deco wares known as geometrics,

introduced in the late 1920s when Susie Cooper was Chief Designer (Plate 17.6). These patterns, including the most well-known pattern, *Cubist*, were painted in bold bright colours against black and introduced in 1928. Besides being decorated on general domestic wares such as coffee and tea sets, the pattern was also used on a range of advertising wares for Ross Tonic Water and Grapefruit Drinks. The pattern range, which included *Moon and Mountain* (see Frontispiece), represents some of the most dramatic art deco patterns ever produced by the company (Plate 17.7). *The Pottery and Glass Record* of 1928 described them as 'blobs of colour and streaks with blues, greens and reds violently contrasted'.[5] From a practical point of view geometric wares were unsatisfactory as the large blocks of enamel colour tended to flake; this is especially true with blue.

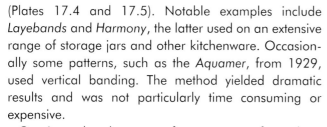

Plate 17.4. A group of earthenware pots with hand-painted banded decoration in various colours including a coffee pot (7670), designed by Susie Cooper, c.1928, a teapot and coffee can and saucer. Height of tallest item 7½in. (19cm).

Plate 17.5. Two earthenware Paris jugs decorated with hand-painted wavy bands, patterns 8332 and 8721, c.1928-1929. Height of tallest item 4½in. (11.4cm).

Plate 17.6. A part earthenware coffee set decorated with a geometric pattern (8215) designed by Susie Cooper, c.1928. Height of coffee pot 7½in. (19cm).

Plate 17.7. A group of earthenware pots decorated with hand-painted geometric patterns including a Cubist coffee pot (centre), box and cover and pin tray. Oval dish (left), pattern 8071, c.1928, a Moon and Mountain Paris jug (7960), c.1928, a coffee can and saucer (8333), possibly designed by Susie Cooper, and a Paris jug decorated with pattern 8872, c.1931. Height of tallest item 7½in. (19cm).

Plate 17.8. Examples of hand-painted floral patterns by Gray's. Paris jug decorated with pattern 9432, water jug (9058) and Paris jug (9344). All date from c.1930-1931. Height of tallest item 7½in. (19cm).

Susie Cooper

Susie Cooper met Gordon Forsyth at the Burslem School of Art, whilst she was studying. He suggested that she attend daytime art classes and in 1919 she received a full-time scholarship. Initially intending to study fashion design at the Royal College of Art in London, she soon discovered that scholarships were only given to those already working in the decorative arts. Forsyth, therefore, arranged for her to work at the Gray's pottery for a period of time in order to qualify. Susie Cooper started working at Gray's, as a decorator, in June 1922. She was soon helping Forsyth with his *Gloria Lustre* range with particular responsibility for painting the heraldic lions that typified the range. Gordon Forsyth and Edward Gray were important figures in Susie Cooper's life and they were very much her 'mentors'. In about 1923 she was promoted to the position of resident designer. Her early pieces used simple floral groups in stylised form that emphasised the brush strokes and left much plain ground; a typical example is 2866 – thought to be her first design from 1923 – painted with flowers in red, green, blue and orange enamel colours. Of the range of Susie Cooper patterns shown at the British Industries Fair in 1926, the trade press noted that 'many of the patterns exhibited a tendency towards the futurist, if only in a mild form'.[6]

Susie Cooper developed a wide range of hand-painted patterns that helped to build her reputation. Her popularity grew and at some stage, thought to be about 1927, she was given her own backstamp with the words 'Designed by Susie Cooper' – an unheard of honour at this time for a woman and a significant achievement for such a young person – an indication of the high regard for her work. Furthermore, she was given the opportunity to design a coffee pot shape as well as a teapot, milk jug and sugar bowl. It is thought that when Susie Cooper left Gray's in October 1929 to establish her own pottery business pattern numbers had reached around 8500.

Plate 17.9. An earthenware part tea set decorated with a hand-painted pattern (A273), c.1933-1934 and a Paris jug decorated with a stylised abstract pattern (A941), c.1933. Height of jug 5in. (12.7cm).

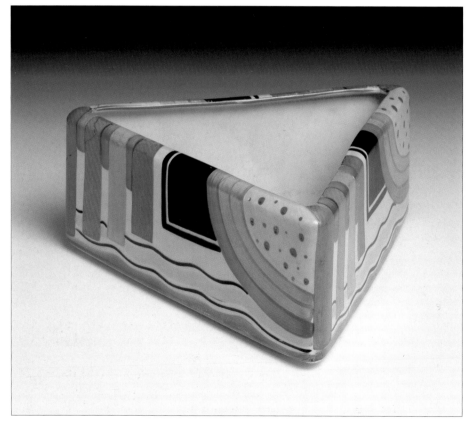

Plate 17.10. A triangular shaped planter decorated with a hand-painted abstract pattern (9413) c.1931. Height 3½in. (9cm).

Plate 17.11. Three earthenware lamp bases decorated with stylised patterns A1142, c.1933, 9677, c.1932 and 9318, c.1930. Tallest item 5½in. (14cm).

Gordon Forsyth (1879-1952)

Through his experience as a ceramic designer, painter and influential educator Gordon Forsyth became a freelance designer of lustre wares for Gray's resulting in his *Gloria Lustre* range. He brought his great knowledge, ideas and style into his pieces, employing various metallic glazes, which required perfect preparation and firing conditions for success. His excellent reputation was gained at the important Pilkington (Royal Lancastrian) Tile and Pottery Company, at Clifton Junction, near Manchester, where he oversaw the design department from 1906 until 1920. The first lines of lustre ware were produced from 1906. In 1920, aged forty-one, he had become Superintendent of Art in Stoke-on-Trent and played a key role in promoting the relationship between art and industry by linking the School of Art with local businesses.

Other Designers

Throughout the '20s and '30s Edward Gray built up a team of talented and influential designers and skilled painters who put his ideas into practice. During the '30s the company produced a striking range of patterns in the art deco style including a series of lamp bases (Plate 17.11) as well as a rare line decorated with golfers and jockeys (Plate 17.13).

One of the first designers to be invited to work for the company after Susie Cooper had left was Dorothy Tomes. Not much is known about her as a designer, but it is assumed that she was responsible for the wide range of stylised floral patterns that were applied to large plaques and decorative ware (Plate 17.12). These all-over patterns, which featured a number of art deco motifs, were decorated in a range of bold colour combinations and stand out as some of the best art deco styled patterns produced by Gray's during the '30s. This range of patterns, however, is often wrongly attributed to Susie Cooper although she explained some years later that she didn't produce all-over patterns, preferring to leave some space around the motif. This probably

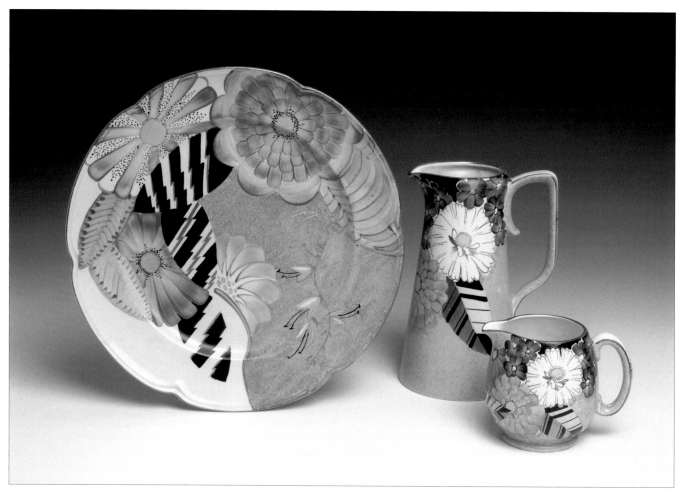

Plate 17.12. A group of patterns including a charger (A2160) from 1934, a water jug (A2448), c.1934, and a Paris jug (A2448) c.1934. Height of tallest item 12½in. (31.8cm).

explains why she wasn't keen on her geometric patterns. Dorothy Tomes left Gray's in 1932, just before the factory moved from Hanley to Stoke.[7]

In 1931 the *Pottery and Glass Record* reviewed, in some detail, the London showroom in Hatton Garden and the latest art deco designs that were on display. In particular the article explained how the owner of the showroom had uncovered the original panelling from 250 years ago. This was complemented by oak panels on the other walls with one wall being decorated with drawings of stylised flowers and gazelles, possibly the work of Susie Cooper. The latest pottery was displayed on unpolished oak tables as well as oak cubes and triangles. The article noted the new modernistic pattern called *Radio* which was made up of yellow, orange and black colours and the *Persian* pattern,

depicting fan-shaped flowers. Within the showroom was an inner room dedicated to the many lustre designs for which the company had become known. These various lustre patterns and styles were applied to a range of tea wares, cigarette boxes, ashtrays, vases and lamp bases including the pentagon shape. A notable item, probably for display only, was a large plaque depicting a knight on horseback decorated entirely in silver lustre except for a little mauve and blue, with red plumes in his helmet and in his boot.[8]

One of the most important designers from the '30s through to the post-war period was Sam Talbot. He joined Gray's in about 1925 and was responsible for some of the most important patterns of the period. Unfortunately, it is rather difficult to know which patterns

Plate 17.13. An earthenware lamp base, height 5½in. (14cm), decorated with a stylised hand-painted golfer scene (A301), c.1932.

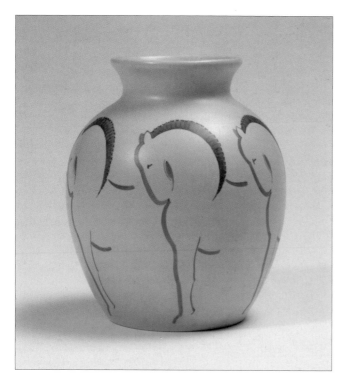

Plate 17.14. *An earthenware vase decorated with a hand-painted stylised horse design, mid-1930s. Height 6½in. (16.5cm).*

he designed as his name was not included on the backstamp despite receiving some acknowledgement in the trade press and other design publications. particularly in the post-war period. It can be assumed, however, that he was responsible for a majority of the latest patterns or at least that he played an important role in the success of the company during the '50s. One of his acknowledged patterns was *Stella,* which featured raised spots, launched in about 1937. In the *Decorative Art Studio Year Book* of 1943-1948 no fewer than five different patterns were illustrated with his name included in the caption: a stylised strawberry and green leaves pattern in bronze lustre, a ground-laid border of grey and green berries, a pattern depicting a basket of fruit, a set of vases decorated with stylised lustre patterns and a simple motif of a tree, in gold and browns. Whilst

these may not be in the art deco style, it does show how important he was within the pottery trade.

Gray's showed a number of hand-painted patterns at the important *British Industrial Art in Relation to the Home* exhibition in 1933. The trade press noted that 'one of the best, for true simplicity of effect, was the No 986. This consisted of brown bands and brown dashes and green spots upon a yellow glaze'.[9] Other patterns included silver lustre designs with hand-painted decoration. The same article commented that 'it must be acknowledged that modernity of outlook characterises the whole of these patterns'.[10]

New patterns, launched at the British Industries Fair in 1934, included *Tartan,* a banded design of various colours. The same display included the new stoneware beer and lemonade sets, which were decorated with stylised hand-painted motifs, and proved popular. Gray's also produced a similar range of decorative wares such as vases decorated with simple motifs (Plate 17.14). Probably some of the latest pottery on display was the work of the freelance designer, Nancy Catford, who modelled a series of wall masks including a fisherman called 'Old Salt', a young boy entitled 'Sunny Boy', an owl, a fox and a budgerigar group found with different colouring. She also produced life-sized garden ornaments including a toucan, penguins, owls and a rabbit; these had very little decoration. In 1935 Gray's showed a number of wares at the British Art in Industry exhibition staged at the Royal Academy of Art in London. One particular coffee set featured platinum banding to the base of the wares and on the lids with handles painted in black. By the mid-'30s Grays introduced a new range called *Sunbuff,* which featured the name on the backstamp. This range contained many different hand-painted patterns, many stylised floral patterns, and proved popular. Towards the late '30s transfer-printed wares became more abundant.

The factory continued to produce high quality decorations, especially lustre wares influenced by the Sunderland factories. In 1959 A.E. Gray & Co Ltd was purchased by Susan Williams-Ellis, owner of the Portmeirion Pottery.

1. Company advertisement, *The Pottery and Glass Record,* June 1915.
2. For further information on Edward Gray see: P. Niblett, *Hand-Painted Gray's Pottery,* City Museum and Art Gallery, Stoke-on-Trent, 1982.
3. A range of *Gloria Lustre* items was illustrated in *The Pottery and Glass Record* in September 1925, p.339, and in *Pottery Gazette,* 1 April 1926, p.603.
4. *Pottery Gazette,* 2 April 1923, p.656.
5. Pottery and Glass Record, April 1928, p.77.
6. *Pottery Gazette,* 1 April 1926, p.602.
7. Information from P. Niblett, op. cit.
8. *Pottery and Glass Record,* October 1931.
9. *Pottery Gazette,* 1 July 1933, p. 842; pattern illustrated on p.841.
10. Ibid.

18.

Susie Cooper

Andrew Casey

THROUGHOUT HER PROLIFIC AND INFLUENTIAL career, both as designer and owner of a pottery company, Susie Cooper's quick response to the latest fashions and market trends kept her ahead of her competitors in an ever shrinking market. She produced a number of striking art deco designs during the late '20s for A.E. Gray & Co Ltd (Gray's) and then, for a limited period, for her own factory from 1929.

It was at Gray's that she gained an understanding of the possibilities and limitations of hand-painted decoration that would stand her in good stead when she finally established her own factory at the end of the '20s. It also gave her an important insight into the pottery trade, the current market and the sorts of patterns that sold. Despite being promoted to the position of Chief Designer, she still had to respond to what the owner Edward Gray thought would be popular. He suggested that she should develop a range of geometric patterns during the late '20s in response to the increasing

Plate 18.1. An earthenware coffee set decorated with a less well-known Susie Cooper 'modernist' pattern. Originally produced at the George Street Pottery, this example was entered into the pattern book as E/69 from 1929/1930. Height of coffee pot 6¾in. (17.5cm). The Susie Cooper pattern book refers to this design as 'modernist'. The Fife shape coffee set was supplied by Grimwades.

153

Plate 18.2. An earthenware coffee can decorated with coloured bands, E/51, bearing the Tunstall backstamp, c.1929/1930, and a Dutch jug, E/50. Height of jug 4in. (10.5cm). This was the first pattern entered into the new pattern book for the Chelsea Works and it is clear that it is a colour variation of the early banded design.

popularity of peasant pottery, the over-glaze brightly coloured pottery that was coming on to the market from Europe. The designer was not keen on the execution of the patterns as they were thickly painted and would often flake or rub. Furthermore, the company did not manufacture their own wares and Susie Cooper became frustrated by the various shapes that they bought in, with many not matching, even in sets. With growing confidence she decided that she wanted to become an independent designer with the opportunity of making her own statement in ceramic design. She left Gray's in 1929,[1] having realised a few years earlier that if she stayed with them she would be a decorator rather than a designer.

With financial help from her family, Susie Cooper decided to set up in business, initially renting rooms at the George Street Pottery in Tunstall with a few decorators. She secured the invaluable assistance of Albert Richardson, a well-established potter, who kindly offered to assist her with technical difficulties in producing her first pottery. Sadly, without any warning, the landlord foreclosed and Cooper was forced to seek new accommodation. According to the designer, only one firing was done at the George Street Pottery[2] and the pattern book from this period is thought not to exist. The limited range of patterns that were fired are known only from extant examples such as the striking modernist pattern that demonstrated Susie Cooper was aware of European art trends, applied to a coffee set (Plate 18.1), and a banded pattern (Plate 18.2). These wares were stamped with the words 'A SUSIE COOPER PRODUCTION TUNSTALL ENGLAND'.

New premises were soon located at the Chelsea Works in Burslem and the Susie Cooper Pottery began production in March 1930. The designer knew the

Plate 18.3. An earthenware coffee pot (shape name and manufacturer unknown) decorated with a geometric pattern (E/110) from c.1931, a beaker (E/276) decorated with a colour variation of E/110 from c.1933, and a lemonade jug decorated with a geometric pattern (8215) from the Gray's period, c.1929. Size 7½in. (19cm).

market very well and understood that there was a gap between the expensive bone china coffee wares and the lower end of the market that used cheap rubber standing or banding. Given her intuitive understanding of the mood of the day, and the demands of the customer, the designer created a wide range of free-hand art deco styled patterns, but these were produced amongst a whole range of floral and banded patterns to please all markets, as demonstrated in the first illustrated range of her work in the trade press in 1930. The article featured a selection of wares, such as a teapot, cheese dish and milk jug decorated with a simple brushwork floral pattern called *Bronze Chrysanthemums* (E/96) alongside a series of abstract patterns decorated with bands, half circles and spots on a range of wares including a vase, coffee pot, biscuit barrel and tea wares.[3] The trade press commented:

she has paid particular attention to the trend in modern design as applied to particular channels of the pottery trade – especially the more exclusive departments.[4]

It was the designer's aim to introduce a varied selection of early morning sets, sandwich sets, ashtrays, bon-bon dishes, some dinnerware and a series of banded jugs, all in earthenware, with the intention of introducing bookends and figures later when she could manufacture her own shapes. This was not possible, however, until a new connection was made with Wood and Sons the following year. Until that important arrangement was finalised, Susie Cooper had to be satisfied with buying white wares from various suppliers, such as Grimwades and Grindley, but soon found that those manufactured by Wood and Sons were of a better quality. On occasion,

Plate 18.4. *An earthenware square plate and Dutch jug, supplied by Wood and Sons, decorated with a geometric pattern, E/237, c.1933. Height of jug 4¾in. (12cm).*

Plate 18.5. *A group of simple hand-painted patterns. The larger plate is decorated with the Scarlet Runner Beans pattern (E/241) from 1932; the candlestick is decorated with the Symphony pattern (E/153) from 1931, milk jug (E/119) and plate (E/155).*

Plate 18.6. A rare tall earthenware Console shape vase decorated with an abstract pattern, possibly E/184, from 1931. Height 6in. (15cm).

however, the selected shapes were incongruous with the sort of patterns that were being applied to it, as is the case with an elegant styled shape that she used thought to have been supplied by Grimwades (Plate 18.3).

Her art deco designs were generally similar to those that she created at Gray's Pottery but with an increasingly varied palette. Her abstract and geometric patterns used blocks of on-glaze colour sparingly around the ware rather than the whole surface (Plate 18.4). This new approach to patterning had as much to do with the limitations of her workforce as an awareness of modern art. Her new enterprise had a staff of about six or so young decorators who were not, on the whole, skilled enough to undertake sophisticated patterns. These young women were trained by the designer how

to space the design and how to apply colour so simple spots were used to decorate the ware and, as they became more proficient, spots became buds, feathers and beans (Plate 18.5). To some extent her patterns were created to meet the abilities of her decorators and, as the business grew, further young girls were recruited, often direct from the local schools of art.

Often referred to as 'modernistic' and 'abstract' in her pattern books, her art deco designs were essentially confined to the first three or four years of production at her works (1929-1933). Probably the most adventurous of these was a series of abstract cogwheel-like patterns applied to various shapes, but in particular the *Console* shape (Plate 18.6). Recorded in the pattern book are other similar patterns and shapes that included *The*

Plate 18.7. An earthenware Cube shaped part tea set decorated with a hand-painted geometric pattern, c.1933. Height of teapot 6½in. (16.5cm). The ware was supplied by Wood and Sons Ltd.

Storm (E/174) and *Citrons* (E/194) with many other patterns described but unknown today.[5] A number of abstract patterns were applied to the *Cube* shape, a bold angular shape that was very much of the period (Plate 18.7), including *Galaxy* (E/225). The *Cube* shape, supplied by Wood and Sons, was also used for a limited range of pictorial patterns. Susie Cooper used another shape called *Wedge* for a series of slightly modernistic patterns as well as a number of floral designs (Plate 18.8).

A number of her art deco designs were produced purely for commercial reasons as there was a clear demand for patterns that nodded to the popularity of the country cottage scenes issued by many other manufacturers. Susie Cooper used patterns such as *The*

Homestead, *Panorama* and *Caravan* and other similar designs for a new set of short order sets that were ideal for young married couples or smaller families who didn't want to buy extensive dinner services like their parents had (Plate 18.9). She was also commissioned, probably at one of the British Industries Fairs, to produce a series of ashtrays for hotels (Plate 18.10).

The breakthrough for Susie Cooper came in 1931 when Wood and Sons offered her space at the Crown Works in Burslem, part of the Bursley Ltd factory that had been empty for some years having previously being occupied by both Charlotte Rhead and her father Frederick. Importantly, Harry Wood offered to manufacture her shapes as well, thus providing her with the complete control she so desired. Susie Cooper set

Plate 18.8. An earthenware Wedge shaped trio decorated with an abstract pattern (E/559), milk jug (E/533) from c.1933 and a saucer (E/278) from c.1932. Height of cup 2¾in. (7cm).

Plate 18.9. A group of hand-painted earthenware short order patterns. Left to right: Dutch jug decorated with The Seagull pattern, c.1931; the Panorama (E/306) pattern applied to a Cube shaped cup and saucer, c.1932; The Homestead pattern decorated on a stepped jug, height 5½in (14cm) c.1931.

Plate 18.10. A pattern book entry illustrating patterns for ashtrays, c.1933.

about creating a new range called *Kestrel* which was launched at the British Industries Fair in 1932. A practical and functional shape that was easily cleaned, poured well and could take all manner of decoration, it

was used for a series of brightly coloured banded patterns as well as many hand-painted floral patterns. The *Kestrel* range was extended to other shapes, importantly the tureen, launched in 1933 and praised for its sheer practicality in that the lid could be used as a separate serving dish. Another less well-known shape was *Curlew*, a bird-like form launched in about 1932. It was used for a limited number of patterns and was phased out within two years (see Plate 18.6).

One of the most popular motifs of the art deco period was the leaping deer that first appeared on the official poster, designed by Robert Bonfils, for the 1925 Exposition Internationale des Arts Décoratifs et Industriels Modernes. This motif was used by a number of British designers such as Harold Holdway for Spode in 1936, John Adams for Carter, Stabler and Adams in the 1920s and for a textile design by Gregory Brown for W. Foxton Ltd in 1931. Susie Cooper utilised this motif throughout the '30s from her first trade advertisement in 1930, in her publicity material, as a table centre from 1936, and as her backstamp from 1932 through to the '50s. Furthermore, it was selectively used for a number of hand-painted plaques such as those for advertising,

Plate 18.11. An earthenware plaque decorated with a hand-painted stylised leaping deer, c.1932.

Plate 18.12. A hand-painted original drawing of a tiger (E/974) for a service plate from the Susie Cooper pattern book, c.1935.

Plate 18.13. A period photograph of a group of earthenware hand-painted pieces decorated with stylised animals such as a leaping deer, monkey and pig, c.1933.

(Below) Plate 18.14. A hand-painted earthenware face mask of a young woman, thought to have been a self portrait of the designer, c.1933. Height 8½in. (22cm).

(Below right) Plate 18.15. A rare hand-painted earthenware face mask of an older woman, c.1933. Height 11¼in. (28.7cm).

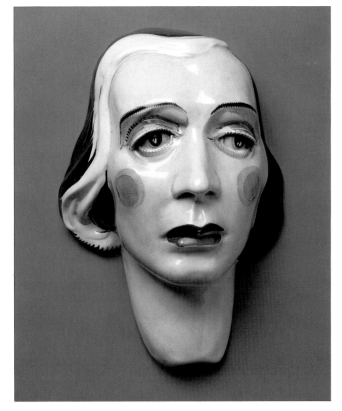

Plate 18.16. An archive photograph of the Susie Cooper trade stand at the British Industries Fair, 1933, illustrating her Curlew shape (left), elephant napkin rings (centre) and a number of Kestrel shaped wares.

often displayed on her trade stands and in her London showroom (Plate 18.11).

During the art deco period Susie Cooper used several animal motifs for her patterns, not only for a series of early hand-painted nursery wares but also for a range of decorative service plates featuring individual centres such as a fox, leopard, grazing deer and a tiger (Plate 18.12). She also produced a range of unique pieces that were often used to decorate her trade stands and included hand-painted ginger jars depicting a variety of animal designs (Plate 18.13) used at the important trade shows and exhibitions. Susie Cooper responded to the popularity of face masks on the market and developed a limited range that included a young woman (Plate 18.14), a Chinaman, judge and one of an older lady (Plate 18.15). These were displayed both in the London showroom and at the British Industries Fair in 1933 (Plate 18.16).

Susie Cooper was always looking forward rather than

back to her previous triumphs so when the art deco style began to lose favour with the British pottery market she began to experiment with new decorative ideas such as crayon and aerographic decoration. Besides developing a popular range of wash banded patterns in subtle colours that were very different from the strident art deco colours, ultimately Cooper turned to transfer-printed patterns that would enable her to compete on the international market. Patterns such as *Dresden Spray, Nosegay* and *April* were typical. Nick Dolan commented that:

> Although the design theory that informed her work was essentially modernist it was not the bleak and stark modernism of the continental model but one that was adapted to encompass the best traditions of the English industry and the need that she correctly perceived in her market for good quality patterns.[6]

---

1. Interview with Susie Cooper in the *Designer* magazine, March 1979.
2. B. Youds, *Susie Cooper An Elegant Affair*, Thames and Hudson, 1996. The first range of patterns were given an A prefix and were recorded

in the description book.
3. 'Buyer's Notes', *Pottery Gazette*, 1 April 1930, p.593.
4. Ibid.
5. Information from the Susie Cooper pattern

books held at the Wedgwood Museum.
6. Quote taken from *Susie Cooper: A Pioneer of Modern Design*, Antique Collectors' Club, 1992, p.54.

19.

Crown Devon

Peter and Brenda Aspinall

THE STORY OF FIELDING'S CROWN DEVON and the family whose members created and ran the firm over four generations is a fascinating one. In 1878 Simon Fielding combined with three other people working in the Stoke Potteries to open a new pottery manufacturing business, Railway Pottery in Sutherland Street. Five years earlier he had purchased the controlling interest in a small colour mill where his son Abraham was serving as an apprentice colour maker. He placed Abraham in charge of the new pottery venture, which began trading under the name of Fielding, later to become S.F. & Co from the late 1880s.

It was sound business sense on Simon Fielding's part to set up this further new business to support his colour mill, ensuring that all the necessary materials needed for pottery production were purchased from the mill. However, his good business acumen seemed to stagnate from that point in time as he left the day to day running of the business to his three partners, preferring to pursue his passion for breeding game birds and gun dogs.[1] By trading on his society connections Simon Fielding still managed a reasonable living, acquired capital and eventually gravitated to being a manufacturer of pottery. His dreams of further advances in the pottery industry were shattered when court bailiffs took possession of the premises in 1879.

Abraham Fielding made a surprising decision to buy the company and pay off the debts. Despite having scant knowledge of pottery manufacture, working at the colour mill had given him a basic grounding in the pottery industry and he had made many valuable connections with certain other pottery manufacturers. His hard work helped him to establish in the ensuing years a thriving and extremely profitable business.

In 1883 Fielding's Railway Pottery sustained the first of four disastrous fires, leaving only the walls of the pottery

standing and the loss of up to £4,000. Undeterred, Abraham began reconstructing a larger more modern pottery only to suffer again with another calamitous fire in 1888.

Many lesser men would have been destroyed by the occurrence of two such damaging fires, but within the space of five years Abraham began reconstructing his pottery. Using new concepts and principals he installed new plant and machinery that was much more efficient and cost effective than any used in pottery manufacture up to that date. The business progressed and prospered, quickly establishing a reputation for being a family company who treated an ever-growing staff with consideration and care. They provided the workforce with working conditions that were far ahead of their time.

By the early part of the twentieth century the company enjoyed great commercial success. They became a limited company in 1905, the same year that the founder of the company died. S.F. Fielding & Co. specialised in high quality pottery decorated with patterns typical of the period alongside other new lines such as Soleilian Ware launched in 1904.

In the late 1920s art deco mania engulfed the British pottery industry, with Fielding's *Crown Devon* becoming a main producer of wares in the latest styles. In particular, Howard Carter's discovery of the boy Pharaoh Tutankhamun's tomb, with all its amazing treasures intact, gave an added impetus to the art deco craze and led to many pottery manufacturers producing new lines with designs inspired by the artefacts discovered.

In an era of deep economic depression, Abraham Fielding was now being assisted by his son Alec Ross Fielding and his grandson Reginald Fielding. They were an important factor in the continued success and

Plate 19.1. An
earthenware ginger jar
and cover decorated with
a stylised pattern printed
with some hand-painted
decoration and based on
the Orient design, 1930s.
Height of jar 17in. (43cm).

Plate 19.2. An earthenware coffee set decorated with the Orient pattern, 1930s.

advancement of the business, as was the acquisition of two new employees, Enoch Boulton and George Barker. Enoch Boulton was given the job of Design and Decoration Manager and George Barker the position of Sales Director. They worked in conjunction with Director Reginald Fielding and revolutionised the company's product portfolio enabling Fielding's Crown Devon to compete successfully during a time of recession.

The pottery was famous for the many styles and finishes utilised in its varied and prolific production. Many items were hand painted and attention to detail was uppermost in the patterns and shapes produced. The most important pieces were those in *Lustrine, Mattajade, Mattita* and particularly items that were heavily decorated in brightly coloured enamels with an abundance of gilding. Lustreware items included vases, jugs, wall plaques, tea and coffee sets, candlesticks, table lamps, even chamber pots, and were decorated with dragons, butterflies, stylised flowers, birds,

galleons, castles, fairies and mermaids. One of the most important art deco designs was the *Orient* design (Plate 19.1). Flamboyantly decorated in rich enamels in red, black, gold and green, this was a 'top seller' and even today rightly commands high prices when it comes up for sale (Plate 19.2).

Lustrine items were originally introduced in 1917 but this range was expanded in the '30s with the public clamouring for even more art deco designs and eventually over one hundred patterns emerged. *Lustrine* referred to the background colour which, as the name suggests, was in a lustre finish and was available in green, orange, purple, ruby, blue, yellow and pink, amongst others.

The *Mattajade* range (Plate 19.3) was launched in 1932, featuring a wonderful mottled deep turquoise hue, and many fantastic heavily enamelled and gilded designs were applied to items bearing its backstamp.[2] Dragons, flowers, birds, trees and spiders' webs were

Plate 19.3. An earthenware vase decorated with stylised trees and butterflies, pattern M192, a vase decorated with Mattajade pattern M757 and a Mattajade bowl, pattern no 2342 and a Mattita tube-lined vase, pattern M83. Height of tallest item 7½in. (19cm).

Plate 19.4. A group of decorative vases. Left to right: a Mattajade handled jug decorated with the Fairy Castle pattern 2406, a tube-lined Vogue shaped vase, pattern M169, and an earthenware jug, pattern M45. Height of tallest item 9¾in. (25cm).

Plate 19.5. Two hand-painted earthenware plaques decorated with the Mattita *plaque (left), pattern M35, and pattern no: M409. Diameter of plaque 7⅞in. (20cm).*

used to dramatic effect, and perhaps the most famous pattern of all was *Fairy Castle* (Plate 19.4) which depicted a wonderful red roofed turreted castle perched high above a woodland scene with a meandering footpath leading up to it. This particular design received the royal seal of approval from Queen Mary who purchased several items in the range at the British Industries Fair of 1932.

Following the success of *Mattajade* Fielding's produced further items with a matt design including *Mattita* and *Mattatone*. Items bearing the *Mattita* backstamp were decorated with colourful abstract designs similar to those by Clarice Cliff (Plate 19.5). One of the most popular patterns of the time (1932) was a *Mattita* item with a predominantly bright yellow background depicting a cottage with a bright red roof. Stylised poplar trees and red capped toadstools were

often incorporated into these designs too.

One of the most striking and attractive of the art deco designs produced by Fielding's was a design called *Fantazia* (Plate 19.6). It is a scene of magic and fantasy, hence the pattern name. This particular design and others were copied from book illustrations with *Fantazia* being adapted from illustrations by the well-known Irish artist Henry Clarke for an edition of Hans Christian Andersen's *Fairy Tales* produced by Harrap in 1916. It is interesting to point out that Carlton Ware also produced a design they called *Fantasia*.[3] Perhaps this is not surprising as designers went from pottery to pottery and obviously plagiarism was rife if a particular design was popular with the public.

Another success for Fielding's was the range of bright coloured geometric designs mostly applied to a black background and decorated with circles, triangles,

Plate 19.6. A group of Crown Devon decorative items. Left to right: a small enamelled vase decorated with butterflies, pattern 321, a blue enamelled Vogue shaped Fantazia vase, pattern 444, a blue enamelled powder bowl, pattern 2069, diameter 5½in. (14cm), and a hand painted Vogue shaped vase decorated with a hand painted floral design, pattern A60. Height of tallest item 7¾in. (19.5cm).

Plate 19.7. An earthenware tea for two featuring a hand-painted geometric design with the words 'painted by Hylda Cooke' on reverse. Height of teapot 4¾in. (12cm).

Plate 19.8. A group of Crown Devon jugs (which usually came in sets of three). Left to right: a stylised floral pattern (A11), a similar floral design (A294) and a geometric pattern (A17). About 1928. Height of tallest item 5⅛in. (13cm).

Plate 19.9. Examples of hand-painted tableware. Left to right: a coffee pot decorated with pattern A132, an Era Ware beaker, pattern E120, a preserve jar with cane handle and pattern A131 and a coffee pot (centre) and jug decorated with pattern A195. Height of pot 7⅞in. (20cm). The Windermere can was specially made for T.H. Winder & Co, Windermere.

Plate 19.10. A hand-painted earthenware plaque decorated with a stylised floral pattern, late '20s. Diameter of plaque 7⅞in. (20cm).

oblongs and, indeed, any other geometric shape they could find, decorated in bright yellow, red, blue and green (Plates 19.7 to 19.10).

Crown Devon also produced a popular range of art deco figurines that were clearly influenced by European manufacturers such as Goldscheider (Plate 19.11). These new figures were designed by Kathleen Parsons, Walter Lamonby and later Olga Hartzeg who had started working at the factory during the late '30s. Most of these were created in the true art deco style and

Plate 19.11. A period leaflet illustrating some of the range of Crown Devon figures, 1930s.

included dancers, flapper girl figures in the fashion trends of the day and nudes. But, as reported in 1936:

...in other types, fantasy had a strong appeal in pose and in some stances pertness, of the dance subjects, as seen in the Sutherland series; altogether there being fifty to sixty different models on view. Done in a variety of colourings, hand painted, fine modern character studies expressed by Miss Parson's designs, especially the Windy hat Girl, charming Balloon Flyers Girls, notably the best possibly Betty, good scheme of figure, and the best possibly in character modelling, Janita, a Spanish type.[4]

One amusing story tells of the various salesmen employed by Fielding's being very reluctant to take samples of these nudes home in case they got into trouble from their wives! Nude figurines were still very daring and avant-garde at that time.

With the outbreak of the Second World War austerity descended on the pottery industry. The production of fancy goods was severely restricted with export only rules applying for all but utilitarian items. However, export rejects were provided to United Kingdom retailers on a strict quota basis. Fielding's continued to produce items for the home market during the war but these were not of the same quality as in pre-war days. Items such as novelty cruet sets, dinner and tea ware featuring tree landscape patterns and other simpler designs, jam pots in all shapes and sizes, souvenir ware and comical dogs and cats were all churned out to keep the business turning over.

Once the war was over Fielding's stepped up production but never again produced the wonderful designs of the art deco period for which they were well known and for which a demand still exists today. The Fielding connection with the pottery ended in 1967 and it eventually closed its doors in 1982.

1. Cockfighting was now illegal in England but certain members of the upper classes still staged illicit cockfights and there was a lively trade in game birds. Simon Fielding had risen to prominence in this so-called sport when working for the Duke of Sutherland on his Trentham Hall estate.
2. *Mattajade* was the name given to the background colour of the pieces.
3. Note that Carlton Ware spelt their design with an s whilst Crown Devon used a z.
4. *The Pottery and Glass Record*, March 1936, p. 61.

20.

Empire Porcelain Company

Miranda Goodby

THE EMPIRE PORCELAIN COMPANY was founded in 1895 by the London and New York based import company, Lazarus & Rosenfeld. Operating from the Empire Works, Shelton, Stoke-on-Trent, it rapidly expanded, building a second factory next to the original works and employing over six hundred people by 1898.[1] The firm only produced semi-porcelain – or earthenware – rather than the bone china that its name implies.

The company prided itself on its use of the new printing technology of chromolithography bought in from specialist printing firms to decorate its pottery.[2] Despite this, for the first two decades of the twentieth century its wares were predominantly in an eighteenth century revival rococo style, competing with popular Continental wares and decorated with aerography and bright gilding in addition to lithographs.

In the late 1920s the company underwent a change of direction. It modernised the style of its backstamps, started adding the month and year of production to its marks, and introduced a variety of new ranges, styles and decorations (Plate 20.1). It continued to make its lithographed wares, but in a much more contemporary

(Above) Plate 20.1. An earthenware coffee service decorated with a stylised floral pattern, 1932.

Plate 20.2. An earthenware cup and saucer decorated with a transfer-printed crinoline lady surrounded by gold stamping, 1939. This lithograph was an open stock pattern and used by other factories.

Plate 20.3. Butterdish and cover in the form of a thatched cottage and painted in underglaze colours, 1936.

Plate 20.4. An earthenware covered box, candlestick and footed dish decorated with mottled glazes. All with printed marks. Candlestick and dish from 1934 and candlestick from 1937.

Plate 20.5. A pair of stepped candlesticks decorated with a mottled green-blue glaze, c.1935. The base has a paper label that reads 'Empire Art Ware/England'.

style. Instead of relying on pastiche eighteenth century rococo styles the firm introduced modern designs which, by the end of the 1930s, included large quantities of fashionable 'crinoline lady in a garden' patterns (often augmented by gold stamping) and the popular floral chintz designs (Plate 20.2). Some of these printed patterns were unique to Empire while others were open stock, with the same subjects also appearing on other firms' wares.

The company also began to make a considerable use of other types of decoration. Empire's version of the popular moulded cottage design tea wares with painted details, made by so many firms, was produced under the trade name *Tudor Cottage* from the early 1930s (Plate 20.3). This period also saw the introduction of 'Empire Art Ware', a wide range of ornamental wares from vases to candlesticks and bookends decorated with semi-matt 'art' glazes predominantly in shades of blue and buff or orange and buff (Plates 20.4 and 20.5).

Hand-painted tea wares and fancies also became an important part of the factory's output and ranged from the conventional to the determinedly art deco (Plates 20.6 and

20.7). While in many instances the painted patterns were applied to comparatively standard shapes, the firm also introduced modern, geometric shapes for some of its wares (Plate 20.8). A small series of figures of elegantly dressed women and girls was also produced. The trade names 'Ivory Glaze', 'Ivory Ware' and, in particular, 'Shelton Ivory', introduced by 1936,[3] were incorporated into the backstamps of many of the firm's wares (Plate 20.9).

Never a company in the forefront of fashion, Empire adapted itself successfully to the prevailing tastes, concentrating on producing highly saleable wares aimed at the mass market and reflecting, rather than leading, the fashion. The firm did not set out to be a trendsetter. It scarcely advertised in the *Pottery Gazette* in the 1920s and 1930s. It did not show at the 1930 Modern Pottery Exhibition in Stoke-on-Trent, nor at the annual British Industries Fairs until 1937.[4] The *Pottery Gazette*, describing Empire's stand at the British Industries Fair in 1937, wrote:

The concern in question is an old-established one, and one

Plate 20.6. An earthenware trio decorated with a hand-painted floral pattern with brown shell edge to rim, 1940.

Plate 20.7. An earthenware handled dish decorated with a stylised pattern, 1940.

that is identified with a world-wide trade. The whole of the wares exhibited, we are given to understand, will fall within the strictly competitive zone.[5]

In 1938 their comment was:

The shapes and decorations are invariably such as will prove satisfying to the average taste and the extensive scale on which the wares are produced implies keen conditions of marketing.[6]

Relying on the established markets of the British Empire and North America that its parent company Lazarus & Rosenfeld dealt with, Empire had a worldwide trade. It exported particularly to the United States (where the crinoline lady patterns were very popular) and to Australia, with printed patterns such as *Mimosa* and the chintz design *Golden Wattle* being produced especially for the latter market.

Although not one of the leading firms producing art deco wares, Empire knew its market well and was highly successful. Its concentration on supplying 'the average taste' meant that it appealed to a wide audience, while the inexpensive nature of its brightly printed or simple painted wares made them very affordable.

In the wartime Board of Trade regulations of 1942 (which continued until 1952) its export trade ensured that it was one of the 'nucleus' firms that continued in production throughout hostilities.[7] Despite this it did not exhibit at either the post-war Britain Can Make It or Festival of Britain shows, both of which were aimed at a domestic audience. Instead it concentrated on its export market, which by the early 1950s comprised almost thirty countries from Iceland to South Africa and included North and South America as well as many Commonwealth countries. The firm was taken over by Qualcast in 1958 and closed in 1967.[8]

1. *Pottery Gazette*, May 1898, pp.378-9.
2. Advertisements in the *Pottery Gazette,* January 1896 onwards and editorial September 1896, pp.709-710.
3. *Pottery Gazette Diary*, 1937.
4. *Pottery Gazette,* February 1937, p.250 and April 1937, p.549.
5. Ibid., February 1937, p.250.
6. Ibid., February 1938, p.248.
7. Ibid., October 1941, November 1941 and supplement.
8. *Evening Sentinel*, 31 March 1967.

Plate 20.8. A jam dish and spoon decorated with a hand-painted stylised flower design, 1934.

Plate 20.9. An earthenware teaset decorated with a hand-painted floral pattern with banded decoration, 1940.

21

Royal Venton Ware

David Steventon

JOHN STEVENTON & SONS LTD, under the Royal Venton Ware label, was just one of many small to medium sized family owned firms producing tableware in Burslem during the art deco period of the '20s and '30s. However, production of hand-painted and decorated pieces ended with the company's move to tiles, fireplaces and sanitary ware in the mid-1930s. According to the late G.M. McKenzie, who joined as an accountant from Michelin in the early 1930s, this change took place in 1934 although some ceramic experts claim alternative dates.[1] Certainly by 1937 the company was producing sanitary ware from the new Middlewich factory, acquired from British Salt in 1936. Production of art deco pieces was therefore limited but stands comparison with the larger factories and the better-known designers.

The company was first formed as a partnership in about 1896/97 between Mr William J. Brown, Mr W. Lees and Mr John Steventon. They were to produce earthenware under the name Brown Lees and Steventon, the names being taken in alphabetical order. The first factory in Bournes Bank was rented but the Hill Pottery, Victoria and Hill China Works site in Burslem was purchased at auction in September 1900.[2]

Mr Lees withdrew after a short period and the partnership continued under the name of Brown & Steventon until about 1913/14 when a private limited company was formed. It was to be known as Brown & Steventon Ltd with Mr W.J. Brown Snr, Mr W.J. Brown Jnr, Mr John Steventon and Mr William Horace Steventon on the Board of Directors and with Mr Reginald John Steventon being appointed at a later date as Secretary. William and Reginald Steventon were the sons of John Steventon. In 1923 W.J. Brown Snr and W.J. Brown Jnr resigned from the company and the Board became John Steventon (Chairman), W.H. Steventon and R.J.

Steventon, hence the name of John Steventon & Sons Ltd.

It is understood that sales were originally mainly to markets but they were also made through mail order catalogues, particularly in the United States of America. They were mostly in commercially available lithographic print designs including *Willow* pattern and a reproduction of a Rogers design, with the Brown & Steventon backstamp.[3] It is also understood that the name Royal Venton came about after a purchase by a member of the Royal Family at an Ideal Home Exhibition. A later effort to discredit the use of Royal was discounted by the fact that the company had used it for several years. Throughout the many years of production the company used a number of backstamps with the first bearing the simple statement 'Steventons Ltd', followed by a mark that incorporated the sun logo, used by Brown & Steventon, but updated to John Steventon & Sons Ltd, followed by the crown mark concluding with a larger and more elaborate version of that mark. The last version featured included the EST 1897. In between there were several variations of this mark, usually associated with named patterns such as *Autumn, Carmen, Kato, Marigold, Poppy* and *Carmen* positioned above or below the main mark.

In the absence of an archive of pattern books, it is impossible to catalogue the full range of the output from the company and difficult to be certain of the correct attribution of pattern to designer. Three people, however, were clearly major contributors to the quality and variety of output: Harold Holdcroft, Gladys Scarlett and Frank Phillips, each of them having their own backstamp (Plate 21.1).

Harold Holdcroft, born in 1904, was a student at Burslem School of Art and was appointed lecturer there at the early age of eighteen. He would therefore have

Plate 21.1. Standard backstamps used by the company designers Harold Holdcroft, Gladys Scarlett and Frank Phillips.

had an influence on other pottery designers and artists attending the school during the 1920s. He had certainly joined John Steventon & Sons Ltd by 1928, with Royal Venton ware pieces bearing his backstamp featuring a lion passant with his signature, produced either in a lustre finish or in a matt, mottled pink background.[4] The lustre finish pieces are typically with a light ochre background and decorated with boldly coloured bunches of fruit (Plate 21.2) or with a white background and executed in geometric designs (Plate 21.3). The boldly coloured bunches of fruit designs feature too on the mottled pink background pieces, as do designs based on a stylised bird (Plate 21.4). The designer also used variations of the stylised fruit border (Plate 21.5).

Intriguingly, one of the other designs found on a recent purchase of a pair of lustre finish vases with the Holdcroft backstamp is of art deco poplar trees, fields and houses. This calls into question the attribution of this type of design to Gladys Scarlett (see below).

The lion passant was also included in the backstamp for an Olde English Inns set of designs (thought to feature about twenty different historic inns) but is assumed to have no connection with Holdcroft. The best known, and certainly the most highly priced, of Holdcroft's work in Royal Venton Ware on the market today is the nursery ware elephant tea set.[5] The teapot, milk jug and sugar bowl were produced both in a plain mottled grey and in a highly decorated design with a circus or pirate theme. The teapot has the trunk for a spout and a masked monkey as the finial mounted on the lid (Plate 21.6). Harold Holdcroft moved on from John Steventon & Sons Ltd to T.C. Wild in 1934,

Plate 21.2. An earthenware ginger jar decorated with a pattern of bold coloured bunches of fruit on a beige lustre glaze, designed by Harold Holdcroft, c.1928. 8in. (20.3cm) high.

Plate 21.3. A group of decorative vases. Centre vase decorated with bold stylised floral motifs on a white background with a lustre finish and gold outline, marked 2254, c.1930. Pair of matching vases decorated with bold abstract motifs on white background with a lustre finish, c.1930. All designed by Harold Holdcroft. Height of tallest item 9½in. (24.1cm).

Plate 21.4. An earthenware vase decorated with a hand-painted stylised lyre bird on a lightly mottled matt pink background, designed by Harold Holdcroft, late 1920s. 9½in. (24.1cm) high. Note the painted shadow of the bird.

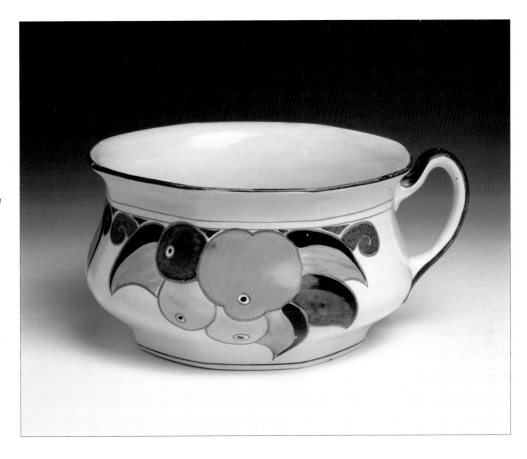

Plate 21.5. An earthenware chamber pot, decorated with a hand-painted pattern of stylised fruit, designed by Harold Holdcroft, c.1930. 9in. (22.9cm) diameter.

eventually to produce the *Old Country Roses* design for Royal Albert.

Gladys Scarlett was a talented paintress, leaving school to go straight to work at A.J. Wilkinson Ltd. Initially set to work there with Dolly Cliff, she was soon the first to be moved across to work with Clarice Cliff. Whilst Colley Shorter sent Clarice Cliff to the Royal College of Art, Gladys continued both painting and designing. Scarlett worked with Clarice Cliff for five years but, having been passed over for promotion when the first 'Missus' of the Bizarre paint shop resigned and failing to secure a wage increase, she was prompted to seek employment elsewhere. She doubled her wages on joining John Steventon & Sons Ltd in 1932, shortly before her twenty-first birthday. She was to work as a paintress with the modeller Frank Phillips, leaving for Maddock's only when Royal Venton moved over to tiles, fireplaces and sanitary ware.[6] Her back stamp at Royal Venton incorporated a painter's palette, accentuating the hand painting involved in producing her designs.

Typical of her patterns is *Autumn Leaves*, hand-painted with the shading on the leaf ranging from reddish

Plate 21.6. A part teaset in the form of an elephant, designed by Harold Holdcroft.

Plate 21.7. A group of hand-painted earthenware tea wares: a teacup, saucer and plate decorated with a stylised 'blossom on twigs' pattern designed by Harold Holdcroft, marked 2984, about late 1920s, and an octagonal plate decorated with the Autumn Leaves pattern designed by Gladys Scarlett, marked A536, c.1932. Diameter of largest plate 8½in.

orange through pale green to an autumnal yellow (Plate 21.7). Similar designs that cannot directly be attributed to her, but are clearly influenced by her, are autumn leaves with berries, water lilies, crocus and various other brightly coloured flowers. The crocus design in particular is more delicately executed than the equivalent Clarice Cliff design, with a bluish grey wash for the sky above the flowers to complete the picture.

One of her plainer designs was banding around the piece in several concentric rings in slightly different shades of blue. There were also banded designs in various shades of green and brown on art deco mouldings, having two or rarely four fins on the rims, presumably influenced by her but again not carrying her backstamp (Plate 21.8). These were offered on a full range of dinnerware and tea sets. Included in the range was a rectangular plate with a circular depression in the

centre very similar to one of the Bizarre pieces and decorated with a variety of scenic and floral designs. Royal Venton was perhaps the only other company to produce such a shape (Plate 21.9).[7] Although none of these rectangular pieces found so far has Gladys' backstamp, they must have been influenced by her and her experience at A.J. Wilkinson. On the purchase of such a piece in a deco poplar trees and fields design at an antique and collectors' fair at Harrogate in 1997, the vendor's comment to the author was 'poor man's Clarice Cliff'.

As a modeller, Frank Phillips was responsible for the Floretta Ware range (Plate 21.13). This was launched in February 1932 with a full colour advertisement in the trade press.[8] Certainly the range was very extensive, being produced in over 120 different shapes.[9] These had a brilliant glaze and were presented in several colour-

Plate 21.8. A part earthenware coffee set, shape name unknown, decorated with bands of brown with ochre lines in a large hatchwork design attributed to Gladys Scarlett, c.1932. Coffee pot 6½in. (16.5cm) high.

Plate 21.9. A group of hand-painted earthenware plates. From left to right. Rectangular plate decorated with the Laburnum pattern, marked 5269, c.1932; a similar plate decorated with the Poplars and Poppies design, c.1932; both of these plates are attributed to Gladys Scarlett. A dinner plate decorated in the Sunrise pattern, marked 3803, c.1930 and a smaller plate decorated with the Regent design of green flowers and banded decoration, late 1920s. Diameter of largest item 10in. (25.4cm).

Plate 21.10. *An earthenware dinner plate decorated with the print and enamelled Poppy pattern, late 1920s. 9in. (22.9cm) diameter.*

Plate 21.11. *An earthenware vase decorated with an art deco inspired pattern on a white background, marked S344, c.1930. 8½in. (21.6cm) high.*

Plate 21.12. *An earthenware water jug, hand painted with stylised flowers and leaves, marked 292, c.1930. 6½in (16.5cm) high.*

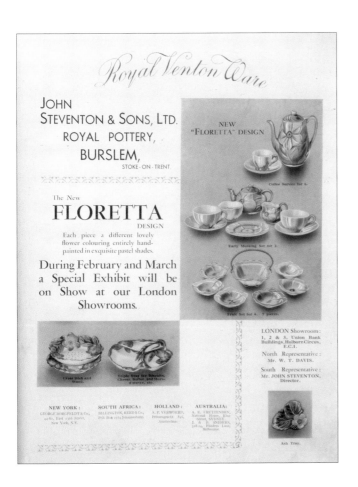

Plate 21.13. A period advertisement for the new Floretta range designed by Francis Phillips, 1932.

Plate 21.14. A part earthenware, Classic shape, dinner set comprising a dinner plate, fish plate, tureen with cover and small tureen with base plate, cover and ladle, decorated with a broad sand-coloured band and straw-yellow and brown grass pattern with detailing in orange, marked A447, c.1933. Diameter of dinner plate 10in. (25.4cm).

Plate 21.15. A part earthenware, Classic shape, tea set decorated with a hand-painted pomegranate design, c.1933. Height of teapot 3½in. (8.9cm).

ways in pastel shades, typically mauve and lilac, yellow and cerise, and pale green and yellow. They were moulded as flower petal shapes or with flower petals in relief on a smooth background. Particularly striking are the candlesticks. Although not obviously a functional design shape, they fit easily into the clenched fist and the candle itself remains vertical. The Floretta Ware backstamp featured the designer's name, either signed as Francis Phillips or as Van Phillips, although many pieces used only the standard mark.

It is clear in retrospect that it was the modelling of the earthenware shapes for dinner, coffee and tea as well as the decoration on them that followed the art deco movement (Plate 21.14). Not only were there the fins on the flat pieces produced in the banded designs, but there were also ziggurats for the finials on the teapots and vegetable tureen lids such as in the *Classic* design (Plate 21.15).[10] Overall, the impression from reading *Buyer's Notes* in the *Pottery Gazette* from the 1920s onwards is that there was a steady improvement in the quality and variety of output from John Steventon & Sons Ltd, with a full but short-lived flowering of art deco work in the early 1930s.

1. G. Godden, *Encyclopaedia of British Pottery and Porcelain Marks*, Barrie & Jenkins, London, 1964 gives the use of the main backstamp as 1923 through to 1936 and V. Bergesen, *Bergesen's Price Guide*, Barrie & Jenkins, London, 1992 gives the date as 1931 to 1940.
2. The Hill Pottery is a historic site, being in use at least as far back as 1736, and used in turn by John Mitchell, Aaron Wood, Samuel Alcock, Thomas Ford, Alcock & Diggory and Burgess & Leigh, among others.

3. This plate is illustrated in G. Godden, op. cit., reference number 654.
4. This range is illustrated in *Pottery Gazette*, 2 April 1928, p.627.
5. This range is illustrated in E. Bramah, *Novelty Teapots: Five Hundred Years of Art and Design*, 1992.
6. For further information see G. Slater, 'Some Ceramic Works by Gladys Scarlett', *The Agora*, Vol 1, No 3, February 1997 and L. Griffin, 'The Bizarre People – the Tale of Gladys Scarlett', *Clarice Cliff*

Collectors Club Review, Autumn 1983.
7. G. Slater, 'Gladys Scarlett', *The Agora*, December 1997.
8. This information was quoted in J. Spours, *Art Deco Tableware*, Ward Lock, 1988.
9. Information from *Pottery Gazette*, 1 January 1932, p.59.
10. This range is illustrated in the *Pottery Gazette*, 1 January 1933, p.55.

22

Crown Ducal Ware

Sue Taylor

EARTHENWARE MANUFACTURERS A.G. Richardson & Co Ltd were established in 1915 and named after their first Chairman, Albert Goodwin Richardson. Two other members of the Richardson family were also directors of the company which initially traded from the Gordon Pottery in Tunstall, Stoke-on-Trent. They adopted the trade name Crown Ducal and their products were favourably reviewed by the trade press in October of that year.[1] The following year two additional directors joined the company – John Harrison, whose background was in pottery manufacture with Johnson Brothers, and Joseph Rushton, who had sales experience with Bourne of Denby and Wood & Sons.[2] In 1919 A.G. Richardson left to run the Regal Pottery in Cobridge, manufacturing under the trade name Regal Ware, leaving Harrison and Rushton to develop the future production of Crown Ducal ware.[3]

In the early years the company produced a range of good quality earthenware similar in design and decoration to many of the other earthenware manufacturers in the Potteries. Early advertisements describe their range of vellum and silverine wares; black and rose decoration; white and gold ware; hand-painted and ground-laid effects in all colours.[4] This description did not change to any great extent between the first advertisements of 1915 and the later ones of the early 1920s.

The North Staffordshire Chamber of Commerce export catalogue of 1921 shows examples of the range of goods on offer (Plate 22.1). In addition to the decorative techniques described above there are examples of chintz lithographed patterns and Crown Ducal *Carnival Ware*, featuring a black matt ground with painted floral decoration.[5] The goods on offer strongly resemble the productions of Richardson's competitors such as S. Fielding & Co (with their Crown Devon vellum wares), Wiltshaw and Robinson (with Carlton Ware) and Thos.

A. G. RICHARDSON & CO., LTD.

Gordon Pottery, Tunstall, Staffs.

xvii

Plate 22.1. A page from the Chamber of Commerce Export Bulletin of 1921 showing a selection of the company's early products.

Forester & Sons (Phoenix Wares). Indeed, the *Pottery Gazette* drew attention to the fact that the company laid no claim to novelty in their offerings to the trade.[6] The styles are still reminiscent of the Victorian age and show no move towards a modernisation of design (Plate 22.2).

Messrs Harrison and Rushton brought some innovative ideas to the Crown Ducal range. In 1921 they introduced a range of self-coloured tea wares using the technique of aerography, later claiming to have been pioneers of this type of ware in the Potteries (Plate 22.3).[7] These were illustrated in 1923 on the new *Gem* shape[8] where the solid coloured grounds emphasised the strong shapes of the new wares. This, combined with printed and enamel painted patterns, heralded a change in style. This was noted in the *Pottery Gazette* report of the 1921 British Industries Fair which commented that many of the newest Crown Ducal pieces were:

> right away in type from anything the firm has previously produced. It is refreshing to see that amongst the current samples use is being made of fresh and less conventional styles of decoration and a more intensive use of colour is being resorted to.[9]

The new wares were a great success and by 1923 the

Plate 22.2. Examples of Crown Ducal ware which used solid coloured grounds shown in the British Pottery Manufacturers Standard Exporter, about 1921.

Plate 22.3. A collection of self-coloured wares including a coffee pot and candlestick. Height of coffee pot 7½in. (19cm).

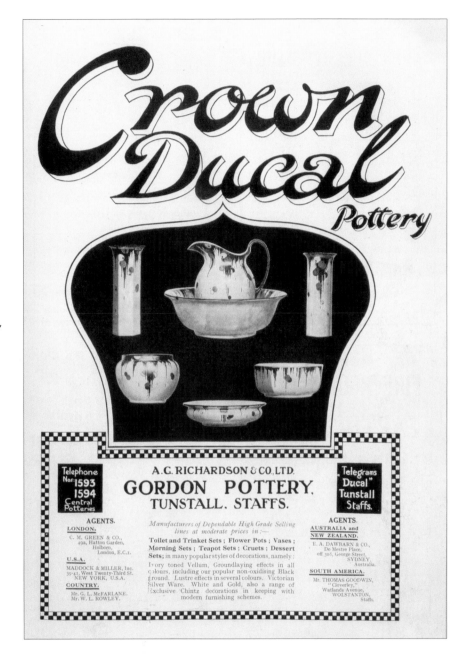

Plate 22.4. *A period Crown Ducal advertisement illustrating the Cairo pattern, March 1923.*

company employed twenty full-time aerographers, this at a time when other companies were reportedly laying off staff.[10] At the British Industries Fair of that year their stand was a positive blaze of colour. The solid coloured grounds were available in yellow, orange, tomato red, kingfisher blue and jade green. This was described as a courageous outburst.[11] Around four hundred patterns were produced in the period 1920-1924.

Company pattern books survive, but it is not possible to attribute the designs accurately to a particular designer. The company modeller Cornelius Machin, who worked between about 1915 and 1940, was probably responsible for the shapes produced during this early period, whilst Decorating Manager W.B. Johnson would have overseen the early designs.[12] It has been suggested that Norman W. Keates was the designer of many of the early printed and enamel painted patterns from around 1922 to 1930.[13] Keates had trained at the Royal Doulton factory and worked there for many years. It is possible that he was employed on a freelance basis for

Plate 22.5. Examples of the Red Tree *pattern decorated on a number of wares including the* Tankard *shaped coffee pot, teapot and plate. Height of coffee pot 7½in. (19cm), 1925.*

Richardson's, as this was a fairly common practice among pottery designers.

It certainly appears that around the 1923-1925 period the company had access to the services of one or more imaginative and forward looking designers who produced a new look for tea wares and fancies. They utilised the skills of the large number of hand paintresses now employed to work on the printed and painted patterns which had become the mainstay of production. The *Cairo* pattern (Plate 22.4) is a good example of how this traditional method of decoration was given a more modern treatment with lustre grounds and geometric shapes. In common with other companies, pattern names reflected the contemporary interest in Eastern matters with *Cairo* and *Luxor* appearing in 1923.

In 1925 the company produced a full tableware service in a new and ground-breaking design, which has since been attributed to Norman Keates.[14] They exhibited this at the 1925 Paris Exposition Internationale des Arts Décoratifs et Industriels Modernes.[15] Deceptively simple and adaptable to many shapes, the *Red Tree* pattern (no. A1211) (Plate 22.5) was described by the trade press as fresh in its very impulse and:

> both in the matter of spacing and colouring quite unlike anything we remember having seen previously in English pottery.[16]

This stylised pattern was a bold attempt by the company to create a new and modern design which would stimulate international interest at the Paris exhibition. Its stark lines and unusual shape contrast with traditional English floral or rural patterns, but it retained the tried and tested technique of underglaze printing and enamel overglaze painting. It is unfortunate that a more innovative range of shapes was not designed specifically for the pattern as this would have confirmed its status as a totally modern art deco product.

Now also known as *Orange Tree,* the pattern was applied to a huge variety of shapes. The designer had to graduate and engrave the pattern for around two hundred different shapes of ware, including the normal range of tea and dinner wares, tureens, jugs, cheese and butter dishes, eggcup sets. Although the pattern appeared on modern shapes, such as *Tankard* and *Octagon,* it was also used on existing traditional shapes, such as *Gem,* thus creating some unusual mixtures of contemporary and traditional pieces in the same set. In the same year the company had produced the *Octagon* multi-sided shape in response to what the *Pottery and Glass Record* described as modern demand for plates and dishes 'with corners'.[17] The success of the A1211 pattern kept the company financially viable through difficult times and the range remained in production until the 1960s.

1927 saw the introduction of a new range of lustre wares, called *Radiance.* Described by the trade press as 'West End style',[18] these were designed by an ex-Burslem School of Art student, Roland Heath, who only worked briefly at Richardson's from around 1926-1928.[19] The bold printed and painted patterns of natural forms, such as plants and butterflies (Plate 22.6), show the influence of the earlier art nouveau style, but the bold and lustred treatment given to them by Crown Ducal places them in the more luxurious art deco period.

The lustre productions were soon followed by a range of flambé wares, the production of which was overseen by Edward R. Wilkes, for whom the company provided a separate studio.[20] Art wares of this type would have been popular export wares for the company's expanding market and would have competed against the flambé ranges of Charles Noke at Royal Doulton and Pilkington's *Royal Lancastrian* lustre wares. Wilkes had worked as a painter with the Stoke potter Bernard Moore, famed for his flambé and lustre productions, and then he had moved to the Crown Staffordshire Porcelain Co where art director Reginald Tomlinson hoped to develop a range of flambé wares to rival those of Moore.[21] This venture was not a success and so it seems probable that Wilkes was invited to utilise his skills at A.G. Richardson and there he created the *Rouge* and *Golden Spectria* flambé ranges in the mid- to late

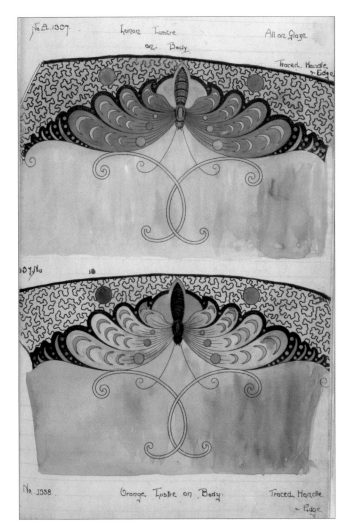

Plate 22.6. A pattern book extract illustrating the Butterfly *pattern (A1337/A1338) printed underglaze and painted overglaze on lustre grounds, part of the* Radiance *range, and designed by Roland Heath, 1926.*

1920s, along with other crystalline and lustre effects.[22]

In spite of the success of the distinctive *Red Tree* pattern, and the above mentioned art wares, A.G. Richardson were not at the forefront of modern ceramic design in the immediate aftermath of the 1925 Paris exhibition. Their tableware shapes and patterns remained fairly traditional, probably with their North American customers in mind. The success of this market meant that, around 1930, additional designers had to be brought in to cope with the demand. Harold Holdcroft, previously with Royal Venton and better known for his later work with Royal Albert, designed for the company, whilst his friend William Ruscoe was

Plate 22.7. The Granada pattern applied to an earthenware plaque. Designed by Charlotte Rhead, about 1933. Diameter of plaque 10⁷⁄₁₆in. (26.5cm).

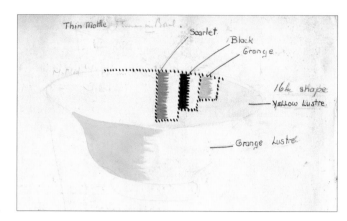

Plate 22.8. A pattern book entry showing the drawing for the Stitch pattern (3274), designed by Charlotte Rhead, about 1933-1934.

Plate 22.9. The tube-lined Wisteria pattern (4954) applied to a tall jug (shape 227) with a snow glaze. Designed by Charlotte Rhead, 1937. The tube-lined decoration was done by Rose Dickinson.

employed on a freelance basis to assist the long-standing company modeller, Cornelius Machin, who was unable to keep up with the demand.[23]

In 1932 an important new designer arrived at Richardson's.[24] Charlotte Rhead had previously worked for Wood and Sons Ltd and for Burgess & Leigh Ltd and, with these companies, had gained a reputation for new and artistically pleasing designs, many of which employed the handcraft technique of tube lining. Richardson's no doubt recognised that she could help them expand into new styles and ranges.

Tube lining was a decorative technique new to the Crown Ducal range and the trade press described it as a smart type of treatment appealing to those of cultured taste.[25] They reported dozens of new Charlotte Rhead patterns which were bright and cheerful, and colourful without being garish. One of her first designs produced by the company in 1933 was Byzantine, a boldly tube-lined floral pattern which brought a new dimension to Richardson's existing shapes.[26] Rhead's designs combined geometrical and classical borders and motifs with bold, colourful floral patterns, quite unlike the company's other lithographed floral patterns (Plate 22.7).

Plate 22.10. An earthenware plaque tube-lined with the Golden Leaves *pattern (4921), designed by Charlotte Rhead, 1937. Diameter of plaque 10⁷⁄₁₆in. (26.5 cm).*

Perhaps with an eye to economy and faster production, she also designed a range of patterns which featured a tube-lined 'stitching' as a highlight feature around rims and handles and as a pattern border. This was applied to both decorative and table wares, giving them a unique and modern look. The best known of these patterns are probably *Stitch* and *Patch*, both of which continued in production for many years (Plate 22.8). Rhead made use of the company's existing skill in aerography, utilising this technique on some of these less intricate designs. She also developed new glazes to complement the tube-lined patterns, producing mottled and 'snow' glazes as a background to the patterns. These, combined with some

of the more unusual Crown Ducal shapes, created a fresh and modern look (Plate 22.9).

Rhead was a prolific designer and demand was such that, in 1934, the company opened a second factory at the Britannia Pottery in Cobridge, Stoke-on-Trent.[27] It is difficult to determine which of the hundreds of Crown Ducal designs in the surviving pattern books are hers. The tube-lined wares can almost certainly be attributed to Rhead, but we are left to speculate as to which other designers were responsible for other patterns. Attempts were made to adapt some of her well-known patterns, such as *Golden Leaves* (4921) for tablewares (Plate 22.10). Some designs, although resembling her work,

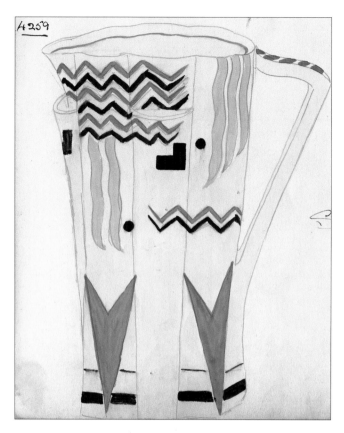

Plate 22.11. An abstract design in the art deco style for a flower jug as illustrated in the A.G. Richardson pattern book. The designer is unknown.

appear rather too garish for such a stylish artist (Plate 22.11). Although Charlotte Rhead left the company around 1942, it continued to produce many of her designs after the war. Later productions lack the technical skill and flair of the earlier pieces.

Patterns dating from 1934-1935 show how, almost ten years after the Paris International exhibition, Crown Ducal designs were finally reflecting the modern styles first seen on the Continent in the 1920s. Freehand painted tableware designs incorporate Egyptian hieroglyphic symbols, broken geometric shapes, zig-zag patterns and bands and platinum highlights (Plate 22.12). We may never know how many of these designs were put into production, but their simple patterns would have been easily copied by the team of paintresses, producing different colourways and adaptations as required.

Whilst these innovative developments caught the eye of the trade and public, the company continued production of a full range of earthenware goods for home and hotel. Open stock lithographed patterns were

being purchased from the big suppliers such as Ratauds and the Universal Transfer Co, mostly of traditional floral or rural designs,[28] and the popularity of printed chintz patterns continued. Production of printed and enamel painted patterns continued throughout and, in 1933, a new range of shapes was introduced with the *Sunburst* pattern (2649) (Plate 22.13). Its modern angular and lobed shapes featured a traditional pattern that led the *Pottery Gazette* to describe the designs as not being 'extravagant or freakish'.[29]

This description could be used to sum up the Crown Ducal approach to the art deco style. Keeping an eye firmly on financial matters, the company never entirely departed from its traditional market and conservative design requirements. This economic cushion afforded it the security needed to encourage the modern designs of Charlotte Rhead for which it is now best remembered and which were its main contribution to art deco.

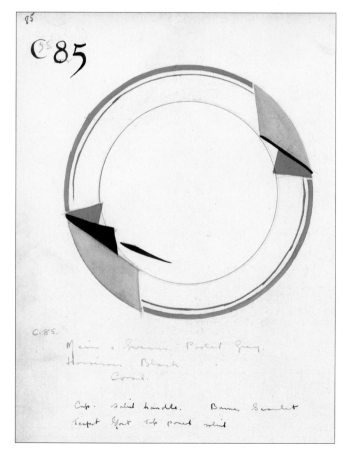

Plate 22.12. A design for an art deco styled pattern as illustrated in the A.G. Richardson pattern book.

Plate 22.13. A collection of wares decorated with the Sunburst pattern from the early 1930s. Height of teapot 5½in (14cm).

1. 'Buyers' Notes', *Pottery Gazette*, October 1915, p.1089.
2. Gerrard Shaw, 'The history of A.G. Richardson's Crown Ducal production 1920-1940 and an assessment of its place in the progressive approach to design witnessed in the Staffordshire pottery industry in the inter-war years', dissertation submitted as part of the requirement for the degree of Master of Arts in History of Art and Design, University of Central England 1993, pp.19 and 26.
3. 'Trade Notes', *Pottery Gazette*, December 1919, p.1350.
4. Company advertisement, *Pottery Gazette*, March 1923, p.385.
5. North Staffordshire Chamber of Commerce, *Comercio ed Industrie di North Staffordshire 1921*, p.xvii.
6. 'Buyers' Notes', *Pottery Gazette*, October 1915, p.1089.
7. 'Messrs. A.G. Richardson & Co. Ltd. Tunstall: An Enterprising Firm', *Pottery and Glass Record*, November 1925, p.419.

8. 'Buyers' Notes', *Pottery Gazette*, February 1923, p.263.
9. 'The British Industries Fair', *Pottery Gazette*, April 1921, p.602.
10. 'Buyers' Notes', *Pottery Gazette*, February 1923, p.261.
11. 'At the British Industries Fair 1923', *Pottery and Glass Record*, April 1923, p.662.
12. Shaw, op. cit. p.125.
13. Ibid. p.27.
14. Ibid. p.46.
15. 'Pottery and Glass at the Paris Exhibition of Decorative Arts', *Pottery Gazette*, July 1925, p.1092.
16. 'Buyers' Notes', *Pottery Gazette*, May 1925, p.759.
17. 'Messrs. A.G. Richardson & Co. Ltd. Tunstall: An Enterprising Firm' *Pottery and Glass Record*, November 1925, p.419.
18. 'Buyers' Notes', *Pottery Gazette*, February 1927, p.261.
19. Shaw, op. cit. p.55.

20. 'Buyers' Notes', *Pottery Gazette*, July 1927, p.1095.
21. Gordon Elliott, *Potters: oral history in the Staffordshire ceramic industry*, Churnet Valley Books, 2004, p.106.
22. Company advertisement, *Pottery Gazette*, July 1927, p.1095.
23. William Ruscoe, 'A Potter's Lot', unpublished autobiography, c.1986.
24. Andrew Casey, *Twentieth Century Ceramic Designers in Britain*, Antique Collectors' Club, 2001, p.62.
25. 'Buyers' Notes', *Pottery Gazette*, March 1933, p.323.
26. Bernard Bumpus, *Collecting Rhead Pottery*, Francis Joseph Publications, 1999, p.88.
27. 'The story of Crown Ducal', *British Bulletin of Commerce Survey Part 2*, December 1954, p.20.
28. A.G. Richardson pattern books.
29. 'Buyers' Notes', *Pottery Gazette*, March 1933, p.323.

23.

Paragon China

Frank Ashworth

IN THE ART DECO ERA THE MARKET for delicate bone china tea wares with modern shapes and bold enamel decoration was a highly competitive one dominated by a small number of Staffordshire manufacturers. Paragon was one of the more prominent names appealing to a discriminating middle and upper middle class market in Britain and the overseas Dominions. As the trade press observed in 1931:

Paragon possesses the rare ability of interpreting the public's taste in china and creating designs which are pleasingly familiar yet distinctively modern.[1]

Paragon became noted for tea wares in a quintessentially English interpretation of the art deco style and for nursery wares whose public appeal was enhanced by royal patronage.

Established at the St Gregory's Works, Longton, in 1897,[2] the company began trading as the Star China Co after the move to the larger Atlas Works in 1903 and marketed the wares as 'The Paragon of Excellence'. Under the management of Herbert James Aynsley, a member of the Aynsley china family,[3] the company prospered. By 1919 the Atlas Works were described as 'one of the largest all-china factories in Longton, and certainly one of the most up-to-date', with a well-equipped painting and gilding shop.[4] Hugh Irving, married to Herbert Aynsley's daughter, joined the company in 1910 and later became governing director.[5] The Star China Co, better known to the public through

Plate 23.1. Nursery ware bowls decorated with patterns by Eileen A. Soper and showing her facsimile signature. Diameter 5⅝in. (14.4cm).

Plate 23.2. A Derby shape cup and saucer, a souvenir from the British Empire Exhibition at Wembley in 1924. Height of cup 2¹¹/₁₆in. (7cm).

Plate 23.3. A Modern shape cup and saucer, milk jug and sugar bowl decorated with pattern G1745/2. Height of milk jug 2¹³/₁₆in. (7.2cm).

the Paragon designation given to the wares, became the Paragon China Co in 1919 and the following October the name was registered as a trademark. Paragon China Ltd was registered as a private company in 1930[6] and by 1935 had some 350 employees.

The company had a tradition of innovation. In 1916, reflecting the new influence of silent films from Hollywood, Paragon nursery wares portrayed Charlie Chaplin. The work of the well-known children's book illustrator Chloë Preston[7] featured on other nursery wares, while Louis Wain's[8] famous cats were reproduced in 1918. From the 1920s new and established names, many from outside the industry, were commissioned to bring their skills and creativity to pottery design. Frances Clayton[9] was employed as a designer at Paragon while she trained at the Burslem School of Art under Gordon

Plate 23.4. A Duchess shape cup and saucer, side plate, bread and butter plate, milk jug and sugar bowl decorated with the Wheatear pattern (X2020). Width of bread and butter plate 10⅛in. (25.6cm).

Forsyth from 1919 to 1924. After introducing new patterns and distinctive shapes at Paragon, she left to take up a scholarship at the Royal College of Art. John Hassall,[10] well known for his holiday poster 'Skegness is so bracing', was a children's illustrator whose drawings first appeared on Paragon nursery wares in the Edwardian period and retained their popularity into the later 1920s. A notable innovation was the use of shapes described as true to their purpose, with extended bases so that a young child would not upset them. A nursery series by Beatrice Mallet featured original rhymes to accompany refined, but rather quaint, drawings of subjects such as 'We's looking for Santa Claus' and 'Pam's Washing Day'. Constance Grace created *The Alphabet* design shown at the British Industries Fair in February 1930. For the Christmas trade in 1930 Paragon launched a *Mickey Mouse* series, having secured exclusive world rights to reproduce the famous drawings of Walt Disney.[11] This followed the success of

the first Mickey Mouse film, *Steamboat Willie*, which had been released in 1928. A series of twelve illustrations conveyed a story showing the adventures of Mickey and his friends, bold colouring giving an impression of great liveliness. Production of the Mickey Mouse series continued until about 1934. The following year the introduction of Eileen Soper's delightful and delicately drawn vignettes of children at play made her Paragon's most important artist on nursery ware (Plate 23.1).[12]

In the inter-war period Paragon not only made 'inroads into the better class markets',[13] but also gained an enviable reputation as 'a progressive factory'. By the close of the 1920s the company was cautiously experimenting with an open, freer style of pattern on oval tea sets. The new *Modern* shape was then introduced to wide critical acclaim and acknowledged the changes in taste of the early 1930s associated with the style then known as 'Jazz Modern'. Designed by J.A. Robinson,[14] a former pupil of Gordon Forsyth and a full-

Paragon China

Plate 23.5. A number of Ascot shaped wares (registered 780094) decorated with the Hydrangea pattern (G870). Width of bread and butter plate 8%in. (21.7cm).

Plate 23.5a. A period leaflet promoting the latest Paragon patterns including the Hydrangea pattern on the cover.

Plate 23.6. An Ascot shape sugar bowl decorated with a floral pattern (G4252). Diameter of bowl 4⅛in. (11.3cm).

time designer at Paragon from the mid-1920s, the *Modern* shape (Plate 23.3) featured an inverted cone design with a useful handle, which was described as 'decidedly original without being ultra modern'.[15] Matching cream jugs had long, broad open tops, while teapot lids were characterised by a diamond-shaped finial. *The Studio* magazine in early 1932 illustrated an example of J.A. Robinson's new conical design, with the caption 'a cup and saucer of particularly graceful shape'.[16]

The same art deco influences were employed on the patterns, which were hand painted, often within a printed outline. There were new brightly coloured flower patterns such as *Salon, Primrose* and *Summertime*, many shown on the *Modern* shape. The rich colours might be set off by a groundlay of deep ivory, as found with the

Crocus design in freehand painting featuring 'a finely realistic mauve flower, hanging on a ground-laid ivory band.'[17] The *English Flowers Suite*, a series of eighteen flower designs on the *Modern* shape, was described as:

a type of pattern which is thoroughly English in character, and of a Modern design which will enjoy wide popularity in this Country'.[18]

The range comprised tea sets for six or twelve persons, coffee sets, morning sets for two, fruit sets, supper sets and breakfast sets. In contrast to the delicate floral designs, there were 'a few decidedly futuristic designs with rather jazzy colour effects.'[19]

The *Duchess* shape (Plate 23.4) continued the fashion for conical outlines, 'modelled as if in a series of steps',

Plate 23.7. A Modern *shape coffee pot, milk jug, cup and saucer decorated with the* Hydrangea *pattern. Height of coffee pot 6½in. (16.5cm).*

while flower handles emphasised the floral theme.[20] The new *Ascot* shape (Plates 23.5 and 23.6), introduced in 1933 and illustrated in *The Studio* later that year, was somewhat bulbous in outline and characterised by a stylised foot and handle decoration evocative of the Odeon cinema.[21] Royal Paragon China sales literature from 1933, illustrating in colour the *Hydrangea* (Plate 23.7), *Iceland Poppy, Clematis* and *Honesty* (Plate 23.8) patterns, set out the company's aspirations to be seen as a fine china producer of the first order:

PARAGON CHINA has a world-wide reputation built upon an ideal which is ever before the producers. This ideal is the determination that the imprint of the name shall identify PARAGON CHINA in every detail of its production with that extra touch of exclusiveness and beauty brought of extra care and thought.[22]

Paragon tea sets were available in a number of shapes and patterns covering the price range. A tea set in *Wild Violets*, pattern number G1025, retailed at 35s. The most expensive, at 81s., was the *Hydrangea* design, pattern number G870, on the *Ascot* shape. The *Iceland Poppy* pattern on the *Modern* shape (Plate 23.9) was available as a tea set for six or twelve persons, a morning set or as a coffee set, priced from 42s.6d. to 82s. Especial emphasis was given to designs supplied to the Queen or the Duchess of York.

Much of the credit for the company's new vigour must be attributed to the inspired appointment of Thomas Fennemore[23] as Paragon sales manager in 1929. Fennemore, 'a Londoner having a special and intimate experience of modern methods in connection with salesmanship',[24] worked in advertising from 1919 to 1926.[25] A marketing specialist with progressive ideas, he believed that manufacturers were increasingly aware of the importance of design. As part of 'a new sales policy',[26] he got together with Colley A. Shorter at A.J. Wilkinson Ltd to organise an 'exhibition, unique in its character and topical in its interest'[27] at the First Avenue Hotel, High Holborn in September 1929. These joint presentations were repeated in 1930 and 1931 and showed new designs from Wilkinson's young designer Clarice Cliff and the latest Paragon wares. The 1931 exhibition at High Holborn included table settings arranged by well-known editors of national women's magazines and model window displays to educate retailers in the art of selling on 'modern lines'.[28]

Plate 23.8. A mustard pot and cover decorated with the Honesty pattern (G1090), one of many floral designs offered in 1933. Height 3⅟₁₆in. (7.8cm).

Exhibitions were seen as an important way to reach the more affluent customers patronising the many new department stores established in the inter-war period – Derry & Toms, Dickens & Jones and Barkers of Kensington being notable names – an arrangement later extended to leading stores in provincial towns and cities. The Paragon management invited leaders of society, royalty and aristocracy, politicians and topical personalities to publicity events linked to charitable causes, events widely reported in the national press. Queen Mary toured the Paragon exhibition held at John Barker & Co, Kensington, in the autumn of 1931 and 'expressed her admiration of the beautiful china ware displayed'.[29] At the British Industries Fair for 1932 Paragon had a bright, well-arranged stand, which included real cakes with icing decorated to match the china and the tablecloths, one cake being in the form of Sir Malcolm Campbell's racing car which inspired the

Plate 23.9. A Modern shape cup, saucer and side plate decorated with the Iceland Poppy pattern. Width of side plate 5⅞in. (14.9cm).

Plate 23.9a. A period leaflet illustrating the Iceland Poppy pattern decorated on the Modern shape.

popular *Blue Bird* pattern.[30] An exhibition of Paragon China at Harrods opened by Lady Elibank on 10 October 1932 brought together an array of society ladies, among them the Duchess of Sutherland and Mrs. Stanley Baldwin. Advertisements appeared in women's magazines such as *Modern Woman* and *Modern Home*, appealing directly to a new generation of women influenced by articles on modern interiors. These newly enfranchised consumers sought to emulate the taste of fashionable personalities of theatre and film. Paragon later exhibited at the prestigious Royal Academy Exhibition of British Art in Industry at Burlington House, Piccadilly which closed in March 1935. A highlight of the display was a Paragon service decorated with a motif of black arabesque ornament designed by Agnes Pinder Davis[31] and illustrating the point made in Gerald Crow's publication, *The Conquest of Ugliness*,[32] that beauty need not involve extra expense to the public.

Royal patronage was a further element in Paragon's success and soon earned the company a reputation as producers of wares for royal occasions (Plate 23.10). The links with royalty really began to flourish from the early 1920s. Paragon received an order to equip the nursery of Princess Mary's household in 1923. Following the birth of Princess Elizabeth in 1926, the Duchess of York purchased and authorised the reproduction of a specially designed nursery set for the young princess, *Two for Joy* (Plate 23.11) designed by the Decorating Manager, a Mr Austin, an old gentleman who took many of his pattern names from musical shows then running in the West End.[33] The pattern was described by Queen Mary as 'perfectly sweet'[34] and was decorated entirely by 'the girl students of the factory who were receiving instruction in the City Art School'.[35] In 1929 the company introduced Princess Elizabeth nursery ware consisting of cups and saucers, mugs, milk beakers, baby plates and porridge plates. It was made by special permission of the Duchess of York from a photographic portrait by Marcus Adams supplied by the Duchess. A special pattern was authorised after the birth of Princess Margaret in August

Plate 23.10. A group of commemorative wares. Left to right: a Marcus Adams plate, registered no. 720255; a commemorative mug with handle as a lion rampant; a Coronation plate, pattern G3963. Diameter of plate 9in. (22.8cm).

1930 (Plate 23.12). The pattern included the two love birds, a traditional emblem in the Strathmore family, the marguerite, the rose and the heather, finished in duchess blue. Incorporated with the design was the royal coat of arms.

In 1933 Queen Mary visited the Paragon stand at the British Industries Fair and purchased a dinner service. A few months later, in April 1933, the Queen conferred upon Paragon China the royal warrant of appointment as 'China Potters to Her Majesty the Queen'. In the same year the Duchess of York purchased from Paragon China for her new home, White Lodge, and for her own personal use, three complete services of Paragon China. At the British Industries Fair for 1934 the latest 'Royal Paragon' pattern, G1686, was described in the trade press as 'original and modernistic' and featured a chequer border in apple-green and grey, with a little black, one of the Queen's many purchases for that year.[36] J.A. Robinson designed a selection of souvenir items to mark the Silver Jubilee of King George V and

Queen Mary in 1935. A design, heraldic in character, embodying the rose, shamrock and thistle, as well as the flags of the Empire surrounding portraits of the King and Queen, was selected by the royal family from a number submitted by artists in the Potteries. Each piece was inscribed 'By the Special Approval and Permission of THEIR MAJESTIES THE KING AND QUEEN'. A year later, the accession of Edward VIII was the occasion for a new range of coronation commemoratives which were regarded as among the most ambitious and distinctive in the industry:

Produced on entirely new and very dignified shapes, with designs embodying the highest form of Heraldic art, and many intimate details, the pieces are beautiful specimens of craftsmanship, well worthy to be a memento of so great an occasion.[37]

This was unexpectedly followed by the new king's abdication and appropriately modified designs were

Plate 23.11. A Windsor shape cup and saucer, side plate, milk jug and fruit dish decorated with magpies and flowers and inscribed 'Two for Joy', with a turquoise blue rim, pattern F43. Width of side plate 6⁷⁄₁₆in. (16.3cm). 1927.

Plate 23.12. Three side plates. Left to right: plate with printed mark bearing the Royal Paragon name, coat of arms and the inscription: 'By Appointment. Replica of Service Produced for H.M. The Queen'; plate inscribed 'Hand Painted China By Paragon England', made some time between 1929 and 1933; plate decorated with yellow and green budgerigars, sprays of heather and pink rose to celebrate the birth of Princess Margaret Rose at Glamis Castle etc. Width of centre plate 5⁹⁄₁₆in. (14.1cm).

prepared for King George VI and Queen Elizabeth. At the British Industries Fair of 1937 Paragon received the largest combined order ever placed at a single stand by the royal family and company output for the year reached record levels. In 1938 the new Queen conferred her royal warrant on the company, the only pottery manufacturers so honoured. Later in the year, with foreign events dominating the political scene, a special issue of Peace commemoration china bearing a signed photograph of Neville Chamberlain celebrated his return from Munich.

A comparative newcomer without the long traditions of the fine china companies of Stoke, Worcester and Derby, Paragon prospered in a highly competitive environment, even during the most dismal times of economic gloom and depression between the wars when less imaginative competitors were reduced to producing promotional china or closing their doors for the final time. Under the management of Hugh Irving and his sons, Paragon went on, in the post-war period, to become the only Staffordshire china company with three royal warrants of appointment. Not surprisingly the special qualities of Paragon china from the art deco period are increasingly appreciated. Collectors particularly seek the more distinctive tea ware designs and the extravagantly decorated commemorative wares originated by J.A. Robinson.

1. *Pottery Gazette*, 1 January 1931, p.5.
2. The early partnership of Coggins and Illingworth at the St Gregory's Works registered their first designs in July 1897.
3. Herbert James Aynsley (1851-1929) was the eldest surviving son of John Aynsley, china manufacturer, who founded the Portland Works, Sutherland Road, Longton. He joined William Illingworth at the St Gregory's Works in 1898 and retired in 1927.
4. *Pottery Gazette*, 1 April 1919, pp.383-4.
5. Hugh Irving, born in 1875, married Hilda Aynsley, the youngest of Herbert Aynsley's three daughters, at Forsbrook, on 19 November 1907.
6. The new company, with a registered capital of £25,000, had H.U. Irving as governing director and F.P. Holgate as sales director (registration no. 247811).
7. Beatrice Zöe (Chlöe) Preston (1887-1969) was from a privileged background and educated privately. Her first book, *The Peek-a-Boos*, was published in 1910. She was best known as a children's illustrator.
8. Louis Wain (1860-1939), an artist famous for his drawings of cats, studied at the West London School of Art from 1877 to 1880. He was a prolific illustrator of books from the 1880s and first drew cats in 1883, his humorous portrayals of them in human guise becoming very popular by the 1890s. *Louis Wain's Annual* ran for many years after its inception in 1901. Star China brought out a new range of Paragon nursery wares with Louis Wain illustrations displayed at the British Industries Fair in April 1918.
9. Frances Clayton (1903-1985) was born at Burslem and educated at St Paul's School, Burslem. In August 1924 she was awarded a scholarship at the Royal College of Art where she studied until 1927. She later taught pottery and design at the Camberwell School of Art, marrying the well-known artist, C.G. Richards in 1929.
10. John Hassall (1868-1948) was educated at Newton Abbot College and on the Continent. He exhibited at the Royal Academy and then embarked on a career as a poster artist. In 1901 he was elected as a member of the Royal Institute of Painters in Water Colours and began work as an illustrator of children's books.
11. *Pottery Gazette*, 2 June 1930, pp.949 and 951;

LV, 1 December 1930, p.1845.
12. Eileen Soper (1905-1990), born in Enfield, Middlesex, was educated at home and studied under her father, George Soper RE, who was a painter and illustrator. Eileen Soper exhibited at the Royal Academy and the Royal Society of Arts. As an artist, she specialised in angelic children, later illustrating the works of Enid Blyton. She also wrote and illustrated several books including *Where Badgers Wake* (1955) and *Muntjac* (1969).
13. *Pottery Gazette*, 2 August 1926, p.1207.
14. J.A. 'Jack' Robinson (c.1910-1987) originally came from Liverpool, an orphan. While visiting an aunt in the Potteries he decided to stay and enrolled at the Burslem School of Art where he was a pupil of Gordon Forsyth. Working at first at the Carlton factory, he joined Paragon at about fourteen years of age, designing nursery, tea wares and commemorative pieces in the 1920s and 1930s. He became Decorating Manager at Paragon on the departure of Mr Austin in about 1932. He remained at Paragon until after the war and then left to work at other china factories. *Pottery and Glass Record*, XVI, October 1934, p.260.
15. *Pottery and Glass Record*, July 1931, p.210.
16. *The Studio*, January-June 1932, p.280.
17. *Pottery and Glass Record*, September 1930, p.270; July 1931, p.210.
18. *Pottery Gazette*, 1 March 1932, p. 295. *English Flowers Suite* patterns included *Blue Hydrangea* (also in pink, grey and green), *Yellow Crocus* (also in blue and green), *Pink Almond Blossom* (also in orange), *Tulips, Shirley Poppies* and *Flowers*.
19. *The Pottery and Glass Record*, July 1931, p.210.
20. *Pottery Gazette*, 1 October 1934, p.1226.
21. The *Ascot* shape was selected to illustrate Harry Trethowan's 'Modern British Pottery Design', *The Studio*, July-December 1933, p.182.
22. Royal Paragon China sales literature (The Horace Barks Reference Library, Stoke-on-Trent).
23. Thomas Acland Fennemore F.R.S.A. (1902-1955) became Managing Director of E. Brain & Co in 1932. As a leading authority on industrial design, he then became Registrar of the National Register of Industrial Art Designers established by the Board of Trade in the 1930s on the recommendation of the Council of Art and Industry to maintain and improve the standard of industrial design. Many of the most eminent ceramic designers of the period registered.

24. *Pottery Gazette*, 2 December 1929, p.1909.
25. J. Spours, *Art Deco Tableware*, 1988, p.84.
26. *The Pottery and Glass Record*, October 1929, p.207.
27. Ibid., September 1929, p.286.
28. *Pottery Gazette*, 1 October 1931, pp.1395-7.
29. *The Pottery and Glass Record*, November 1931, p. 28.
30. Sir Malcolm Campbell (1885-1949) broke the land speed record nine times between 1924 and 1935. Paragon registered the Blue Bird design, no. 772063, to commemorate his achievements. Sir Malcolm approved this design a few days before he broke the world speed record in 1932.
31. Agnes Pinder Davis NRD studied art at the Byam Shaw School of Art, Campden Hill and at the St John's Wood School of Art. She then studied sculpture under John Skeaping at the Central School of Arts and Crafts, Southampton Row, and watercolour painting with Leonard Walker. She specialised in flower painting and the creation of designs with flower motifs and turned to commercial art and industrial design early in her career. Harry Trethowan at Heals introduced her to some of the leading pottery and glass firms. She was commissioned to design decorative features for the Cunard liners the *Queen Mary*, the *Queen Elizabeth* and the *Mauretania*. After the war, in 1946, she became a design consultant to the Bristol Pottery and in the 1950s she modelled chinoiserie figures for Royal Worcester.
32. Gerald Crow's *The Conquest of Ugliness*, a study of William Morris' life and work, was published by Methuen in 1935.
33. *Wild Violets* and *Lilac Time* are examples of Paragon pattern names taken from London musicals of the time.
34. *Pottery Gazette*, 1 April 1927, p.640.
35. Ibid., 1 February 1927, p.265, the correspondent continuing: 'A rejuvenation of individualistic styles of pottery decoration was becoming sorely needed in the trade, and one does not hesitate to forecast that the future success of the English pottery trade is likely to rest very much upon the furtherance of handcraft, as distinct from the purely mechanical aids to decoration.'
36. *The Pottery and Glass Record*, March 1934, p.61.
37. *Pottery Gazette*, 1 September 1936.

Plate 24.1. Ginger jar, earthenware, Tut pattern designed by Enoch Boulton, c.1925.
12½in. (32cm) high.

24.

Carlton Ware

Helen Martin and Harvey Pettit

THE ART DECO PERIOD was a high point in Carlton Ware's history. One of the strengths of this illustrious pottery was that it not only adopted the trends of the day but often led them. The owner, Cuthbert Wiltshaw, allowed his designers free reign resulting in the introduction of many innovative and original wares. One fashion that wasn't followed was the use of the designer's name on wares as was the case with Susie Cooper, Charlotte Rhead, Clarice Cliff and many others. Cuthbert wanted Carlton Ware's name to be made from its products rather than the names of those who had designed them.

Carlton Ware was made by Wiltshaw and Robinson formed with the partnership of James Frederick Wiltshaw and the brothers J.A. and W.H. Robinson. About 1890 they began making pots at the Copeland Street Works in Stoke-on-Trent. The partnership ended in 1911, leaving James Frederick as sole proprietor until his untimely death in 1918. His eldest son, Cuthbert, took over the reins on returning from war service, running the pottery until an illness ended his life in 1966. A year later the works was sold to Arthur Wood Ltd and was subsequently managed by Anthony Wood whose tenure also saw the introduction of many exciting new wares. In 1987 he sold the works to County Potteries, a holding company with little or no background in ceramics. Two years later Carlton Ware went into receivership. The factory buildings were sold and their contents divided into lots and sold by tender. Grosvenor Ceramics Hardware purchased the trade name, some moulds, shape and pattern books and goodwill, re-launching Carlton Ware in 1990. Within a few years Carlton Ware had lost impetus and became dormant. In 1997 Frank Salmon bought the trade name and, having no potting experience, he commissioned Peggy Davies Studio and Bairstow Manor Pottery to make Carlton Ware for him.

The first designer of art deco patterns for Carlton Ware was Enoch Boulton, who began to work for the pottery in the early '20s. One of his first remits was to extend the highly successful designs featuring Oriental landscapes with pagodas and temples introduced by his predecessor, Horace Wain. This was to include the star of the 'Orientals', the *Chinaland* pattern. Boulton is also believed to have designed the fabulous *Tut* pattern inspired by the discovery of the tomb of Tutankhamun (Plate 24.1). The exploration of the tomb popularised all things Egyptian. This pattern can loosely be interpreted as an art deco design since ancient Egyptian civilisation had a strong influence on the style. Boulton continued to devise many other exotic gold printed patterns that today we regard as belonging to the art deco stable.

In the latter part of the '20s Wiltshaw & Robinson bought the Vine Street china works of Birks, Rawlins & Co, which was subsequently run by Cuthbert's younger brother, Douglas. The new venture saw the introduction of many highly original art deco china patterns, but it was not to last. In the early '30s difficult trading conditions and bad handling of both manufactories by the bank led to the sale of the china works and eventual administrative receivership. Judicious management and economies, however, resulted in a return to solvency and the saving of the Copeland Street works. The difficulties of the time were compounded by Enoch Boulton's departure to Fielding's, a nearby competitor. This move is believed to have been instigated by Fielding's, makers of Crown Devon, who had poached Carlton Ware's key salesman a year or so before.

Fortuitously, Cuthbert had employed a young designer to help Enoch Boulton after the china works had been bought. Her name was Violet Elmer. Miss Elmer busied herself with china patterns and, to her surprise, when Enoch Boulton left she was asked to take on the much

Plate 24.2. *Conical vase, earthenware, decorated with the* Bell *pattern designed by Violet Elmer, c.1934. 8in. (20.5cm) high.*

Plate 24.3. *An earthenware vase decorated with the* Floral Comets *designed by Violet Elmer, c.1930. 6in. (15.5cm) high.*

Plate 24.4. *An earthenware biscuit box decorated with the* Persian Garden *pattern designed by Violet Elmer, c.1936. 6¾in. (17 cm) high.*

larger task of creating earthenware shapes and patterns. With considerable verve she took on this heavy responsibility and within a short time many of her exquisite designs were in production (Plates 24.2-24.7). Violet was helped by another budding designer, Olive Kew (Plate 24.8). Alas, Miss Kew had to leave as a consequence of the receivership, for the luxury of two resident designers could not be afforded. In the latter part of the '30s Cuthbert's eldest daughter, Betty Wiltshaw, joined Vi Elmer, but left to marry shortly before the Second World War.

Much of the women's work incorporated what we now regard as classic art deco elements. Lightning flashes,

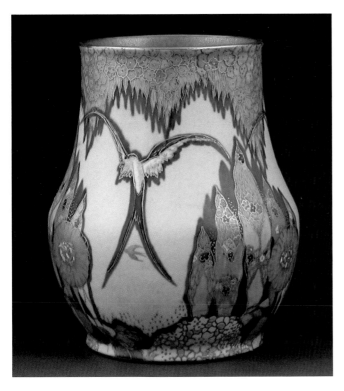

Plate 24.5. *An earthenware vase decorated with the Fantasia pattern designed by Violet Elmer, c.1930. 6in. (15.5cm) high.*

Plate 24.6. *An earthenware biscuit box and cover decorated with the Crested Bird & Waterlily designed by Violet Elmer, c.1932. 6¼in. (16cm) high.*

Plate 24.7. *A Diamond finned earthenware dish decorated with the Devil's Copse pattern designed by Violet Elmer, c.1935. 10in. (25cm) wide.*

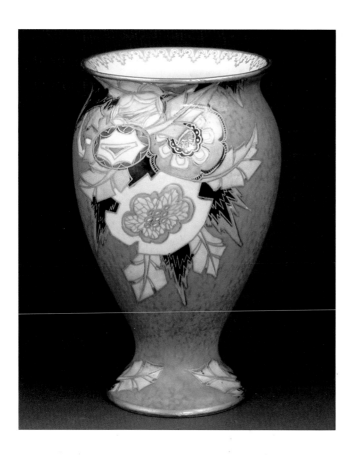

Plate 24.8. *An earthenware vase decorated with the Jagged Bouquet pattern designed by Olive Kew, c.1930. 6in. (15.5cm) high.*

Plate 24.9. *A selection of Modern Ware shapes comprising, left to right: conical bowl, diamond finned dish, candlestick and mug, earthenware. Designer unknown although pattern devised by Violet Elmer, c.1936.*

Plate 24.10. *The* Lightning *pattern applied to an earthenware vase, from the* Handcraft *range designed by Violet Elmer c.1934. 7in. (18cm) high.*

strong French influence. Freehand painted decorations became very popular at the time and many manufacturers supplied the demand for them. The *Handcraft* range was a departure from highly refined, precisely printed and enamelled delights that were often lavished with gold and which Carlton Ware had made its hallmark. Most *Handcraft* utilises a delicious soft matt glaze, although in total contrast some of the art deco examples are highly glazed, such as the *Lightning* and *Chevrons* patterns (Plates 24.10 and 24.11).

Not all designs went into production. The decision as to which shape or pattern would be made was agreed between Cuthbert and his salesmen in the presence of the designer. The influence of the salesmen was considerable. They had their fingers on the pulse of public taste, being in direct contact with retailers whom they frequently visited. The team's decisions often led to a tour de force with the introduction of wares that can only be described as extraordinary pots. Their production was only made possible by the highly-skilled and dedicated work of those who made and decorated the wares.

Violet Elmer left to marry in the late '30s to be replaced by Rene Pemberton, yet another talented designer. Rene continued the style and forms now characteristically Carlton Ware until all was curtailed by World War II. Miss Pemberton had a tall act to follow but she did so with ease, no doubt helped by her training at

geometric symbols, fans, stylised flowers and explosions abounded, all perfectly executed on the canvas of the high quality earthenware which at times was so fine it was taken for bone china. The elaborate decorated wares were balanced by ranges of modernist shapes with simple but sophisticated decorations, most notably from the *Modern Ware* range as it was called (Plate 24.9). From the '30s onwards many floral and fruit embossed salad ware ranges were also introduced, usually in a style that is now synonymous with Carlton Ware. The output of Wiltshaw and Robinson in this heyday of British ceramics was inventive and prolific.

In 1928 Carlton Ware introduced a series of freehand painted decorations called *Handcraft*. Initially these were influenced by the work of Dutch potters and probably Carter, Stabler and Adams and Gray's. By the early '30s the range included many striking art deco designs with a

Plate 24.11. *An earthenware covered box decorated with the* Chevrons *pattern designed by Violet Elmer, c.1933. 5in. (12.5cm) wide.*

Plate 24.12. An earthenware bowl decorated with the Flower & Falling Leaf designed by Violet Elmer, c.1937. 8in. (20.5cm) diameter.

Gray's Pottery under Susie Cooper and her long attendance at the Burslem College of Art.

Whilst the art deco designers created both patterns and shapes, none of them modelled the shapes they devised. Wiltshaw & Robinson, like many others, employed its own modeller and sometimes used freelance modellers. Their vital contribution to a pot bank is usually and sadly overlooked. From the mid-'30s Ronald Hopkinson was responsible for modelling most shapes. He worked closely with Miss Elmer and Miss Pemberton; his skills were second to none. Ronald had trained at Minton, eventually moving to Wedgwood where he modelled some of the cast Keith Murray shapes under Arnold Austin. Unfortunately little is known

about who undertook this essential part of producing a pot before Hopkinson's appointment.

As far as the design of ceramics is concerned, the decade of the 1930s clearly belongs to women; so many potteries depended on their highly imaginative creations. It is impossible to say if this was deliberate on the part of the manufacturers. Surely some realised that at this time pottery was mostly bought by women. Who better to determine what would be desirable to them than another woman? Whatever the reason for their employ, the pottery ladies' contribution to these pinnacle years of British twentieth century ceramics is immeasurable and Carlton Ware's unsung designers were up there with the best of them.

25

Myott Pottery

Andrew Casey

DURING THE LATE '20s and '30s several small, middle market, pottery manufacturers became aware, through the various trade shows and trade press coverage, of the growing fashion for bold, hand-painted patterns decorated on angular shapes that we know today as art deco. Rather than having a deep desire to embrace modernity, the move towards producing art deco wares had more to do with sales figures as this type of ware was proving very popular. As a result many of the smaller manufacturers quickly rushed to replicate the art deco style in order to gain part of the market. One such example was the Myott Pottery which, although established within the industry as a quality maker of

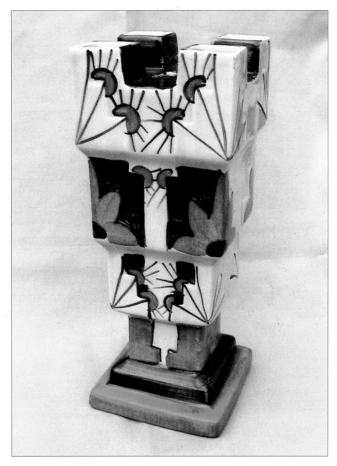

Plate 25.2. An earthenware castle shaped vase decorated with the Orange Flowers pattern (8942), 1933. Height 8½in. (21.7cm).

Plate 25.1. An earthenware jug featuring a moulded cat, hand painted in various colours, 1933. Height 9¾in. (24.5cm).

general pottery goods, suddenly changed direction and introduced its own examples of art deco ceramics.

Myott Son & Co was established in 1898 after James Myott bought the Alexander Pottery, based in Wolfe Street in Stoke-on-Trent, a small earthenware

Plate 25.3. Two earthenware plates decorated with hand-painted abstract floral designs, 1930s.

Plate 25.4. An earthenware diamond shaped planter decorated with the hand-painted Hollyhocks pattern, c.1933-34. Width 10½in. (26.5cm).

manufacturer operated by George Thomas Mountford from 1888. The son of James Myott, Ashley, worked there as an apprentice and when the owner died he took over the running of the business, probably with financial help from his father. Ashley was assisted by his brother and eventually they moved the business to larger premises in Cobridge in 1902. With the installation of new machinery they were able to extend their production which, during the early part of the twentieth century, included toilet wares, dinner ware, jugs and flowerpots; many shapes had previously been used by the late owner. In 1903 an agent was established in Canada for the much needed export market with new showrooms in Liverpool and Manchester. By the early '20s the company had representatives in many countries including Australia, America and South Africa.[1]

Also by the early '20s the trade press noted that Myott were producers of semi-porcelain of the first grade for domestic wares. Like many middle market companies of the period, the range of patterns and shapes was fairly traditional with patterns such as the mazarine blue band and gilt decoration proving very popular in the export markets. In 1928, however, the trade press noted:

a range of bright and lively coloured patterns such as can only be obtained through the medium of brushwork.[2]

Suddenly in 1933 a staggering range of brightly painted art deco style vases, jugs and plaques burst on to the rather conservative British pottery market (Plates 25.1 and 25.2). They were clearly introduced to compete in the new fashionable market of hand-painted pottery pioneered so successfully by Clarice Cliff. Myott's dramatic shapes were angular and, painted in colours such as orange, yellow and browns, were in total contrast to anything the company had produced earlier. Unlike other factories, Myott clearly made a considerable effort to manufacture a whole range of art deco styled pots which must have been a costly exercise given that there was no guarantee that these new lines would be successful. The new shapes, decorated with a diverse range of hand-painted patterns, were applied to a soft honey glaze, often covered in blocks of colours with both stylised flowers and abstract leaves (Plate 25.3), often complemented by colourful banding. Although these patterns were very striking they were not painted to the high standards of many other pottery manufacturers, with some examples of Myott pottery being rather crudely executed (Plate 25.4).

Unfortunately nothing much is known about the company as the pattern books and information on the key staff and the designers were probably destroyed in a fire at the works during the late '40s. The only contemporary evidence is the article in the trade press and a limited number of company advertisements that give some insight into the history of Myott. A number of shapes were noted in the trade press who commented:

a vase in a unique shape is called the Tower and in spite of its eccentricity (or because of it) it has already been very favourably noticed by buyers.[3]

The same article mentioned new jug shapes such as *Tunisian, Persian, Algerian* and *Egyptian*. A company advertisement from this period illustrated the *Fan* and *Moderne* vase (Plate 25.5), which were very similar to each other, with clear reference to both the Aztec and

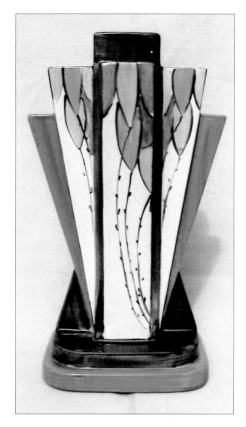

Plate 25.5. An earthenware Moderne *shaped vase decorated with the* Pencil Trees *pattern (9112), c.1933-4. Height 8½in. (21.5cm).*

Egyptian styles. Some of these shapes, such as the *Beaky* and *Torpedo,* simply ignore any of the concerns for practicality or functionalism being discussed at the time.[4]

These highly colourful wares were not restricted to flower jugs and vases but included morning sets, fruit sets and a range of fancies such as the *Duchess* set for the dressing table, consisting of a tray, two modernistic candlesticks and a puff bowl.[5] The *Dante* jug was a popular shape as it was less angular and could take all forms of decoration; as a result it was still in production after the Second World War. A number of simple hand-painted patterns were applied to tea and coffee wares as well as posy rings (Plate 25.6). The *Jubilee* cider set, launched in 1935, was decorated with several striking patterns.[6]

With a good understanding of the pottery trade and market needs the company continued to produce the popular traditional lines alongside the art deco wares. These included the *Georgian* shape, featuring an embossed edge, and the *Conway* tea for two sets, both from 1933, with patterns such as *Chelsea Bird* and *Bouquet.* In 1935 the company did issue new dinner

Plate 25.6. An earthenware side plate decorated with a simple floral pattern, 1930s.

ware patterns, possibly on the *Conway* shape, including *Swallow* and *Acorn* which were, according to the trade press:

> both of modernistic treatment, well designed to fit in with modern furnishings, but in no sense over advanced.[7]

In 1937 the company launched the *Queens* shape as well as some rustic ware, matt glazed wares and a new hand-painted pattern called *Iris*.

At some stage during the late '30s the company decided to stop production of the modern wares and return to the production of traditional lines. This was also the case with many other pottery manufacturers. No doubt Myott were aware that customer tastes had changed again and wanted a different product range from the Myott Pottery.

Plate 25.7. An unusual earthenware owl bookend, c.1933-34. Height 6½in. (16.5cm).

1. A. Myott, and P. Pollitt, *The Mystery of Myott – A History of the Myott Pottery Stoke-on-Trent 1898-1991*, 2003.
2. 'Buyers' Notes', *Pottery Gazette*, 1 November 1928, p.1757.
3. 'Around the London Showrooms', *The Pottery and Glass Record*, 1933, p.254.
4. More recently Myott collectors have given new names to some of these shapes.
5. 'Buyers' Notes', *Pottery Gazette*, 1 November 1935, p.1383.
6. This set and other new wares were illustrated in *Pottery Gazette*, 1 November 1935, p.1383.
7. 'Buyers' Notes', *Pottery Gazette*, 1 November 1935, pp.1383-85.

26

Royal Winton

Susan Scott

ROYAL WINTON enjoyed great success throughout the '20s and '30s yet, surprisingly, very few examples of pure art deco shapes and patterns are seen today. Winton manufactured for the mass market rather than pursuing innovative design. They focused on products that would generate mass sales, like their signature chintz and pastel ware lines, but even within these lines

Plate 26.1. An illustration of toilet ware produced by Grimwades, c.1926.

deco influences can be seen in shapes that one would never have expected to find covered with 'all-over floral' transfers.

Grimwade Brothers was founded in 1885 at the Winton Pottery, Stoke-on-Trent by Leonard Lumsden Grimwade and his brother Sidney. From a single shed they grew quickly and over the next thirty years acquired Stoke Pottery, Upper Hanley Pottery, Atlas China Works, Heron Cross Pottery and in 1913 the Rubian Art Pottery. At its height Grimwades Ltd employed over one thousand workers and produced a wide range of goods for the middle-class market (Plate 26.1).

Between the wars there were over four hundred firms in Staffordshire vying with one another for a share of the marketplace. They tried to come up with new patterns and styles for every British Industries Fair and were not slow to copy other companies' successes. Although the 1920s were for some the Jazz Age, the age of the vivid, the exotic and art deco design, for many this was a time to recover from the horrors of the First World War and the Russian Revolution. An American advertisement for English chintzes described them as 'bordering on the sensational…novel indeed and radically different, but not Bolshevik'. It would be fair to say that Royal Winton were not revolutionaries in the world of Staffordshire ceramics. Chintz was meant for the seaside cottage and the country kitchen and not the avant-garde house in New York or the stylish flat in London.

A.J. Wilkinson Ltd dabbled in chintz, which was noted by the trade press:

> We should regard this pattern [Maytime] as a good provincial or suburban line. We do not suggest that it will sell briskly in the city, though one never knows.[1]

Of course A.J. Wilkinson, owned by Colley Shorter, went

Plate 26.2. A coffee pot decorated with the printed Jazz pattern, c.1930.

Plate 26.3. An example of Grimwades' foray into art deco, a hand-painted Delhi pattern teapot from 1930.

on to produce the ultimate in British art deco ceramics, Clarice Cliff. Grimwades went in a totally different cosier direction with the introduction of *Marguerite* chintz in 1929, followed by *Springtime* and *Summertime* in 1932. Canada did not embrace art deco design in ceramics and vastly more chintz was found in Canada than Clarice Cliff or Susie Cooper's more deco designs. Since Winton was a major exporter to Canada, Australia and New Zealand, it is not surprising that art deco design was a footnote rather than a major theme at Grimwade.

The most recognisable art deco design produced by the factory was the colourful hand-painted *Delhi* pattern introduced in 1930 (Plate 26.3). The pattern depicts a stylised tree with an arch of leaves against bright yellow and reddish orange rays of sunlight. This pattern was often applied to rounded rather than angular shapes to rather strange effect. Although Winton incorporated the names of their chintz patterns into the backstamps, few deco patterns had recorded names: *Persian*, *Delhi* and *Forrester* are the best known.[2] The *Pottery Gazette* made frequent mention of the Winton chintz patterns, the relief-moulded ware and the pastel ware, but there is remarkably little mention of any art deco shapes or patterns produced by Royal Winton between the wars except for the occasional company advertisement with

Plate 26.4. An earthenware trio, possibly Ascot shape, decorated with the art deco styled Wheels pattern, c.1930.

Plate 26.5. Banded decoration applied to the Hastings shape, c.1930.

Plate 26.6. A group of Royal Winton wares decorated with stylised floral and landscape patterns, from a company advertisement about 1936.

one listing the *Norman* shape and the *Beverley* pattern with pattern number 1355.[3]

Although Grimwades modelled the very angular *Norman* shape for tableware in 1932, it is more often found covered in chintz than deco patterns. In 1937, when chintz was not as popular as it was in the early 1930s, Grimwades ran several advertisements in the trade press for 'distinctly novel treatments, certain to appeal',[4] including the very deco shape *Bude* decorated with a lustre landscape. These pieces were expensive to produce; one might speculate that they were not great sellers because they do not turn up often and the deco shapes once again came to be covered in chintz by the late 1930s. This resulted in a rather split personality sharp-edged cosy-patterned piece satisfying neither deco nor chintz buyer (Plate 26.7). Clearly deco was not

a large part of Grimwades' exports. A 1936 Export Catalogue discovered recently in New Zealand does not offer a single piece of deco Grimwades among the many pages of chintzware, salad ware, moulded relief ware, toilet sets and 'hygienic' hospital, table and kitchen ware.

From a review of the *Pottery Gazette* from the '30s it is evident that when Grimwades sought new lines they turned less to deco design than to a new chintz pattern or cottage ware or pretty floral-handled pastel ware. In 1930 the *Pottery Gazette* reported:

Grimwades Ltd. are thoroughly 'in the ribs' of the market so far as medium-priced useful and fancy goods are concerned.[5]

Plate 26.7. Examples of how the chintz patterns were unsuccessfully applied to art deco shapes, the art deco Norman shape range.

In 1932 they commented:

Winton have always applied themselves very assiduously to supply pottery dealers whose interests are associated with the masses and middle classes.

Finally in 1936 they repeated:

this is a house which can cater in an exceptional way for what are known as bread-and-butter lines, a fact which at once places them upon the current list of almost every dealer who has a call for middle-class goods.

During the depression, as firms struggled to survive, they would obviously continue to produce what would sell best for them. For most of the 1930s Grimwades were able to market pretty wares to the masses and their attempts to compete with other Staffordshire firms in the more deco markets were not particularly successful. Very few books on twentieth century design or art deco ceramics even mention the name of Grimwades' Royal Winton, although some of their deco pieces are comparable to the deco designs of leading English factories of the time.

1. 'Buyers' Notes', *Pottery Gazette*, September 1926.
2. These patterns were illustrated in *Pottery Gazette*, 1 November 1930, p.1739.
3. Company advertisement placed in *Pottery Gazette*, 1 July 1933, p.783.
4. Company advertisement placed in *Pottery Gazette*, 2 September 1935, p.1061.
5. Buyers' Notes, *Pottery Gazette*, 1 November 1930, p.1739.

27

Greta Pottery

Andrew Casey

THE STORY OF THE SHORT-LIVED GRETA POTTERY IS a fascinating account of how the skilled designer Grete Marks from Germany arrived in Britain and, despite many obstacles and challenges, was able to establish her own factory which brought an authentic European design aesthetic to the British pottery industry.

The Greta Pottery was established in Stoke-on-Trent in 1938 by Grete Marks. Born Margarete Heymann in August 1899 in Cologne, she studied at the Cologne School of Arts and at the Düsseldorf Academy. In November 1920 she enrolled on the preliminary course at the Bauhaus School of Arts in Weimar. The Art Director was the influential designer Walter Gropius who proposed a modernist approach to design which supported mass production and modern technology.[1] In order to achieve this he wanted every student to be trained by two teachers in every subject – an artist and a craftsperson. Margarete Heymann studied under Johannes Itten and later studied pottery design for sixth months with Gerhard Marcks. In 1921 Grete left the Bauhaus to work at a pottery workshop in Frechen and later taught pottery to children.[2]

Following her marriage to Gustav Loebenstein in 1923, the couple established their own pottery, Haël-Werkstätten für künstlerische Keramic (for artistic ceramics) in Marwitz, near Velten, north of Berlin. The company soon became a member of the Deutscher Werkbund – known for its commitment to progressive design. The designer created a wide range of vases, bowls, lamp bases and teawares decorated with coloured glazes which were progressive and modern, echoing the teachings of the Bauhaus (Plate 27.1). Many of these were illustrated in the company's catalogue from 1924. The business was successful with wares being sold across Germany and in England, with the London department store, Heals, importing her ware. This small concern employed over one hundred and twenty workers at the height of its success.[3] In 1928 her husband was killed in a car accident but despite this she continued the running of the factory, participating at the annual Leipzig trade fair in 1929 and 1930.

By 1933 the commercial success of the pottery business was suffering due to the deteriorating economic situation in Germany and the increasing Nazi hostility towards Jews. When her factory was forcibly purchased by the National Socialists in 1934 Grete and her children fled Germany for England. Other designers such as Marcel Bruer, Walter Gropius and Moholoy-Nagy had also come to Britain. Ambrose Heal, the owner of Heals, assisted her in making the journey to

Plate 27.1. An earthenware dish decorated with an abstract pattern, designed by Grete Marks. Diameter 14⅝in. (37.2cm).

Plate 27.2. An earthenware vase decorated with rouletted bands with a semi-matt glaze and overglaze painted bands. Designed by Grete Marks for Minton, Stoke-on-Trent. Height 4¾in. (12cm).

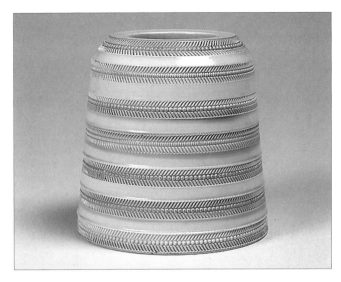

Plate 27.3. An earthenware vase decorated with bands of rouletted decoration with a semi-matt glaze and overglaze painted bands. Designed by Grete Marks for Minton, Stoke-on-Trent. Height 3¾in. (9.7cm).

England. She was given a one month visa and had to find a job in order to stay in the country.

It was inevitable that Grete would eventually move to Stoke, the centre of the British pottery industry, in order to secure work. Gordon Forsyth, the well-respected Superintendent of Art Education, helped Grete establish herself in the Potteries by arranging an exhibition of her pottery and paintings at the Burslem School of Art. From this she was contracted to teach for one term at the school of art.

Shortly afterwards the prestigious pottery Minton offered her the opportunity to run an independent studio within their factory, starting in September 1937. It is difficult to understand why Minton, of all the pottery manufacturers in the Stoke area, would have invited her to work for them. There were many other more progressive pottery companies such as Josiah Wedgwood and Sons Ltd and Royal Doulton that had embraced the new modern look, whereas Minton were renowned internationally for their classical, traditional and heavily gilded wares which were out of reach of the general ceramic buyer. Previously the company had hired the designer Reginald Haggar in 1930 whose new ideas for contemporary patterns the company thought were too avant-garde. He left after five years and was replaced by the designer John Wadsworth who had worked there before.[4]

With the opportunity to develop her own shapes and patterns Grete was able to recreate some of her earlier shapes as well as creating new ones such as a range of vases (Plate 27.2). She must have been seen by the company as an important designer as she was given her own backstamp which read 'Greta Pottery at Minton'. The problem for the factory, however, was how to market these European inspired ceramics that were at total odds with anything being produced in the British pottery industry at the time, although her work was sold at the London stores Heals and Fortnum & Mason (Plate 27.3). Despite some artistic success the relationship with

Plate 27.4. Two earthenware bowls decorated with contrasting semi-matt glazes with moulded geometric handles. Designed by Grete Marks for Ridgways, Shelton, 1937-1940.

Plate 27.5. Two earthenware plates decorated with a semi-matt glaze with an overglaze printed and painted stylised floral motif. Designed by Grete Marks for Ridgways, Shelton, c.1937-1938. Diameter 6½in. (16.7cm).

Plate 27.7. A period photograph showing the range of bought-in shapes decorated with simple patterns. Designed by Grete Marks 1937-1940.

Plate 27.6. An earthenware plate decorated with hand-painted decoration, designed by Grete Marks for E. Brain & Co Ltd about 1937. Diameter 6½in. (16.7cm).

Plate 27.8. An earthenware teapot decorated with a semi-matt glaze with an overglaze abstract pattern. Designed by Grete Marks 1937-1940. Length 18⅛in. (46cm).

Minton broke down after only sixth months and Grete left the company.[5]

Soon afterwards Grete secured work at Ridgways where she designed both patterns and shapes, including her conical tea wares with disc handles, which were similar to her early work in Germany (Plate 27.4), alongside simple stylised floral motifs (Plate 27.5). She also worked on a freelance basis and in particular with Freda Beardmore at E. Brain & Co, designing bone china tableware and printed designs that were picked out in hand painted enamels (Plate 27.6). In 1938 she married Harold Marks, an extra-mural tutor for Oxford University working with the Workers' Educational Association.

Having tried her very best to introduce new shapes and patterns at the various British pottery firms without much success, Grete decided to set up her own small pottery

Plate 27.9. An earthenware plate decorated with a semi-matt glaze with overglaze painted stylised spray of flowers and leaves. Designed by Grete Marks 1937-1940. Diameter 6⅞in. (17.4cm).

works with her husband. In 1938 the Greta Pottery was established in part of the Cleveland Tile Works in Summer Street, Stoke. As this small pottery didn't have facilities to manufacture blank wares the designer had to use bought in wares from various suppliers (Plate 27.7). Grete clearly selected a range of modern shapes which she supplemented with a number of moulded wares she made herself. The range of pottery offered was very similar to her early work which also used a range of matt and semi-matt glazes, often coupled with the minimum of decoration (Plate 27.8), but she did use simple floral motifs which were rather abstract (Plate 27.9) and sometimes slightly more realistic (Plate 27.10). The shapes that she did model were rather striking and included a candlestick decorated with semi-matt glazes (Plate 27.11) and a series of banded plates (Plate 27.12). In total contrast to her modern shapes she also produced some nursery style patterns (Plate 27.13). The wares produced by the pottery were usually marked with a hand-painted G P and were sold in many of the important department stores such as Heals and John Lewis (Plate 24.14). In 1940 her latest productions were illustrated in the *Pottery Gazette*. Sadly, after only a few

Plate 27.10. An earthenware vase decorated with a semi-matt glaze and an onglaze stylised floral pattern. Designed by Grete Marks 1937-1940. Height 7½in. (19.2cm).

Plate 27.11. A striking candlestick decorated with semi-matt glazes. Designed by Grete Marks 1937-1940. Height 6½in. (16.6cm).

Plate 27.12. Two earthenware side plates decorated with semi-matt glazes and different coloured centres. Designed by Grete Marks for the Greta Pottery, 1937-1940. Diameter 7in. (17.7cm).

Plate 27.13. An earthenware plate decorated with a matt glaze nursery subject and an overglaze painted design of two girls ice-skating. Designed by Grete Marks for the Greta Pottery, 1937-1940. Diameter 6¼in. (16.2cm).

years and with the Second World War looming on the horizon, the factory, like many others, closed in 1940.

By the late '30s the British pottery industry had yet totally to embrace the modernist approach to design, although some factories were making some effort with the modern works. Cheryl Buckley commented that:

Due to lack of opportunities, Marks was unable properly to develop her pottery designs in Britain, although arguably she was one of the most capable of proposing a truly radical modernist aesthetic in pottery by drawing on her Bauhaus training and her experience of the German pottery industry.[6]

During the war Grete concentrated on her painting whilst her husband served in the army. By 1945 they had moved to London where Grete continued to paint and, interestingly, began to make studio pottery and pottery pictures, combining specially made pieces with broken pottery.[7] Grete Marks died in London in November 1990, aged ninety-one.

Plate 27.14. A period photograph of the range of vases and bowls decorated with simple patterns from the late '30s. Designed by Grete Marks for the Greta Pottery, 1937-1940. Diameter of plate 6¼in. (16.2cm).

1. Information from the Potteries Museum, Stoke-on-Trent.
2. For a more in-depth history of the designer and her life see: U. Hudson-Wiedenmann and J. Rudoe, 'Grete Marks, Artist Potter', *The Decorative Arts Society Journal*. No. 26. 2002.
3. Ibid.
4. For further in formation see Chapter 8 and J. Spours, *Art Deco Tableware*, Ward Lock, 1984.
5. Buckley, C., 'Women and Modernism: A Case Study of Grete Marks (1899-1990)' published in *Women Designing. Redefining Design in Britain between the Wars* (edited by J. Seddon and S.
Worden), University of Brighton, 1994, pp.104-109.
6. Buckley, C., *Potters and Paintresses: Women Designers in the Pottery Industry 1870-1955*, The Women's Press, 1990.
7. Author in conversation with Frances Marks, October 2006.

28

Less Well-known Manufacturers

All essays in this section are written by Andrew Casey except:
John Aynsley & Sons by Frank Ashworth, Candy Pottery by Ian Turner,
George Clews by Hilary Calvert, Crown Staffordshire by Sue Taylor

DURING the '20s and '30s hundreds of small family run pottery works were in operation, many of them less well known than the most successful companies operating within the industry, both in Stoke-on-Trent and across Britain. The information for these short essays has been gathered from a number of sources but chiefly the *Pottery Gazette* and the *Pottery and Glass Record*. Trade reviews, Buyers' Notes and company advertisements have all been used to build up a picture. Please note that not all the examples of new pottery introduced by the various manufacturers were illustrated in the trade press and therefore some information on the new pottery may not be in the art deco style.

The author has selected a number of factories that are less well known but there were many other smaller pottery works in operation during the '20s and '30s that did not receive much, if any, coverage in the trade press. There are also a few pottery manufacturers included in this section who are better known for their product ranges from a different period. For example, the 'contemporary' pottery produced by W.R. Midwinter Ltd during the 1950s is very well known, but less has been recorded or published about their productions from the art deco period.

Following a general survey of the trade press, it is clear that the less well-known companies who found it harder to respond quickly to the new fashion for art deco styled pottery began to introduce their own versions from about 1931, but the style was more prevalent from some two years later. According to a reliable source, the *Pottery Gazette* tended to review and illustrate the products of those manufacturers who advertised extensively in the journal.

Other important sources
P. Atterbury, E. Denker and M. Batkin, *Twentieth Century Ceramics: A Collector's Guide to British and North American Factory Produced Ceramics*, Miller's, 1999
J. Spours, *Art Deco Tableware*, Ward Lock, 1988
G.A. Godden, *Encyclopaedia of British Pottery and Porcelain Marks*, Barrie and Jenkins, 2003

ADDERLEYS LTD
Daisy Bank Pottery, Longton

Formerly William Alsager Adderley & Co, 1876-1905, Adderleys Ltd were established in 1906 in Longton. They concentrated on the production of a wide range of goods including bone

Plate 28.1. A large earthenware jug decorated with banded decoration, Adderleys, c.1930.

china and earthenware tea and coffee sets, dinner wares, toilet wares and a selection of household goods, including practical kitchenware, for the home and export market. Adderleys were noted for their up to the minute and stylish transfer prints that nodded to the interest in brightly coloured wares from the late '20s. In 1928 they introduced the *New Octagon* shape as well as a range of underglaze hand-painted patterns and some enamelled designs. In about 1929 the company backstamp hinted at a new approach to modernity by including the words PORCELAINE MODERNE.

By 1930 the company took out an advertisement to promote the new *Troy* pattern that was featured in the trade press for most of the year. In about 1931 they introduced a striking *Electric Blue* body used for a variety of wares such as tea, dinner and toilet wares. A new pattern depicting a Viking ship with gold and green sails was introduced in 1931. During the same year three bone china cups and saucers, available in white or ivory and decorated with stylised landscape designs, were used in a company advertisement that included the *Watteau* pattern on the *Stafford* shape and *Orchard* and *Bourton* decorated on the *Brompton* shape.[1] By the early '30s they had agents in the United States of America, Holland, South America, South Africa, Australasia and New Zealand with a London showroom based at Charterhouse Street.

In order to maximise potential sales the company offered a wide range of new modern patterns, many on the new stylish shapes such as *Marina* from about 1934, alongside traditional printed patterns such as *Wild Rose* on the *Avon* shape and *Pansy* on the *Teck* shape. Probably their most art deco styled shape was *Princess*, launched in 1935, which was conical with triangular shaped handles. A wide range of modern patterns, such as 09467, were applied to this striking shape.[2] Another new china shape was *Sussex*, but this was traditionally styled. The company also launched special lines of bone china called *Steelite* for use in hotels and restaurants along with a range of 'crystallite' ornamental pieces in earthenware.

By 1938 the company had launched the *Glade Green* range, a coloured body similar to those by Johnson Brothers in production at about the same time. A year later the *Alphabet* nursery range, depicting various animals including a kangaroo, antelope and cat, was launched. The company was later named Gainsborough Works. They closed down in 1941 for the duration of the Second World War and in 1947 were taken over by the Ridgway Potteries Ltd, but the company name was retained. In 1964 they became part of the Allied English Potteries and were later joined by Royal Doulton.

ASHTEAD POTTERY
Victoria Works, Ashtead, Surrey

This small manufacturer was established in 1923 by Sir Lawrence Weaver in association with the Rural Industries Board as a training centre for disabled ex-service men after the First World War. They produced a range of hand-thrown and moulded wares decorated with various glaze colours and simple banded decoration. They also produced a range of practical wares for the table including breakfast, dinner, tea and coffee wares. Pottery was displayed and sold at the Heals store in London and it was considered at the time to be patriotic to buy Ashtead pottery and to support the ex-servicemen.

Some examples of Ashtead pottery were shown at the British Empire exhibition in 1924. The factory produced a special jar and cover depicting the 'Herrick' lion on the lid.[3] Ashtead was supported by a number of prominent ceramic designers including Percy Metcalfe, a well-known sculptor and stamp designer who created a number of figural pieces such as his blue-glazed sculpture of a lion, originally made for the British Empire exhibition but proving so popular that it was made commercially. Phoebe Stabler, an acknowledged sculptor and wife of Harold Stabler, a partner at Carter, Stabler and Adams Ltd, had her work produced at Ashtead Nursery, as did E.H. Shepard, whose nursery patterns, including *Winnie the Pooh*, were used by the company. Ashtead also produced souvenir pottery for the Portmeirion village in North Wales. The company closed in 1935.

AVON ART POTTERY LTD
Jubilee Works, Longton

This company was established in 1930 and gained, through originality and quality, a good reputation, soon becoming well known for a diverse range of decorative wares such as vases and bowls as well as tablewares. They used the Avon Ware brand name to promote their products and incorporated it into the backstamp. They soon had

Plate 28.2. A collection of Ashtead banded pottery, c.1929-30.

Plate 28.3. An advertisement for Avon Ware, showing the latest products, 1936.

agents in South Africa, Australia, Holland and Canada. Despite taking out full-page advertisements in the trade press throughout the '30s there was very little coverage of their products and scant information on specific pattern names or shapes. At the British Industries Fair in 1934 they displayed a number of new hand-painted designs for table-ware, often decorated on mottled grounds, including an autumn leaves design (3475), a tulip motif and a number of scroll designs. A new range of bowls and vases decorated with embossed motifs was called *Rubena*. The company was allowed to continue production under the Industries Concentration Scheme until after the war, but closed in 1947.

JOHN AYNSLEY
Portland Works, Longton

In 1924 Kenneth Aynsley became proprietor of the Portland Works in Longton. By the First World War the company had a well-established reputation for china tea, breakfast and hand-painted dessert wares. In the changed conditions of the early 1920s ornamental wares featured prominently – trumpet-shaped flower vases, covered vases and bowls with lustre glazes, including a popular butterfly pattern. Kenneth Aynsley was cautious and financially astute. Aware of the commercial value of the company's heritage and registering the Aynsley name as a trademark in 1928, he also saw the innovations being pioneered by rival china companies such as Shelley and Paragon.

By 1930 the company had introduced an 'up-to-date' version of the 'Aynsley China' logo surrounded by stylised bottle kilns. In the new atmosphere of the period they experimented with modern shapes and jazz designs and gave traditional patterns a contemporary flavour. The *Tulip* was a very dainty shape introduced in October 1931 for tea ware, coffee sets or fancies and

Plate 28.4. *The* Tulip *shape was introduced by John Aynsley in October 1931 for tea ware, coffee sets and fancies. The cups feature a large tulip embossed on each side, while the handles are in the form of a butterfly with the wings extended backwards. Illustrated is pattern B1322, produced in a range of colours, green with detailing in black and orange being especially popular. The* Tulip *design, registered no. 765789, was ordered by Queen Mary and some examples are marked 'As Supplied to H.M. the Queen'.*

featured a large tulip leaf on each side of the cup with butterfly handles as the most distinctive visual attribute (Plate 28.4). In the case of the teapot the butterfly formed the knob of the lid. Available in pink, blue, yellow or green, green with detailing in black and orange proved particularly popular. Although based on earlier precedents, the shape and clarity of the flower decoration give a close association with the period. In 1932 the old *Clyde* shape was offered with a flower handle, while the tall *Austral* and the low *Doris* gained a rustic effect handle. The *Classic* was introduced in 1933 as an elegant new shape with octagonal foot and panelled profile and became one of the company's best sellers. The same year the *Betty* nursery wares were displayed, decorated with dainty and lively figures coloured with unusual freshness, showing up well in the *Ring a Ring a Roses* pattern. *Bluebird* and *Blue Bell Time*, purchased by the Queen, were popular patterns of the time.

In 1934 the conical shape of the *Boston* cup provided a radical design departure. The impact of the straight

tapering lines was diffused by a practical curved handle and by a range of understated modern decorations, such as *Arta*, consisting of horizontal bands and small motifs of vertical lines in contrasting colours, finished off with gold or silver.[4] Other patterns included *Elaine*, where flowers were panelled on the wares with geometric ornament and fashionable bold colours, while *Plaza* was a design modern in feeling, the decoration in green and black complemented with gold or silver. Other noteworthy decorations on the *Boston* shape were the *Ascot*, *Heathertime* and *Fleurette* patterns. The company continues to the present day.

BARKER BROTHERS
Meir Works, Longton

Barker Brothers was established in 1876, producing both bone china and earthenware under the Royal Tudor name. During the early part of the twentieth century they produced a wide range of products – plain wares for the kitchen, toilet wares, fluted tea ware and some nursery wares such as the *Teddy Tail* pattern, based on the comic strip by Charles Folkard for the *Daily Mail* from 1919.[5] This set included teacups and saucers, mugs, tankards and beakers supplied in china with porringers and plates in earthenware. A notable new dinnerware pattern was *Bruges*, decorated under the glaze, and later extended to include vases, flower pots and rose bowls. Barker Brothers also enjoyed great success with a chintz pattern.

The company quickly embraced the art deco style and the fashion for modern brightly painted pottery designed by John Guildford (see Plate 4.8), who had previously worked as decorating manager at A.E. Gray & Co Ltd, leaving in about 1922. Bold, hand-painted, geometric patterns such as *Arabesque*, *The Storm*, *Autocrat* and *Moulin Rouge* sound very evocative of the period (Plate 28.5). Some of these

Plate 28.5. Two hand-painted Moulin Rouge plates, designed by John Guildford, 1929.

patterns were illustrated in the trade press which commented that Barker Brothers did their very best to meet the new art deco movement to give the public what it wanted. A new shape, *Mentone*, was introduced in 1929 and decorated with patterns such as *Tripoli*, a hand-painted bird motif, *Fantasie* and *Paradise*. The '30s saw the introduction of the primrose glaze that was used for several popular patterns and new shapes included *Modern* and *Eureka*. In 1932 the company launched the hand-painted *Dolly Varden* pattern depicting a crinoline lady in a garden.[6] Typical patterns included *Pomona* decorated on embossed early morning sets. Following the Second World War the company decided to offer a wide range of traditional and modern patterns. In about 1955 they were taken over by Alfred Clough and were later sold to John Tams. Barker Brothers closed in 1981.

JOHN BESWICK LTD
Britannia Works, Longton

In 1894 James Wright Beswick founded a small pottery called J.W. Beswick Ltd. By the early twentieth century, after some changes, the company was established at the Britannia Works in Longton. Typical production included domestic toilet wares decorated with transfer-printed patterns. The patterns, as illustrated in the *Pottery Gazette* in December 1919, were rather traditional and applied to the *Stella, Rose* and *King* shapes. When the founder died in 1921, his son John took over. He replaced some of the period and dated wares and introduced an interesting and unusual collection of modern wares including appealing vases decorated with exotic birds, Dutch scenes and similar patterns. By 1927 eighty per cent of all production was ornamental.

Beswick responded to the advent of the art deco style with a number of new ideas including an unusual novelty tea set with the teapot in the form of a large equilateral triangle, with a similar hot water and cream jug that fitted on to an irregular tray, from 1931. *The Pottery and Glass Record* of 1931 reported that the London showroom was showing new lines including an egg set with the tray handle in the form of a perky little duckling; a new pattern of a caravan scene with a sunset effect in the background was applied to vases. By 1934 the factory had produced over two hundred shapes for their range of art deco styled vases and jugs (some bearing embossed decoration) decorated with matt glazes (Plate 28.6). They also produced some face masks. At the same time they produced a brightly coloured modern range called Vortex.

Alongside the art deco styled wares Beswick introduced a range of embossed wares such as *Gardena* that included a teapot in the form of a large rosebud and a long celery dish in the form of a basket; these proved very popular. Other new lines included lettuce wares, cucumber trays, beehive honeypots and dishes moulded to resemble pansies. These were similar to Carlton Ware but were more expensive. The most popular line was the *Cottage Ware*, launched in 1934, which featured a teapot and other items moulded as a thatched cottage. This range was very popular (it was still in production in the '70s) and prompted similar ranges such as *Sundial* from 1937.

Following the death of John Beswick in about 1936, new management decided

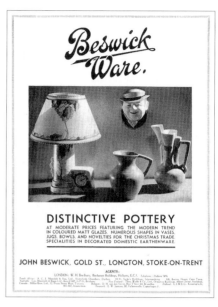

Plate 28.6. A group of Beswick wares, 1935.

that future production would shift from tableware to fancies. Jim Hayward, who had joined the company in 1926, was appointed Decorating Manager. At the same time they sold the Warwick works that was used for bone china production. In 1938 a company advertisement illustrated a wide range of products which included vases, a Laurel and Hardy cruet set and moulded wall pockets. Beswick is known today for their range of detailed and authentic representation of the animal sculptures, especially horses, created by Arthur Gredington. During the late '40s they introduced Beatrix Potter figures and some Disney characters such as Donald Duck, Mickey Mouse and Snow White and the Seven Dwarfs, under special licence from Walt Disney. In 1969 Beswick was sold to Royal Doulton.

BLYTH PORCELAIN CO LTD
Blyth Works, High Street, Longton

Blyth Porcelain, formerly Dresden Porcelain, was established in 1905. Over the years they had gained a reputation for good quality china tea and breakfast wares from stock lines up to higher class product ranges trading under the Diamond China brand name. The company offered bone china wares decorated with all sorts of patterns from elaborate designs to simple enamelled ones but, unlike other manufacturers, none of these featured in their trade advertisements. Instead they promoted the business using a drawing of a large diamond. They declared that they specialised in English bone china tea and breakfast sets.

By 1933 agents were established in New Zealand and Australia. During the early '30s the company introduced a whole range of print and enamelled patterns in the modern style that proved popular with the public. Some of the first, including *Tulip* and *Honesty* from 1932, bore a remarkable likeness to designs by Crown Ducal of the same period.[7] New shapes were developed and old shapes updated with the older *Pearl* shape being given a florally modelled handle. According to the trade press another new shape was in development that would be squarish in outline and possibly called *Diamond*. By the mid-'30s there was a clear move away from the heavy old styles towards lighter and often delicate hand-painted patterns that were applied to modern conical shapes such as *Bute* and *Coral*. The latter was very art deco in form with triangular open handles and, according to the *Pottery Gazette* of 1 February 1936 (p.219), a best selling shape, decorated with outstanding patterns including *Solitude*, which featured a pattern of stylised flowers. They also produced a series of incised floral wares alongside the new *Oxford* shape that featured a two ring handle on the cups.[8] The business was taken over by A.T. Finney in 1935.

BOOTHS LTD
Church Bank Pottery, Longton and Swan Potteries, Tunstall

The company was established in about 1891 and produced a wide range of domestic pottery in line with current tastes. By the early '30s it became apparent to the company that the new modern style was proving very popular amongst the trade and as a result they began to develop their own art deco wares. Perhaps rather reluctantly they produced a limited number of art deco patterns from about 1930, evident with patterns such as *Countryside* (A4130), depicting a country cottage and trees, a stylised floral motif called *Rock Rose* (A3341) from 1930 and *Red Rufe* from 1931. They also issued a series of banded wares applied to art deco shapes, such as pattern 5943, a stylish design featuring a hand-painted *Fly Fishing* pattern (A5743) and a printed pattern of stylised fruit called *Damask*. More unusual ranges included the *Humpty Dumpty* cruet set, the new *Trinity* shaped jug and the new *Mannequin* shape.

By 1934 Booths introduced the new *Ribstone* wares featuring a ribbed body similar to the *Lynton* range by Clarice Cliff (Plate 28.7). Initially produced for decorative wares such as vases, bowls

Plate 28.7. A period advertisement for Booths, 1935.

and lamps, the range was extended due to public demand to include tea and coffee wares. The shape was decorated with several hand-painted patterns such as *Anemone*.[9] Under the new *Silicon China* name, first launched in 1906, the company issued a series of banded and printed patterns, and often a combination of both, that were rather similar to the work of Susie Cooper from the same period and used for hotels and shipping lines. Examples of the pottery were exhibited at the prestigious British Art in Industry exhibition held at the Royal Academy in 1935. Booths was a nucleus firm during the Second World War and later in the '40s they purchased Colcloughs. From 1948 the company was known as Booths & Colcloughs Ltd, based in Hanley.

BOVEY POTTERY CO LTD
Bovey Tracey, Devon

Founded in 1894, this company specialised in the production of domestic earthenware pottery, toilet and hotel wares thought to be designed by William Clayton. During the early '30s they developed a range of tablewares in response to the new style but, from illustrations in the trade press, they focused on modernist shapes with simple banded decoration rather than art deco styled floral patterns. In 1934 they exhibited at the British Industries Fair for the first time displaying the new soft green *Lawn* pattern alongside a modern pattern called *Aurora*, described by the *Pottery and Glass Record* March 1934 (p.64) as being 'a streaky combination of powder red, grey and yellow'. Like many other manufacturers, they also produced a range of embossed toilet wares and a pattern called *Primrose*. The trade press noted new patterns, such as *Sylvan* on the *Bedford* shape, and a range of covered dishes called *Exmoor*, designed by J.F. Price in 1935. This new shape (2095), decorated with green and silver horizontal bands, was illustrated in the trade press. Also on offer was a cabinet toilet set which was available in five colourways: blue, orange, pink, green and lawn green. The company closed in about 1954.

CANDY & CO LTD
Heathfield, near Newton Abbot, South Devon

Candy & Co Ltd were brick, tile and fireplace manufacturers but introduced a range of art pottery hollow ware in the 1920s, partly because they needed to fill voids in their Dressler Tunnel Ovens to secure consistency of firing. The company had been founded by Frank Candy in the 1870s, became a limited company in 1882 and by the end of the century was in the ownership of the Fox family of bankers.

Candy was a large undertaking with a deep ball clay pit and extensive works at Heathfield and, later, a second factory at Nelson in Lancashire where fireplaces were made for the northern markets. The slip-cast art pottery – described by the *Pottery Gazette* in January 1922 (p.67) as 'artistic vases and miscellaneous lines suitable for everyday sale in glass and china establishments' – was launched at the British Industries Fair at White City in 1922 as *Wescontree Ware*. Initially the glazes were muted, glassy, mottled and metallic, but during the later 1920s more brightly coloured cobalt blue and uranium orange glazes were used, sometimes streaked in the manner of Shelley Harmony ware. In 1936 this range was withdrawn and a new range, all hand thrown by a potter called Sid Dart, was introduced under the brand name of Candy Ware.

In the late 1930s these wares included art deco geometric shapes and new bright colours such as 'electric blue' alongside orange, flambé and lustre glazes. A good example of this art deco style is the uranium-glazed lamp base from this period (Plate 28.8). After the war a new range of Candy Ware was

Plate 28.8. A Candy art deco styled lamp base decorated with a bold orange glaze, 1930s.

introduced with few art deco shapes and a more 'contemporary' style but, after producing a range of souvenirs for the 1953 coronation, the art pottery was gradually run down and had ceased altogether by the late 1950s. The company continued to make Candy Tiles at Heathfield until it closed in 1998. All the buildings were demolished the following year and the site is now occupied by British Ceramic Tiles' new automated tile factory.

CIRCLE POTTERY CO
Crown Pottery, Mill Street, Stoke-on-Trent

Little is known about this company which was noted on only a few occasions in the pottery trade press. This is probably due to the fact that they were only in operation for two or three years, opening in 1936 and closing in about

Plate 28.9. Examples of Circle pottery wares, 1936.

1938. Despite this short time the company clearly developed a range of new shapes and patterns for dinner and tea ware (Plate 28.9). Shapes noted in the trade press included the *Royal*, a rather simple form and not really art deco in style, and *Moderne* which, however, was rather deco in style with conical bodies and angular handles, very similar to many shapes produced by other manufacturers during the period.[10] The company preferred to decorate their new lines with hand-painted patterns, such as banding (1170) and wash banding, rather than transfer-printed designs. They also offered a range of matt glazed vases and bowls.

GEORGE CLEWS & CO LTD
Brownhills Pottery, Tunstall

Percy Swinnerton Clews and Harry Preece took a lease on Brownhills Pottery, Tunstall in 1908, two years after the company was formed in 1906, and soon had a thriving pottery business producing teapots in red earthenware. Teapots were to remain the company's volume output, but the Works Manager, Daniel Capper, was interested in glaze chemistry and by 1914 a separate art ware department had been formed. White earthenware was slip cast to make many shapes of vases and bowls that were finished with metallic, crystalline and lustre glazes. The art range was called *Chameleon Ware* and after the First World War was extended to include hand-painted designs (Plate 28.10). All colours were painted directly on to the biscuit fired pottery which was dipped in a semi-matt glaze before firing. Patterns were bold and geometric and covered most of the area of the pot that was always coloured – no areas were left as white background. Colours were pale or dark blue, brown and ochre or a mottled green; in the 1930s a mottled cream was introduced.

A small company such as Clews could easily adapt its designs to suit current

Plate 28.10. An example of Chameleon Ware by George Clews.

fashion. As art deco motifs appeared, the *Chameleon Ware* range was extended to include motifs such as the sunrise, stylised horses and sailing galleons moulded in relief in the slip-cast pottery. Some of the hand-painted designs were sharpened into art deco but, although the new style was offered to customers, the existing patterns were continued, Clews being a very cautious and rather old-fashioned pottery. *Chameleon Ware* was produced for the British and export markets until 1940 when patterned ware ceased and only plain teapots continued in production. After the war, during which Percy Clews died, the art pottery was never revived and only household earthenware and teapots were produced until the company folded in 1961.

JAMES H. COPE & CO LTD
Wellington China Works,
Stafford Street, Longton

Established in about 1887 and trading as Wellington China, this company was well known for its range of high quality bone china tea wares. By the early '30s it had introduced a few designs leaning towards art deco, including a pattern described and illustrated by the *Pottery Gazette* on 2 February 1931 (p.237) as being an 'ultra-modern border design kaleidoscopic style' applied to the *Rena* shape. Other patterns included a simple design of hanging triangles on a green glaze and a series of print and

enamelled designs of various *Crinoline Ladies* (5583). Further note was made of the *Marne* and *Jewel* shapes, but it is not clear if they were newly styled for the art deco period.

In 1932 a number of art deco styled patterns painted in bright colours with gilt decoration applied to the *Clifton* shape were produced along with a number of floral designs with some decorated on a *Cube* shape teacup. The new *Flora* shape was launched in 1933, bearing a hawthorn embossment alongside a series of florally modelled brooches, flower stands and m'lady powder boxes.[11] By the mid-'30s they were developing twenty-one piece boxed sets in the new *Queen* shape issued in 1935, which was rather similar to the *Regent* shape by Shelley. The same year a range of novelties, mirrors and table lamps ornamented with hand-formed and delicately painted flowers were produced, but these have not been seen so may not be art deco. In 1938 the company launched new shapes such as *Ascot* and *Gem* and a new line of children's mugs with pixie handles and a teddy bear mug. The company closed in 1947.

ELIJAH COTTON LTD
Nelson Works, Hanley

This company was established in 1880 and traded as Lord Nelson Ware. They soon gained a good reputation, in the middle class market within the pottery industry, as a specialist in the manufacture of jugs. During the early part of the twentieth century, with the addition of a second factory, they expanded their production to include tea, coffee, toilet wares and kitchenware.

During the early '30s they produced a limited range of art deco patterns, both hand painted and printed, to compete within the market.[12] One notable pattern, *Avis,* depicted a flying blue bird. The trade press noted a number of printed border patterns of fruit for fruit

and sandwich sets and another of stylised flowers called *June*. The new *Hexagon* shaped jug *Leda* was decorated with hand-painted floral patterns in bright colours. Designs such as stylised floral patterns were often hand painted. By the mid-'30s the company had developed and launched the new art deco *Saxony* shaped covered dish (illustrated in *Pottery Gazette* 1 June 1935, p.735) alongside a popular range of Silver Jubilee wares. It closed in 1980.

CROWN STAFFORDSHIRE PORCELAIN COMPANY
Minerva Works, Fenton

T.A. & S. Green, founded in 1847, first advertised under the Crown Staffordshire trade name in 1889 and by 1903 were producing a wide range of bone china products including dinner ware, tea and coffee ware, miniatures, vases, cutlery handles, door furniture and floral china baskets. In the late 1920s Crown Staffordshire pioneered the large-scale production of china floral ornaments and china costume jewellery and it is perhaps for this that they are best known. Throughout the twentieth century, however, they also manufactured fine bone china tea and coffee wares.

Unlike some other companies, they did not develop new ranges of shapes to reflect changes in style but continued to use their traditional tea ware shapes and can shaped coffee cups. These were decorated with imaginative printed and hand-painted designs executed by their large team of talented paintresses, thus producing a modern look at little expense. Surface patterns could be quickly adapted to meet the customers' needs and changing tastes such as the art deco styled pattern 13799 (illustrated in *Pottery Gazette*, 1 July 1933 p.842).

In the 1930s the company introduced the *Pan* range of yellow-glazed tablewares, decorated with hand-painted brightly coloured stylised flowers and birds. This new venture was expected to be a great success, but it transpired that the consumers preferred to see the white body of bone china and so the yellow glaze was dropped. Some unusual modern figure groups featuring children on floral bases were designed by T.M. Bayley in the 1930s, whilst bird groups were designed by Jack Jones. In the latter half of the twentieth century the focus of the company's production moved more towards production of these figures and floral fancies, many of which were destined for the export market. In 1973 the company was taken over by the Wedgwood Group.

DECORO POTTERY CO
Tuscan Works, Longton

This smaller pottery was set up by the parent company R.H. and S.L. Plant Ltd in about 1933. It seems from a report in the trade press that there may have been an earlier Decoro pottery that was bought by Plant's and then moved to their site. The *Pottery Gazette* of 1 June 1935 (p.739) stated.

> the story that we now have to relate is that the manufacture of Decoro's pottery has now been transferred lock, stock and barrel, to a special department of the Forrister Street works at Longton, where there is every prospect of its being sympathetically and progressively extended.

Decoro Pottery specialised in the production of ornamental wares decorated with topical patterns of the day using red-base teapot clay. By 1935 the range included several different bowls, flower jugs, bulb bowls and other shapes decorated with patterns such as *Poppy, Pansy, Floral* and *Autumn*. Another range featured plain glazes in various colours including pink, green and grey. The trade press noted the new Decoro Floral Art Ware range consisting of small giftwares featuring modelled

flowers hand painted in bright colours.

A whole new range of ornamental wares was launched in 1937, including a two-handled vase and new wall vases. Possibly due to the restructuring of the parent company after the Second World War, it was decided to close the Decoro Pottery in 1949. (See Plate 4.10.)

DORIC CHINA CO
China Street, Fenton and later
High Street, Longton

This factory was established in about 1924 by Harry Meigh and Miss Dale. When Miss Dale decided to retire to get married in about 1934, however, a Mr Spanton Reid, the son of the late Harry Reid, joined as a partner bringing with him considerable expertise in pottery management. The company introduced a range of handcraft patterns decorated on the *Marlborough* shape that was also used for the more traditional *Derby* styles. The *Pottery Gazette* of 1 February 1934 noted the new cone-shaped range called *Modante* (p.193). This new shape was decorated with several new stylish patterns such as 455 and 464. In 1935 the company was taken over by Royal Albion China Co.

ELEKTRA PORCELAIN CO LTD
Edensor Works, Edensor Road, Longton

Established in 1924, this company initially produced pottery for the lower end of the market but during the early part of the twentieth century decided to concentrate on the middle class market, at the same time extending their range of shapes. They began by developing a new cellulose-finished glaze that enabled them to price these new decorative wares competitively for the mass market, typified by their new *Zanobia* range first introduced in about the late '20s. Some of the first *Zanobia* wares had four different types of embossment to the body and were

called *Ivorine, Dutch, Oriental Ivory* and *Oriental*. Another range, first shown at the British Industries Fair in 1929, was called *Jettina*; this included vases, flowerpots, powder bowls and several novelties.

The *Zanobia* range encompassed all sorts of decorative patterns and by 1931 included the *Cries of London, Cherry Ripe* and *Chairs to Mend* patterns in the form of an oval plaque on the ware. Some modernistic hand-painted patterns of scenes included an Egyptian boat with a mountain in the background (732) and another imitated the skin of a pineapple. In tandem with these designs they also produced a number of modelled animals including an elephant, finished with a flame glaze to the most striking effect. The trade press noted that there were over seventy different decorations and over four to five hundred shapes available. A similar popular range was called *Vulcan Ware*.

As business increased the company employed a number of new girls to decorate these new hand-painted patterns alongside other decorative techniques such as stencilling, sponging and colour spraying in 1932. Of particular interest was the introduction of tube-lined decorated patterns finished with additional colour; named the *Florina* range,[13] this included iris, plum,

Plate 28.11. *A period illustration featuring Elektra's new crackled ground in fawn with a flower garden pattern (no. 592) applied to a range of shapes and a yacht ornament available in two sizes with many different colourings, 1938.*

daffodil and lily motifs and was shown at the British Industries Fair in 1933. Typical patterns of this period featured stylised motifs painted in bold colours on matt glazes such as 922. New shapes were developed to meet new demands and these were called *Ring* (a wide mouthed jug), *Crown* (a wider bellied shape) and *Aladdin*; the latter was described by the *Pottery Gazette* as 'unique in form: we would even describe it as an extreme and fanciful shape'.

Elektra also issued a number of modelled animals including an Alsatian dog and a bear, with more being considered for production. They showed a number of new patterns at the British Industries Fair in 1934 including a display of scenic decorations such as ships and swimming fish. By 1935 they had agents in South Africa, Holland, New Zealand, Canada and Australia. Two years later they launched a new range of decorated wares called *Ruralia*; stylised trees and cottages were incised into the ware and featured different colour backgrounds – blue, brown and orange – a simple imitation of Clarice Cliff's famous patterns. They were offered in twelve different shapes including *Venice*, *Turin* and *Elin*.

Even as late as 1938 Elektra was still developing new ranges of shapes – rose bowls, posy rings, garden ornaments and wall masks – that were slightly art deco in style. Another pattern called *Roseday* was a stitched style pattern on an oatmeal base. New additions to the *Zanobia* range included modelled bunnies in sets of three or four and a set of modelled yachts. There was also a set of wall ornaments that included flower baskets and jugs as well as one modelled as a heron. The company closed during the 1940s.

ERA POTTERY CO
Sutherland Street, Stoke-on-Trent

The Era Pottery is not well known today, despite being a subsidiary of Crown

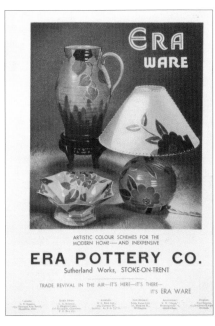

Plate 28.12. An Era company advertisement to promote the latest productions in 1934.

Devon. Era Art Pottery, who used many of the same shapes as the parent company, was set up at the height of the art deco period in about 1930. They traded as Era Ware and by about 1936 the backstamp incorporated a stylised cottage and trees. They had agents in Amsterdam, Australia, Canada and South Africa and a London showroom in Holborn. They soon became well known for decorative wares such as vases, bowls, candlesticks and lamp bases. From period journals it appears that they did not produce tea and coffee wares. One of the first patterns was the *Dream Cottage* pattern from 1932.

The company showed an impressive range of new pottery, including decorative vases, lamps and simple banded jugs, at the British Industries Fair in 1934.[14] The new patterns included *Chrysanthemum*, *Tulip* decorated on a matt black, *Autumn Leaves* and *Cherry* as well as another new pattern featuring a stitched motif on a buff base depicting stylised trees – *Alpine* (663). Another pattern featuring embossed motifs was *Embassy* (677). New patterns for 1935 included *Laburnum*, a stylised tree

design in black and brown with boldly painted floral motifs on lamp bases and bowls.[15] The company also displayed a series of new embossed salad wares including a radish dish moulded as a cabbage leaf. It closed in 1947.

THOS FORESTER & SONS LTD
Phoenix and Imperial Potteries,
Norfolk Street, Shelton, Longton

The company was established in about 1883 with the Phoenix factory being responsible for the production of the art ware side of the business whilst the Imperial factory was concerned with the production of bone china. They had agents in Australia, South Africa, Canada and New Zealand with a London showroom at Hatton Garden.

During the late '20s the company produced a number of new lines that were fairly traditional in style with patterns such as *Korea*, *Osaka* and the free-hand *Kingston* being typical. These were decorated on a wide range of wares including morning sets as well as tea and coffee wares.

In 1928 the trade press mentioned *Raleigh*, the new squarish shape that was perhaps the company's first attempt to create an art deco styled range and reflected the need to meet the new demands for modern shapes and patterns. As early as 1930 the trade press were commenting on the new, slightly futuristic patterns like 6035 being shown to trade buyers. One early example, from 1931, was called *Arboretum*; it featured relief modelling and brushwork and proved to be a great success. This was followed by a similar range, *Lincrusta*, featuring moulded flowers painted in bright colours on a bright yellow ground. Lustre was used for a range called *Arcadia*; one of the patterns, *Poppy*, was a notable example. By 1934 new modern patterns included *Seville*, *Foresta* and a range of blue streaked wares called *Bluevista*.

More important was the new Phoenix

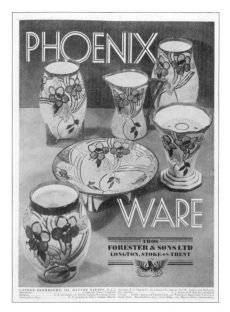

Plate 28.13. A company advertisement for the popular Phoenix Ware launched in about 1934.

Ware launched in about 1934 (Plate 28.13). This range, which encompassed a whole series of patterns and shapes introduced through the decade, made an influential impact on the trade with the bold geometric patterns featuring stylised motifs decorated on a range of art deco styled shapes such as vases, jugs and biscuit barrels. New patterns, for example *Celestine* featuring a striking tree design on a mottled blue and pink ground, *Arcade* in brown, yellow and green and *Radiant*, consisting of green and blue stripes, were launched in 1935.

The company was quick to respond to the changes in taste and moved away from the bright art deco patterns by developing a whole new series of simple shapes, such as the *Saxon* flowerpot, decorated with matt glazes and available in three colours – brown, blue and green. This new range, called *Harmony*, was launched in 1936. They also created a number of incised wares with one example being called *Buda*. Another new shape was *Turin*, more traditional in style, for tea ware. Mention

was also made of a whole series of patterns including *Golden Pompadour, Delta* and *Sheba,* but these were probably more traditional than art deco in style. In 1937 a new matt glaze range called *Egypt* was launched. A year later new patterns, decorated on a new series of shapes, including *Verdant, Velontino, Vandyke* and *Tudor Rose*, were launched alongside other patterns such as *Silver Pompadour* and the hand-painted *Viola*. The company closed in 1959.

GIBSON & SONS LTD
Albany and Harvey Potteries, Burslem

Established by Sydney Gibson in 1875, the company was initially known as Gibson & Sudlow, but by 1885 was called Gibson & Sons Ltd, with two factories, Albany and Harvey, in Burslem. For many years this small company was chiefly involved in the production of teapots of the highest quality; the Albany works was dedicated to manufacture *Rockingham* and *Jet* wares whilst Harvey produced domestic wares. Through the many years of production they used several trademarks including Silvoe Art Ware, Windsor Art Ware, and Royal Harvey (dinner and tea wares). The standard of both design and manufacture must have been outstanding as the company was awarded the Diploma of Honour at both the International Exhibition at Turin in 1911 and two years later at Ghent. In 1930 the trade press illustrated new lines that included an embossed fruit shape called *Sheila*, the traditionally styled *Banff* shape and the comical *Clock* teapot complete with clock face and the words 'Good Morning'.

During the early '30s Gibson issued new patterns and shapes that were stylish but not quite art deco in style. The *Ceres* range, from 1931, featured moulded fruit and flowers in relief with hand-painted decoration on a black ground, whilst a number of new patterns such as *Wedgwood, Globe* and *Melrose*

were applied to teapots. The first art deco pattern, however, known from an illustration in the *Pottery Gazette* of 1 November 1932 (p.1355), was the hand-panted *Crocus* design (9364) applied to plain shaped wares, very much in the style of Clarice Cliff but without the distinctive solid banding that set her designs off well. A range of open-mouthed flower jugs was also launched in the same year along with other similar shapes. The same article also mentioned that some patterns were decorated with tube-lined decoration of a free-hand scroll (0266). For the Silver Jubilee of King George V and Queen Mary in 1935 the company produced an art deco shaped teapot.

In 1935 the trade press commented that the company had extended their range with a series of ornamental wares such as flower jugs with rustic or figured handles alongside some angular and modernistic shapes. These latter shapes bore a striking resemblance to those by the Myott Pottery. In 1936 the new art deco styled pattern *Sunray* was noted in the trade press. The company also produced a range of figures, for example a dancing woman, either as separate items or as a combination of figure flower holders. One of the best selling figures was *Lorna* and the most popular flower holder was *Glasgow*. In about 1947 the company was sold to Mineral Separation and then a few years later to the Howard Pottery Group.

GLOBE POTTERY CO LTD
Waterloo Road, Cobridge,
then at Shelton from 1934

The company was established in about 1914, becoming well known in the export trade for their semi-porcelain table services and vitrified hotel ware. By the late '20s they were exhibiting a wide range of traditionally styled tea wares with gilt decoration including popular Derby styles and Rockingham teapots. By 1935 they had launched a whole new

Plate 28.14. A trade advertisement showing the diverse range of products that the Globe Pottery produced through the 1930s.

series of wares with new art glazes, mottled and arresting marble effects. Over thirty-one new lithographic patterns were also available including a scroll-like motif called *Orient*, painted in blues with banding in black, used for both dinner and tea wares. Some of these new designs were decorated on the popular *Ascot* shaped dinner ware.

Probably the most important range was their new *Renaissant* range launched during the mid-'30s which consisted of a wide range of shapes such as flower vases, trays, bowls, jugs and lamp bases decorated with many different modern patterns, for example *Harmony* and *Sarawaki*. Interestingly, the *Pottery Gazette* of 1 May 1936 (p.679) reported that these outstanding shapes:

> have been specially produced for the firm by a Continental artist who has given particular attention to the trend in regard to modern house furnishing.

This exceptional range, promoted in the trade press with stylish full-page advertisements, was followed a year later by a new bold pattern in green and

tango (bright orange) decorated on the *Kent* shape alongside a new series of moulded jugs including the *Braemar, Fiord, Lysle* and *Ubiqu,* decorated with stylised floral patterns.

T.G. GREEN & CO LTD
Church Gresley, Burton upon Trent

This popular pottery was established by Thomas Goodwin Green in Church Gresley in Derbyshire in 1864. A disastrous fire at the turn of the century necessitated a new factory being built and in 1905 the owner's two sons took over running the family business.

The company is best known for its *Cornish Ware*, a practical range of functional domestic kitchenware decorated with bands of blue and white launched in the early '20s. Not only was it commercially successful, it also set a new standard in the production of kitchenware. A complementary range called *Blue Domino* was introduced in about 1933 and then *Polka Dot* three years later, the latter decorated on a shape similar to *Regent* by Shelley.[16] After some modernisation the range of products was extended to include toilet ware, appliqué ware, vases, cube teapots and various domestic wares. Agents were established in South Africa, Australia and Canada.

Throughout the '20s and '30s, whilst the *Cornish Ware* was selling well, the company continued to introduce new shapes and patterns, with many hand-painted patterns such as *Pomona* from 1933 (a simple Titian style border and advertised as being Handcraft Ware), *Grasmere* and *Crocus* (Plate 28.15). T.G. Green did produce a limited range of patterns and shapes that included some more art deco influenced patterns; launched in about 1932, they included the *Pharos* and *Alpha* patterns, print and enamelled on to the angular earthenware *Obliqué* shape.[17] This modern shape was also decorated with a new print and enamelled landscape

Plate 28.15. A T.G. Green part teaset decorated with the Grasmere pattern. Height of teapot 51.2in. (14cm).

pattern called *Fairy Glen*. In 1932 the trade press mentioned a series of brightly painted jugs decorated on the *Gordon* and *Clive* shapes that were selling well and a new printed pattern, *Woodville*, decorated on the *Richmond* shape.

After the war T.G. Green produced a series of contemporary patterns such as *Samba, Safari* and *Central Park* designed by Colin Haxby. Despite these successes the company struggled during the '60s and in 1965 went into receivership.

W.H. GRINDLEY & CO LTD
New Field Pottery,
Woodland Pottery, Tunstall

Established in 1880 in Tunstall, this company specialised in domestic earthenwares, morning sets, dinner ware, supper sets and various associated items as well as providing blank wares for other manufacturers. They responded quickly to the art deco style by producing a range of patterns and shapes that proved popular. One particular range was *Medina*, featuring a centre floral motif finished with a broad band in green; this was produced from about 1930 with patterns such as *Hazeldene, Georgian* and *Fairfield*. In 1932 they launched the *Lady Mary* pattern alongside a rather conventional *Constable* (probably printed pattern 3031). The trade noted that the *Cecile* pattern was applied to the *Regency* shape.

Plate 28.16. A Grindley earthenware teapot decorated with silver banding, c.1932.

At the British Industries Fair in 1934 the company showed a new range of patterns, many in the modern suites style, with the trade press noting the new hand-painted *Violet* pattern as well as a series of broken banded designs complemented with a floral motif. A year later new modern patterns such as *Nocturne*, the printed *Madeleine* and *Autumn* were launched. Special notice was made of the new embossed tea sets with a very attractive *Narcissus* pattern. The company continued production until 1960 when they were taken over by Alfred Clough Ltd.

HAMMERSLEY & CO
Alsager Pottery, Sutherland Road, Longton

Formed in about 1887, the company was known as Hammersley & Co (Longton) Ltd from 1932. They were well known for the production of bone china tea wares decorated with the more traditional styles popular at the time, but during the late '20s they developed some new shapes and patterns to meet the growing demand for art deco styled wares. Probably one of their first attempts was the new nursery ware line called *Alice in Wonderland* consisting of a mug, cup and saucer and various plates;[18] they obtained exclusive rights to reproduce Sir John Tenniel's artwork. Despite great efforts such as the new *Kew* shape, which featured an embossed

flower handle, the new ranges from 1931 were still rather traditional in both shape and pattern.

During the early '30s a number of handcraft patterns, decorated on the *Kelvin* shape, were issued alongside the new *Tulip* shape which proved ideal for a number of smart enamelled designs that were probably by Fred Clay, designer and decorating manager, who had joined the company in about 1933. At the same time the company continued to produce new designs on their old and best selling shapes such as *Queen Anne* and *Buccleugh*. In 1934 the *Pottery Gazette* noted that a new pattern, *Carnival,* was launched and featured a 'gold print, freely bejewelled with little blobs of enamel, including red, turquoise, orange and emerald green' which sounds rather art deco. In 1935 they launched a new nursery ware set called *Cat Park*. Not much is recorded in the trade press about Hammersley but they continued in production after the Second World War and closed down in 1982.

SAMPSON HANCOCK & SONS
Gordon Works, Stoke and Corona Pottery, Hanley from about 1923

This small factory was established by Sampson Hancock in 1857 and based at the Gordon Works; it was renamed S. Hancock & Sons (Potters) Ltd in 1935. By the late nineteenth century they were advertising their latest handcraft wares, probably designed by George Cartlidge who joined the company in 1890, alongside dinner and toilet wares. In 1900, when the founder died, his three sons Arthur, Harry and Jabez took over the running of the works. One of the most important ranges, each designed by George Cartlidge, was *Morris Ware,* a tube-lined design launched in 1918.[19] This was inspired by the famous designer William Morris who was active at that time. Following the First World War the company increased its

Plate 28.17. A group of Sampson Hancock & Sons vases, including Cremorne, *designed by Molly Hancock c.1930.*

production of ornamental wares which encompassed children's ware such as boxed tea sets and dolls' heads. In the early '20s a new art director, F.X. Abraham, was employed; he was responsible for a wide range of new patterns that may have included *Rubens* and *Titian* wares alongside *Woodland*.

During the early '20s the factory moved to the Corona Pottery in Hanley. A new popular range was Corona Ware. Some art deco patterns, such as the print and enamelled *Springtime* (7990), were created by Edith Gater, as well as some tube-lined wares, though not much is known about her. Molly Hancock, the daughter of Jabez Hancock, produced a series of patterns from 1930 including *Cherry Ripe* and the more art deco inspired *Cremorne* depicting abstract flowers. She also created children's ware. During the mid-'30s the company produced a wide selection of handcraft patterns, such as *Gaiety,* decorated on a range of wares including jugs, bowls, cups and saucers, and a set of flower jugs including the *Venice, Florence, Milan* and *Exeter* shapes. In 1935 a new tea ware shape called *Acme* was launched, decorated with various hand-painted patterns such as *Minuet*. On 1 October 1935 the *Pottery Gazette* (p.1263) mentioned the several new lines, including *Lagoon* with a fish decorated bowl, on display at the British

Industries Fair. Cottage wares were launched at the same time and included plates with relief decoration of cottages and trees, hand painted in bright colours. Following some difficulties the company went into liquidation in about 1937.

HOLLINSHEAD & KIRKHAM LTD
Unicorn Pottery, Tunstall

The company was established in about 1870 in Burslem, but moved to Tunstall c.1876. They soon became well known for their production of useful inexpensive general earthenwares decorated chiefly with transfer-printed patterns. Originally the main body was a white ware but after some time they produced an ivory body for the higher class market with hand-painted decorations that proved popular. On 2 July 1928 the *Pottery Gazette* (p.1089) illustrated a new printed floral pattern that imitated brushwork (643); this was clearly influenced by the art deco style, although the shapes were rather Victorian. At the same time they had introduced a new short order range called the *Maisonette*; suitable for the smaller family, it consisted of a handled supper tray, six octagonal shaped plates, coffee pot, biscuit barrel, six teacups and saucers, milk and sugar. In the late '20s they introduced a series of decorative wares called *Arab Scenes*, applied to

Plate 28.18. A contemporary Hollinshead & Kirkham advertisement showing the latest art deco shapes and patterns for 1935.

various vases and bowls. At the same time the trade press remarked on their high quality toilet wares, noting the *Greek* shape as well as the new *Bute* shape.

It was perhaps in 1932 that the move to produce art deco style patterns began with ranges such as *Lonsdale, Minster, Panola* and *Artesk*. The *Pottery Gazette* of 1 March 1932 (p.339) noted that:

> those dealers who can find a market for the really bright multicoloured decorations in bold, simple brushwork, such as coloured contrasting bands and kaleidoscopic effects, will find something to interest them in this firm's no.1433 decoration.

These proved very popular and over the next few years additional patterns such as *Aloma* and *Sandringham* were added (that do not sound very art deco). Alongside these artistic triumphs the company still created more standard wares, including a printed pattern called *The Lady Fayre* of a woman in a garden decorated on all sorts of wares including a cruet set, cheese dish and preserve pot.[20] The only nod to art deco was the new tea ware shape with a triangular handle, though the shape name is not known. In 1936 the trade press noted the new simple banded dinner wares alongside handcraft designs. Two years later the new Utility range, consisting of a large bowl, four smaller bowls, jug and stand, as well as a new snack set, was launched. The company continued production after the Second World War and was bought by Johnson Brothers Ltd in 1956.

HOWARD POTTERY CO LTD
Norfolk Street, Shelton

Established in about 1925, this company must have made a considerable investment in machinery and staff as by the late '20s they had an extensive range of popular pottery available. By the early '30s, when the art deco style began to

influence the British pottery industry, they were offering a large range of bowls, vases, flowerpots, lamps and novelties decorated with pleasing hand-painted patterns of stylised flowers in various colours under the Brentleigh Ware name. They placed full-page artistic and powerful advertisements, often not including any illustrations of the latest pottery, in the trade press almost every month for some years. They also produced a number of tableware shapes such as *Atlanta, Ryland* and the *Vandyke* shape, which featured an embossed border. These shapes were utilised for a whole new range of patterns including the printed *Stella* design and other striking patterns applied to the *Melba, Lotus, Bognor* and *Olympic* flower vases and flowerpots. In 1931 a new pattern, *Carnival*, consisting of blobs with white flowers on a ground of black or bright blue, was launched.

In February 1935 (p.33) the *Pottery and Glass Record* commented that:

> one is amazed with the vast range of shapes produced and the outstanding originality of the decorations, each of which is designed with due regard to modern requirements and present day furnishing schemes.

The same article noted the new *Pandora* shape, a ball shaped bowl decorated with pattern 568, and the *Oban* and *Brent* shapes. The company's stand at the British Industries Fair of that year featured hundreds of animal figures, both as ornaments and bulb holders, alongside sixty new patterns and forty new shapes. Of particular interest were the figure of a '30s lady talking on the telephone and a Cubist style figure called *Golf lady and caddy*.[21] The trade press also noted the embossed range of plaques and a nursery ware pattern called *Pussy Cat*. The same stand featured a model of a garden with a pond with gnomes fishing and other ornaments included dogs, birds, speckled frogs, a stork and a woman

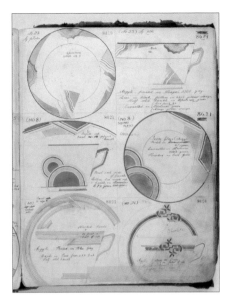

Plate 28.19. An example of an art deco pattern as shown in Howard Pottery's pattern books.

sunbathing.[22] By 1938 the company were offering figures such as dancing ladies, wall pockets, various flower baskets and vases decorated with simple floral motifs. Production continued after the war, though little information is available from this period. In 1974 they were bought by Taunton Vale Industries.

E. HUGHES & CO
Opal China Works, Fenton

This well-known company was established in 1889 and produced pleasing bone china wares. From about 1914 they used the Paladin China brand name and from the '20s they used a new whiter body, called Eusancos china, which sold well for a number of years. They responded to art deco styles as early as 1930 with the new hand-painted *Colorada* pattern in crimson with blue, green, gold and white. The trade press commented, however, that the general production of the factory was still rather on the traditional side and mentioned examples such as the *George, Ayr* and *Arran*, though these

were not illustrated. By 1933 the company had developed a new art deco shape called *Castle*, used for a variety of modernistic patterns, for example 3512 and 3518 which were both hand painted in bold enamel colours such as orange, platinum, yellow and green and depicted stylised leaf motifs, sets of lines and other zig-zag motifs.[23] In 1940 the company was renamed Hughes (Fenton) Ltd. It closed in 1953.

JACKSON AND GOSLING
Grosvenor Porcelain Works,
Gregory Street, Longton

The company was established at King Street, Fenton from about 1866 and by 1909 had moved to Longton. Trading under the name Grosvenor China, they went on to enjoy good business with the reproduction of several Old English styles that met with popular sales. By the late '20s the productions of this company remained rather traditional with a predominance of antique styles, notable patterns including *Shagreen* which was popular with the higher end of the market with the Queen making a purchase. By 1929, however, it was evident that they had made great efforts to produce a new line of modern pottery starting with the elegant *Georgian* shape, coupled with the new *Regent* shape teacup and saucer decorated with a printed design of flowing flowers called *Gay*.[24]

In March 1930 the *Pottery and Glass Record* (p.76) reported that, alongside the main lines of the company, there was a special display at the British Industries Fair of new modern patterns including *Simplicité, Futuria* and *Chanson*. The latter was printed in black and gold with hand-painted decoration in yellow with a blue border. The window display was decorated with examples of the *Rainbow* pattern. Further art deco styled patterns, consisting of simple silver lines of graduating width (8467), were applied to the *Globe* shape and also the popular

Argyle shape that was used extensively by the company during this period. Several designs recorded in the company's pattern books, such as *Woodland* and *Fairy Glen*, are clearly influenced by the latest designs by Shelley. Other art deco styled patterns include *Sporting Scenes*, a series of individual hand-painted motifs of sporting people including golfers, swimmers, footballers and horse riders. Further designs from 1934 included a mixture of printed modern motifs (8497) and others with black and silver banding (8465 and 8466). The company closed soon after being purchased by Shelley Pottery Ltd in the early '50s.

A.E. JONES (LONGTON) LTD
Palissy Pottery, Longton

This well-known company was established in about 1930. Trading as Palissy Pottery, it catered for the middle class market who wanted high quality earthenware pottery. During the late '20s important changes took place, with the quality of the ware being improved. In 1929 it became a limited company and at about the same time purchased the Regal Pottery Co based in Cobridge.

The trade press noted that the company had moved its general production away from the blue-banded designs and gilt that were proving less popular with the market and had developed new modern ranges in the art deco style. The resultant ranges were very striking, both in pattern and shape, with the two most important patterns, *Landscape* and *Futuresque*, being illustrated in *Pottery Gazette* on 1 January 1932 (p.63). The former pattern depicted a landscape with poplar trees and a mass of clouds, whereas the other featured panels of hand-painted zigzags and triangles; both were applied to a geometric shape with triangular handles and knobs, but the name is unknown. Other noted patterns from the same year included *Oakland*, a print and

Plate 28.20. An A.E. Jones trio decorated with a simple stylised floral motif, c.1934.

enamelled pattern decorated with stylised oak trees and, on the larger items, a distant cottage, applied to a shape range that featured an acorn leaf knob. Other similar patterns included *Springtime* and *Poplar*. In 1946 the company was renamed Palissy Pottery and was later taken over by Royal Worcester in 1958. Production ended in 1988.

KEELING & CO LTD
Dale Hall Works, Burslem

Keeling was an old factory that dated back to 1886, established by Mr Stubbs, a contemporary of Spode, Adams and Minton. Over the many years of production the company gained a high reputation for good quality earthenware as well as specialising in hospital and badged wares. They had great success with their Losol Ware trade name launched in 1912, following extensive research by the company to produce a glaze that was safer to use (the lead content of most glazes at that time was very harmful to workers across the entire industry). Furthermore, the factory boasted good ventilated work spaces and comfortable conditions.

From 1920 they reproduced bird and animal figures including a penguin lamp stand. By the early '30s they had a new range of modern shapes and patterns including a series of print and enamelled

designs such as *Mayfair*, *Claremont*, *Westminster* and *Dawnay*. The *Pottery Gazette* of 1 May 1931 (p.677) illustrated two examples of the firm's ornamental wares that were decorated with art deco styled floral designs, possibly using lustres, alongside a moulded flower basket decorated with a similar pattern. Further attempts to be modern were evident in the new *Regent* and *Rita* shapes that were decorated with patterns described by the *Pottery Gazette* of 1 February 1935 (p.209) as being 'very smart without being futuristic'. These new shapes were decorated with a range of brightly coloured print and enamelled designs such as a daffodil pattern (5960) that was interestingly applied to a more traditional shape called *Doris*. The new *Brantique* line was ready for the Christmas market of 1934. After two further years of business, however, the company was closed.

KENSINGTON POTTERY LTD
Statham Street, Hanley, then Burslem from 1937

This popular company, established in 1922, specialised in the production of good quality pottery to suit all markets. In the early '30s they seemed to have embraced the popular art deco market by introducing new shapes coupled with suitable art deco patterns, decorated on ivory ground semi-porcelain. These new handcraft patterns included 1037 and 1039 which were painted in bright colours with some solid gilt decoration on the handles. The *Pottery Gazette* visited the pottery and on 1 January 1934 (p.63) remarked that:

we found the place to be so unlike its former self that we almost wondered whether we had made a mistake and visited the wrong pottery. The atmosphere of the entire place seemed to be different, and the character of the output assuredly was different.

They illustrated two new patterns that featured simple hand-painted floral motifs on the *Elite* shape with octagonal plates. More important was the series of hand-painted ornamental flower vases such as *Gem*, *Elite* and *Saxon* shapes and the *Octagon* bowl painted in bold colours that could be mistaken for an example of Myott pottery (p.61). In the same article the *Gazette* assured the market that Kensington was still supplying their other popular, traditional lines. In 1935 a new square jug, in one size only, and an octagonal shaped vase were introduced alongside a group of new vases and a jug decorated in free-hand patterns such as *Gloria*, a stylised floral motif in green and silver, and a large flower vase and a *Classic* shaped jug. The *Pottery Gazette* of 1 February 1935 (p.209) described the new *Gothic* shape as being 'different in form from anything we have ever seen'.

In 1961 the new company Price & Kensington Potteries Ltd was formed. It is thought that business continued as normal.

JOHN MADDOCK & SONS LTD
Newcastle Street and Dale Hall Potteries Burslem

This company was set up in 1830. They specialised in dinner, tea, breakfast and toilet wares boasting a vitreous semi-porcelain body that sold well and soon gained a good reputation within the industry for quality pottery decorated with pleasing patterns. They had agents in the United States of America, Australia, South Africa, Canada, India and New Zealand and by 1935 new agents in Holland, Belgium and Norway were added. By the late '20s some of the patterns bore a likeness to art deco with patterns such as *Damascus* decorated on the *Marathon* shape.[25] In the early '30s some reorganisation and development took place that resulted in the allocation of space for the production of bone china.

241

In 1931 the company launched the new square shaped range called *Centenary*, named to celebrate the hundred years of the company's history. This popular shape was used for a whole range of patterns including *June*, which bore a slightly art deco styling of a landscape, and the *Belvedere* pattern (3680), with other patterns, for example *Flora* (3779) and *Naples*.[26] A number of transfer-printed patterns, such as those depicting stylised fruit, were applied to the *Minerva* and *Globe* shapes. The trade press mentioned the strongly coloured and modernistic *Gouda* pattern alongside a pattern consisting of stylised trees making a border. The new *Rainbow* pattern (3746) was applied to the *Leeds* and *Tudor* shape. By 1932 the company boasted new art deco inspired shapes; *Earl* and *Venice* both featured open triangular handles that were decorated with a new range of hand-painted on-glaze floral patterns.[27] In 1935 the company illustrated a new art deco style pattern of a repeating border decorated on the *Leeds* shape that was rather traditional with a rosebud knob. A company advertisement promoted the new *Sweet Marie* design, a printed floral applied to the new *Embassy* shape featuring art deco elements, despite the style rather waning by the mid-'30s.[28]

MAYER AND SHERRATT
Clifton and King Street Works, Longton

This factory was set up in about 1906 and used the Melba Bone China brand name. A company advertisement from 1928[29] notes that agents were established in Australia, New Zealand, Rhodesia and the Congo; by the early '30s they had agents in South Africa and the British West Indies and a London showroom in Shoe Lane, Holborn. From the late '20s the company began to introduce hand-painted patterns in line with the popularity for this sort of decoration alongside a range of printed patterns. In 1928 they launched the

Plate 28.21. A Mayer & Sherratt art deco styled Pansy shape tea set featuring flower handles, c.1934.

hand-painted pattern called *Dolly Varden*, designed by Lionel Mayer.

Over the next few years the company launched a series of art deco styled patterns that included the transfer-printed *Dancing Ladies* depicting a stylish interpretation of the crinoline lady, unfortunately on a rather ornate shape, simple hand-painted floral designs and scenic views, the latter similar to the popular designs of Shelley. The new *Holborn* shape, featuring a ring handle, was very similar to the *Regent* shape by Shelley. The *Pottery Gazette* of 1 January 1932 (p.61) described two new patterns, *Fair Days* and *Lightly Speed the Hours*, as being 'decorations of character and peculiar interest'. In 1934 the new shape *Lotus* was introduced, but it was clearly moving back to traditional styling despite the modern shapes such as *Holborn* (illustrated in the *Pottery Gazette* 1 January 1935, p. 57). A year later the company issued a dramatically shaped tea ware decorated with a stylised pattern of trees and a bird and new shapes called *Shell* and *Dawn*.

In 1936 several new tea ware shapes were introduced including *Neon*, which was decorated with many patterns including a print and enamelled design of a sunrise effect in browns and yellows (4419B), and the new taller cup shape named *Tarn*. The factory closed in about 1941.

W.R. MIDWINTER LTD
Albion and Hadderidge Potteries, Burslem

The company was established by William Robinson Midwinter company in 1910, at Bournes Bank in Burslem, Stoke-on-Trent, moving to larger premises in 1914. During the early part of the century they produced various tablewares, dinnerwares, toilet wares and ornamental wares decorated in traditional styles similar to other manufacturers, an example being a banded pattern of underglaze mazarine blue band and two gold lines illustrated in the *Pottery Gazette* on 1 September 1921 (p.1341). They also issued a traditional printed design based on engravings from the late nineteenth century, *Roger*, that became a best seller, and a popular line of all-over silver lustreware for teapots, sugars and creams on the *Georgian* shape, with a black handle.

In the '20s a change of artistic direction took place. New domestic ware shapes such as *Avon, Doric* and *Belle* were decorated with simple and improved lithographs, for example *Dorothy*, depicting a bird and branch design.[30] William Heath Robinson designed the *Fairyland on China* set in about 1928. During the early '30s Midwinter introduced a wide range of hand-painted patterns in the art deco style decorated on modern shapes. Notable was *Windmill*, an asymmetrical design painted in bright red, black and silver, launched from 1934. In 1936 a geometric styled pattern called *The Flower Shop* was introduced alongside other similar patterns that adopted simple art deco motifs similar to the leading manufacturers such as Shelley and Susie Cooper. During the same year the company released the new *Embassy* range, a stylish modern form featuring subtle incised vertical lines on the ware.

Midwinter came to the forefront of the British pottery industry in the '50s and '60s with new shapes and patterns that have been well documented in books and exhibitions. They were taken over by J. & G. Meakin Ltd in 1968 and by Josiah Wedgwood and Sons Ltd in 1970.

MORLEY, FOX & CO LTD
Salopian Works, Fenton

Established in 1906 (although previously known as William Morley from 1879), this company was well known for the manufacture of popular priced earthenware from utilitarian to decorated tableware. Examples of the pottery were illustrated in the trade press in 1928 decorated with fairly typical floral motifs of the period. The *Pottery Gazette* of 2 April 1928 (p.627) noted that they also produced tea and toilet wares, jugs, pudding bowls, pie dishes and ornamental wares. Probably in about 1929 they introduced the *Homeleigh Ware* brand name featuring a stylised cottage and tree as part of the backstamp (an alternative version was issued in about 1939). The factory produced two types of ivory ground and also gained exclusive rights to certain lithographic patterns.

In response to the growing fashion for art deco styled patterns, the company launched a new range of shapes, patterns and sets during the early '30s. New shapes included *Nina* (a dish with a lid featuring a fruit knob), *Panella* (for hand-painted patterns), *Canberra* (a

Plate 28.22. Trees, a Rachel Shaw production for Morley, Fox & Co, c.1930.

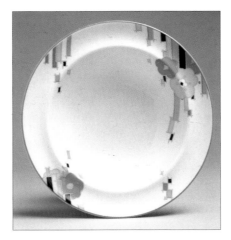

Plate 28.23. An earthenware bowl decorated with the printed Mayfair pattern, Morley, Fox & Co ,1933.

squared dish form) and the *Royal* shape from 1931. The many art deco styled patterns issued during the early '30s included *Crocus* in 1933, *Homestead, Springtime, Arcady,* a fruit design (516) and *Crinoline Ladies.* The latter depicted ladies in the garden in a pink and blue colour scheme, although applied to a traditional shape. Whilst nothing much is known about the designers, one hand-painted pattern called *Trees* (Plate 28.22), depicting stylised trees and landscape in the same vein as the *Autumn* pattern by Clarice Cliff, was designed by Rachel Shaw.

At the British Industries Fair in 1933 the company built a cottage style stand to showcase their many new lines which included several lithographic patterns such as *Florette, Gloria* and *Arlem.* The most important and successful pattern from this period was the printed *Mayfair* (Plate 28.23) available in at least two colourways. This pleasing pattern gained considerable press coverage as well as proving popular with the Queen who, according to the *Pottery and Glass Record* of March 1933 (p.71), bought examples of this pattern at the fair.

Further new modern patterns were shown at the British Industries Fair a year later and included *Ashdown,*[31] *Jewel, Bluebell* and *Narcissus.* It was also

recorded that one new style pattern was called *Jazette,*[32] which so evokes the period. A range of novelties included a model of a cottage for incense burning and a nine-piece strawberry set decorated with bright red fruit. The *Morning Glory* pattern that, according to the trade press, suggested rising suns in bright colours, proved to be a popular seller even though it was a simple design applied to dinnerware, morning and fruit sets. Other patterns included a neat green and silver design (722), a new modern styled shape called *Newlyn* and a number of Jubilee wares. A new pattern from 1935, *Lomond,* was applied to an Ivorine glaze,[33] whilst *Windsor Green* featured a low relief of an oak leaf border. From 1944 the company was known as William Morley & Co Ltd. This new company was in operation until 1957.

NEW PARK POTTERIES LTD
Park Works, High Street, Longton

Within a year of this company's establishment in 1935 they had a stand at the British Industries Fair displaying a wide selection of jugs, vases and bowls decorated with stylised tree patterns, flying birds and floral designs. The company closed in 1957.

THE NEW PEARL POTTERY CO LTD
Brook Street Potteries, Hanley

The New Pearl pottery was formed in 1935 following on from the previous Pearl Pottery which had been established in about 1894. The new company retained the same works, used the Royal Bourbon trade name and continued to use this name in the backstamp. The major change was the type of pottery they produced which was remarkably different altogether. In the year of opening they launched a striking range of overtly art deco shapes and patterns with the bold *Cuba* shape, a cube shaped form with triangular handles, no doubt boosting trade interest. Decorated with brown banding and stylised floral motifs, it was illustrated in the company's advertisement in the *Pottery Gazette* on 1 April 1935 (p.495).

Of interest is the limited series of Edna Best patterns exclusively produced for the retail china shop, Lawleys, during the mid-'30s (Plate 28.24). These art deco patterns were probably not designed by this famous actress, but her name appeared on the base of each piece. (Edna Best was a celebrated English actress who enjoyed great success in Hollywood with parts in films such as the original 1934 Alfred Hitchcock *The Man Who Fell to Earth*.) These bold and colourful hand-painted patterns were decorated on a number of shapes, possibly also specially created for Lawleys, and were clearly influenced by the great success of the *Bizarre* range by Clarice Cliff as some of the shapes were very similar to *Stamford* (Plate 28.24). The known patterns included a banded design in orange and yellow, one that featured stylised vertical banding in green, black and yellow that could easily be mistaken for Gray's Pottery, and one with stylised circles on a honey glaze.

Besides the art deco styled wares the company also introduced a number of

Plate 28.24. An earthenware teapot (missing its lid) decorated with a stylised pattern by Edna Best, New Pearl Pottery, c.1934.

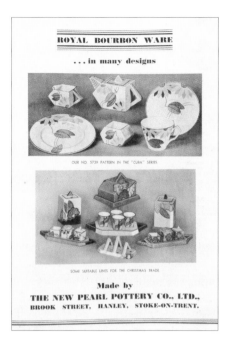

Plate 28.25. A New Pearl Pottery trade advertisement, 1935.

tasteful patterns such as *Marina* and *Primrose*, a modern hand-painted treatment, as well as several printed designs, many applied to the new *Rex* shape which was traditional in style. Nothing much else is known about the history of the company except that in 1936 it was bought by New Hall who in 1947 sold it to William Walker & Sons.

R.H. & S.L. PLANT

Tuscan China Works, Forrister Street, Longton

This family-run company was set up in about 1898, but was known earlier as R.H. Plant & Co, established in 1881. Long associated with the manufacturing of fine bone china under the trade name Tuscan China, over the years they had built up a good reputation with an international clientele. The trade press noted that they were not satisfied by simply producing tea wares but were keen to experiment.

As early as 1930 the company introduced a stylish range of art deco

styled bone china figures that included *The Town Crier*, *In Old Madrid* and *Masquerade* (*Pottery Gazette*, 1 November 1930, p.1733). In addition they produced a new range of modelled human figures, painted in bright colours, that could be used either as ornaments, bookends or lamp bases. Examples included the *Saxon Girl*, wearing a long dress, and *Memories*, a figure of a woman holding a book and available in natural colours or painted in green and black. These were displayed alongside an earlier range of figures, but the date of these is unknown. Attention to tableware patterns continued with the trade press noting that between 1929 and 1930 over three hundred new hand-painted patterns were applied to ivory glazed chinawares, a notable example being *Hollyhock* (9657). Also in 1930 they launched a new range of nursery ware called *Tinker, Tailor, Soldier, Sailor, Rich Man, Poor Man, Beggar Man, Thief* designed by Gladys Peto. It consisted of a teapot, cup and saucer, mug, two plates, beakers, porringer, milk and sugar.[34]

On 2 May 1932 a new range of more art deco inspired wares was illustrated in the *Pottery Gazette* (p.609) including a pattern of flowers and leaves with a butterfly (1736A), decorated on the *Iona* shape, and another more modernistic rendition of flowers (17164) painted in black, gold and green. Interestingly, Plant also produced bone china brooches in the form of a dog and a dog's head. In 1934 the trade noted that a range of new modern patterns was for sale, some applied to the new *Dorothy* shape on an ivory ground. This shape, along with the *Diana* and *Isis* forms, was used for a series of banded designs. Plant took over the Canning Pottery Co in about 1933 and from the information available it seems that they used this site to launch their new Decoro Pottery Co (q.v.).

A new range of lines in 1937 included the *Cromer* shape, wall plaques and loving cups as well as a nursery ware line called *Kiddies in Wonderland* consisting of seven subjects including *Water Babies, Tea Party* and *Jester*.[35] Plant continued production after the Second World War and were taken over by Josiah Wedgwood and Sons Ltd in 1966.

POUNTNEY & CO
Temple Bank, Bristol

The Bristol Potteries were well established during the later part of the eighteenth century. By 1878 Patrick Johnston, a London solicitor, bought the business and in about 1904 his nephew, T.B. Johnston, built a modern pottery works at Fishponds. They produced a wide range of toilet wares, earthenware and semi-porcelain dinner sets that were inexpensive wares, using low cost transfer-printed patterns rather than hand-painted decoration. During the early part of the twentieth century the company exported across Europe, North America, South Africa and Australia. At some stage T.B. Johnston's son, another Patrick Johnston, took control of the company. Cecil Garland joined the company in 1910 and after the First World War was appointed the Artistic and Decorating Manager.

With the advent of the art deco movement they employed a new designer, Jack F. Price. This partnership was a winning success. Price designed the *Academy* and *Dorland* (named after the Dorland Hall exhibition in 1933) shape range in about 1933. At about this time the well-known painter and designer Agnes Pinder Davis worked with Cecil Garland on a number of pattern ideas with some in production during the late '40s. Several examples of the company's wares, many designed by Garland, were shown at the Paris exhibition in 1937 and later at the 'Britain Can Make It' exhibition in London in 1946. Following the Second World War Kenneth Clark headed the design team who produced a number of contemporary lines as well as a number of traditional treatments based on the Victorian period.

PRICE BROTHERS (BURSLEM) LTD
Top Bridge Works, Burslem

This company specialised in the production of earthenware, especially teapots of all kinds of shapes and decorations. The original company was set up in 1896 at the Crown Works in Burslem. In 1934 it was taken over and renamed Price Brothers (Burslem) Ltd with Gerald F. Wood as managing director. The new management invested in modern machinery to speed up production.

One of their first ranges was *Mattona*, a matt glazed series of wares painted in soft colours depicting landscapes and trees with patterns 2022 and 2013 being typical. Of more interest are the new shapes, including the *Modern* vase and *Devon* bowl bearing a striking resemblance to the shapes by Keith Murray for Wedgwood. The popular *Mattona* range was also applied to other shapes such as jugs and biscuit barrels.[36] Another less well-known shape was the *Avon* teapot supplied in a series of six decorations. The company merged with Kensington Pottery in 1962 to form Price & Kensington and by the mid-'80s became part of the Arthur Wood Group.

RADFORD HANDCRAFT POTTERY
Amicable Street, Burslem

The artist potter Edward Thomas Brown Radford, who was born in 1882, came from a long line of pottery artists. His father was apprenticed at Josiah Wedgwood and Sons Ltd, later moving to the Linthorpe Pottery, and Edward learnt his trade from his father, at Pilkington's, before he retired in 1936.

Following the First World War Edward Radford moved to Burslem, Stoke-on-Trent. From about 1920 he was advertising his services as pottery agent in the trade press, attending the various trade fairs demonstrating the art of throwing. In 1930 he set up on his own in a small independent pottery works at

Plate 28.26. *Examples of hand-thrown pottery decorated with various patterns by Edward Radford, about 1933. Height of tallest item 6in. (15.2cm).*

H.J. Wood Ltd at the Alexandra Works, on Amicable Street in Burslem. Under the name Radford Handcraft Pottery he created many bold and artistic wares using all sorts of sources for inspiration. The *Pottery Gazette* commented in March 1933 that:

> Mr Radford's whole time and attention is devoted to the creation of pieces which are genuinely artistic and which will be treasured because of their intrinsic merit. To attain to this position of affairs he goes to the trouble in the first place of producing all his shapes on the wheel: none of them are cast in moulds.

During the art deco period he produced some outstanding patterns, including those featuring stylised angular trees, as well as patterns that bore a likeness to similar designs by the Poole Pottery. He also created a number of sgraffito patterns, mainly of stylised abstract and leaf shapes similar to those by Susie Cooper. His trade card for this new venture read 'Hand made and decorated tableware, bowls, vases, coffee services and nursery ware'.

His modelling work enabled him to produce a range of high quality vases, bowls, jugs and various giftwares, both of traditional and modern forms. Notable lines included simple floral motifs such as anemones often featuring stippled grounds. He also used some of the standard Wood's shapes.

In 1948 Edward Radford retired and

became a teacher of pottery, first in Derbyshire then moving to Manchester in 1954. Unfortunately after he had left the company his name was used on several new lines, such as a whole series of undecorated vases, jugs, ginger jars, flower baskets and candlesticks, which were labelled as his work.

SAMUEL RADFORD LTD
High Street, Fenton

Established in about 1879, this company specialised in the production of bone china tea wares and a range of earthenware. During the '30s they introduced a limited range of art deco styled wares alongside their general production of period styles such as the rich decorations known as Derby styles.

Possibly due to the main production focusing on the more traditional end of the market, their interpretation of the art deco style was rather restrained without being too avant-garde. For example, the new hand-painted rose pattern did have elements of the style whilst the new *London* shape, launched in about 1933, had no resemblance to art deco at all. During the same year the *Regal* shape was introduced and was used for a number of art deco patterns. Banded patterns were shown at their London showrooms in 1935 including 6632 on the *Marina* shape. Other patterns featured hand-painted zigzags and lines with others made up of abstract squares (6048). Another new shape, *Riviera*, was a reworking of the *Regal* shape but with a floral handle and decorated with patterns of stylised flower motifs.[37] Besides a range of hand-painted patterns they also issued several novelty items including moulded wares called *Flora*, a range of embossed wares painted in bold colours, and moulded fruit baskets. The trade press noted a four-piece set consisting of a teapot and stand, hot water jug and honey pot. The company closed in 1957.

RAINBOW POTTERY CO
Green Street, Fenton

This company was established in 1931, but hardly any information is available about it. They took their first stand at the British Industries Fair in 1931 and *The Pottery and Glass Record* reported in March 1931 (p.73) that they showed a range of cellulose-finished wares that included vases, bowls, clock sets, bulb bowls and vases available in two glazes: matt and lacquer. These were complemented with bookends and animal figures such as elephants and birds. The journal commented that 'decorations included those of a modernistic kind'.

Other coverage in the trade press is either non-existent or has not been identified. The factory closed in 1941.

JAMES SADLER & SONS LTD
Wellington and Central Potteries, Burslem

This company was established in about 1882, firstly as Sadler & Co, but from 1899 it was known as James Sadler & Sons Ltd. From about 1899 the company was based at the Wellington Works and from 1920 at the Central Pottery, at which point the early works was closed down. The new site was known as Wellington and Central Potteries. James Sadler & Sons Ltd soon became well known within the pottery industry for the

Plate 28.27. James Sadler & Sons' company advertisement for its Car *teapot,* Pottery Trade Gazette *1 January 1938.*

manufacture of teapots from plain *Rockingham* to *Jet*. Other styles included *Samian, Russett* and coloured pots. Five-piece sets were also popular.

In 1928 Edward Sadler visited the United States of America in order to look at pottery manufacturers and when he returned he started modernising the factory with the first tunnel kiln being installed in 1934. The new kiln gave the factory the opportunity to develop the production of novelty teapots. By the early '30s, when the teapot trade was dwindling, the company reported to the *Pottery Gazette* (1 February 1934, p.189) that they had produced during the last year 'more teapots than we ever produced in any single year during the last half century – considerably more'. In 1930 the company launched the *Handy Hexagon* teapot and a new shape range called *Mayfair*. In 1934 the trade press illustrated the new lines including the new tortoiseshell mottled decoration on the *Stanley* shape. Another en-suite set consisted of teapot, sugar, cream and a covered honey pot with an unusual decorative treatment like crocodile skin, available in four different colours (yellow, pink, amethyst and green).

In 1935 the company launched a range of striking art deco styled ornamental vases suitably named *Nile, Pharos* and *Thebes,* available in two sizes and in a range of modern patterns.[38] In 1938 the company launched the *Ye Daintee Ladyee* teapot modelled as a lady, many of which used silver decoration. Sadler is best known for its popular *Car* teapot (Plate 28.27) launched in about 1938, available in different colours. The registration plate read OKT42. Another design, called the *Football* teapot, featured a footballer as the handle with the knob modelled as a trophy. Other teapots included *Pixie* (otherwise known as *Fairyland*) and *Waverley*. A trade advertisement of 1938 also illustrated the new *Bunny* teapot moulded as a rabbit. Despite expansion, the company went into receivership in 2000. It was purchased by Churchill China.

SHORE AND COGGINS
High Street and Edensor Works, Longton

This smaller company was established in Longton in about 1911 and traded under the Bell China name. From the start of production they specialised in bone china tea wares, often hand painted or printed. By the late '20s, when the art deco style was becoming more popular, the company developed a wide range of patterns such as *Crocus* and *Tulip* launched in 1930. The trade press noticed the change in style and stated that:

> looser patterns which are somewhat a rage just now, Shore and Coggins, can of course, provide such lines.

By 1932 further art deco style patterns, for example *West Moorland* (202), were decorated on the *Lomond* and *Athol* shapes alongside an unusual design of fruit and little dots painted in red (2481) applied to the *Club* shape. Patterns like *Autumn Leaves, Rambler Rose* and *May Blossom* were closer to the art deco style, with the latter decorated on the *Blythe* shape.

Shore and Coggins also produced a series of small sweet dishes in three styles decorated with various patterns, both printed and painted. In 1934 they launched a new art deco styled shape range called *Tudor* available in tea, breakfast and coffee ware.[39] The subtle patterns were print and enamelled and available in six different colour

Plate 28.28. Typical examples of art deco patterns applied to bone china tea plates, Shore and Coggins, c.1930.

treatments to maximise sales potential. The trade press noted a new modern conical shape range called *Troy* alongside the angular shape *Bute*. Some examples of the new patterns, from 1935, were decorated on the new *Opal* shape which was slightly more traditional in form. The company was taken over in 1964 by the Lawley Group, merging with Royal Doulton in 1972.

SHORTER AND SON
Batavia Works, Stoke

This well-known company was founded by Arthur Shorter in the 1870s. In 1878 he joined forces with James Boulton and traded under the name Shorter and Boulton. In about 1885 Arthur Shorter took responsibility for running the A.J. Wilkinson Ltd factory whilst his partner continued to run the former factory. When James Boulton retired in 1897 Arthur Shorter's son Guy took over the responsibility of running the factory. Eventually the business was renamed Shorter and Son Ltd. The company enjoyed a close family relationship with the A.J. Wilkinson company and during the '30s it is thought that Clarice Cliff had some input at Shorters; it is known that the factory also used a number of her art deco shapes.

By the early '20s they had a range of stylish art wares on display at the British Industries Fair and at the same time they realised that the demand for majolica wares, which they specialised in earlier, was in decline. By the early '30s the company decided that they had to produce a new range of contemporary shapes and patterns to appeal to a new market. In order to do this they recruited Harry Steele as Manager and under his direction introduced a new range of lines, shapes and decorative wares. The *Pottery Gazette* commented in December 1933 that:

> in this way a much greater potential market was tapped, and the connections of the house were markedly extended and widened.

Plate 28.29. Collection of Shorter and Son earthenwares including a gravy boat in the shape of a fish, 1930s.

With regard to art deco they developed a number of stylish art deco vases which clearly show the influence of Clarice Cliff, evident in shapes such as *Thisbe, Pyramus, Olwen* and *Rhomboid* finished with stylish glazes which were unlike anything they had ever produced. Another popular line was *Stag Ware*, featuring moulded relief of deer finished with soft matt glazes. The company also produced a wide range of moulded wares.

In 1933 the young designer Mabel Leigh joined the company and produced a distinctive range of wares called *Period Pottery*. These innovative wares, which were unlike any current product on the market, were inspired by the Middle East, Central America and Africa with pattern names such as *Espanol, Moresque, Aztec, Anglo Afrik* and *Medina*. They proved very popular and were continued for many years after the designer had left the company. Following the Second World War the factory continued production and in 1964 they were taken over by Crown Devon.

THE SOHO POTTERY LTD
Soho Pottery, then from c.1904
Elder Works, Cobridge

The Soho Pottery was established in 1901 by Mr S. Simpson. The main brand name was *Solian*, introduced in about 1913. Soho offered a wide selection of goods including coffee wares, trinket sets and general fancies alongside toilet wares and pottery for hotels, restaurants and steamships. From about 1929 they introduced the *Ambassador Ware* and *Homestead Ware* trade names. From the trade press reports it is clear that the company had yet to develop art deco styled patterns, evident by the new traditional style printed pattern range called *The Stately Homes of England* depicting different castles, such as those in Ripon and Windsor, launched in 1930. However, there was a mention of a candlestick modelled in the form of a Spanish lady.

By the early '30s the company were introducing a stylish range of coffee wares with hand-painted patterns of simple stylised florals such as *Briar Rose* and *Rosamund*. Colourful hand-painted patterns issued by Soho include *Merrivale*, a design in black and red with slight touches of green, and the similar *Evesham*. At the same time the company issued a popular pattern, *Davenport Lily*, a more traditional design. In 1933 the new *Reedwoode* shape range featured wicker embossment in low relief. This new shape was able to take various patterns such as the simple plaid design *Chequers*.[40] *Hydrangea*, a pretty art deco style floral pattern, was hand painted on the *Adam* shape. Soho launched a set of square plates with matching coffee cups and saucers decorated with print and enamelled golfing subjects that the trade described as 'distinctly entertaining and attractive'. A range of handcraft patterns were also displayed including *June Rose*, *Maytime* and *Evesham* with the additional patterns including a chequer border called *Homelea* from 1934.

The most striking art deco shape was *Burlington*, launched in 1934. This conical shaped ware, enhanced by spiky triangular handles, was decorated with a wide range of abstract patterns such as a stylised cactus pattern with palm trees,[41] a pattern called *Sunray* hand painted in yellow and brown, as well as several printed art deco floral designs including *Jasmine*. Another shape possibly new that

year was *Victory*, decorated with conventional patterns. In 1936 the trade press noted a series of decorative wares with ribbed decoration in matt glazes in four colours including grey, brown and blue, which included lemonade sets, fruit dishes, beakers and various sized jugs. The company also introduced a series of novelty designs such as a moulded biscuit barrel in the shape of a sweet corn and a series of hand-painted hanging birds and butterflies. In 1944 the company was renamed Simpson's (Potters).

SYLVAC (SHAW AND COPESTAKE)
Normacot Road, Longton

William Shaw established Shaw and Copestake in 1894. Originally known as the Sheaf Art Pottery, they mass-produced pottery such as toilet wares, jugs and some giftware. Shaw purchased a small potbank on Normacot Road in Longton in 1894, moving to a new site on Commerce Street, Longton, two years later. In 1903 William Copestake became a partner in the firm but left after only a few years with his share being bought by Richard Hull. He developed a range of matt glazes in conjunction with local firms. During the early part of the twentieth century typical products included earthenware vases, flowerpots, cheese stands and a number of ornate shapes such as *Unique*, *Holborn* and *York* that were decorated with floral patterns. During the First World War they produced a number of lines and novelties.

When the art deco style caught on they produced a wide range of deco shapes such as candlesticks, flower troughs, vases and jugs moulded as budgerigars, stags and bunnies, in various glazes. SylvaC is better known, however, for the range of rabbits and other animals decorated with matt glaze colours such as green, brown and blue, introduced in the '30s. Although not really in the art deco style, they proved very popular. Sought after ranges included the *Wild Duck* series from 1931, which included

twenty different items, and the *Harvest* and *Poppy* ranges. The new trade name SylvaC was probably introduced in 1936 when the company became limited. In 1938 they merged with Thomas Lawrence Ltd (the Falcon Pottery). During the Second World War the Government requisitioned the SylvaC factory, but part of the other factory was made available to Shaw and Copestake, allowing them to maintain their strong export market. Reginald Thompson, designer and modeller for Falcon, produced new designs for both factories.

TOOTH & CO LTD
Woodville, near Burton upon Trent, Derbyshire

This company, founded by Henry Tooth and William Ault in 1883, was first known as Tooth and Ault but changed to Tooth and Co from about 1887. Trading under the Bretby name, they soon became well known for the wide range of products they introduced from art wares to simple utilitarian wares such as beer and lager sets that were subtly coloured to make them look hand thrown. The company won several awards, including the Silver Medal at the International Health Exhibition of 1884, the Diploma of Honour at the Turin International Exhibition in 1911 and the Grand Prix at the Festival of Empire and Imperial Exhibition held at the Crystal Palace in 1911. During the early '20s new lines including *Carved Bamboo* and *Nerton* were launched. Towards the early '30s the company started to develop a range of art deco styled wares with one of the first probably being the *Aquarius* shape range of vases and jugs featuring a fish modelled in relief alongside a series of wares decorated with mottled glaze effects; this was developed by Mr Swinnerton and sold well. New lines like *Atlantis* featured soft pastel colours whilst *Nina* featured embossed flowers painted in natural colours.

In 1931 the company launched a range

of table lamp figures inspired by the works of Dickens and Shakespeare, including *Sam Weller, Pickwick* and *Jingle* modelled by Mrs F. Rigg, the daughter of the late Henry Tooth (illustrated in *Pottery and Glass Record*, March 1931, p.73). Although these were not really deco in style, another example featuring polar bears around a block of ice and modelled in a Cubist style was very striking indeed. A different range featured moulded floral motifs in relief for a series of vases and bowls. In 1933 Tooth & Co Ltd launched a new series of smart and stylish kitchenwares known as *Imperial Blue* clearly influenced by the great success of T.G. Green Cornish ware from the same period. As popularity grew for this extensive range (it included teapots, jugs, butter dishes, lemon squeezers, rolling pins and napkin rings), it became known as K.K. ware and was extended to include lemonade jugs, eggcups, vinegar bottles and flour dredgers. There was also the self-coloured range that included an early morning set on a ceramic tray, cheese dish and toast rack which was illustrated in the trade press in 1933.

By the following year four new matt glaze colourings – bronze green, old gold, saxe blue and olive green – were prepared; according to the trade press, they felt like satin. The *Pottery Gazette* of 1 December 1934 (page 1451) also commented that:

These will shortly be available in a series of futurist-shaped vases, upon which the firm has been working ever since the early part of the present year, when their first efforts in this direction were so much appreciated.

The company also launched the *Peasant Pottery* range featuring incised decoration and hand-painted decoration of stylised flowers on matt glazes. A number of bowls decorated with relief moulding were available along with several examples of flower jugs. The new *Woodville* tableware range that included morning sets boasted a non-crazing glaze. The trade

press noted examples of garden furniture finished in a bisque pottery known as *Greystone*, including attractive figures naturistically modelled, and illustrated a squirrel, a tortoise and a bird. A striking range of modelled vases bearing panelled sunray shapes, several animal figures including a polar bear series of bookends, and a lamp base with a figure of a woman were produced (illustrated *Pottery Gazette*, 2 April 1934, p.471).

The company closed in 1997.

WEDGWOOD AND CO LTD
Unicorn and Pinnox Works, Tunstall

Wedgwood & Co, established in about 1860, were well-known producers of traditionally styled domestic tableware. By the early '30s they were developing a new range of patterns and shapes to meet the new demand for art deco styled wares. The *Pottery Gazette* noted on 1 May 1934 (p.583) that the current patterns were:

very much less conventional in their treatment, and pencilled bands in conjunction with simple brush work ornaments are to be seen in a big variety of styles and modifications.

The same article noted the *Stuart* pattern, brush worked in shades of brown, and decorated on the *Era* shape shown alongside the *Madeley* (2369) and *Wisteria* on *Ely* shape.

A year later Wedgwood launched the new *Farnol* shape, probably one of its most art deco styled forms, with conical body and triangular handles (Plate 28.30). New contemporary patterns, in typical colours such as green, black and platinum, were created for this shape whilst some earlier patterns were adapted for it as well. The shape, decorated with both 2444 and 2443, was illustrated in the *Pottery Gazette* on 1 April 1935 (p.493). These new lines were on sale alongside a new range of matt or bright glazed wares, some

Plate 28.30. A Wedgwood Farnol shaped earthenware tea set decorated with a stylised hand-painted pattern, early '30s.

decorated with stylised patterns and others featuring incised decoration, such as *Chase* and *Neptune*, offered in glossy green, matt marbled and matt white. Production continued after the Second World War and in 1965 the company was renamed Enoch Wedgwood (Tunstall) and then taken over by Josiah Wedgwood and Sons Ltd in 1980.

WESTON POTTERY
Newport Street, Burslem

The Weston Pottery was newly established in the Potteries in about 1932, based at Newport Street in Burslem which had been empty for a number of years. The trade press noted in 1933 that the small company had introduced 'some useful and attractive productions'. They also specialised in the production of *Samian, Jet* and *Rockingham* that were competitively priced. Typical shapes were a plain shape *Meynell*, a low shape *Crawford* and an octagonal shape called *Lonsdale* that may have been designed to appeal to the art deco fashion. Of interest, but not known today, was a slip-dipped decoration known as *Blue Moon* that the trade noted had a special appeal. In 1934 the company placed a small advertisement illustrating a traditionally formed teapot but with art deco styled flowers and zigzags (Plate 28.31). The

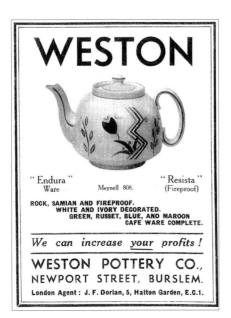

Plate 28.31. A Weston teapot decorated with an abstract pattern, 1930.

same advertisement noted London agents at Stevenage House in Holborn Viaduct. Current teapot shapes included *Endura, Altona* and *Resistas,* the latter being fireproof. In 1934 a new pattern, *Ena,* was launched, though on a rather traditional shape called *Athlone,* and another, *Princess,* that nodded slightly to art deco with a triangle style handle on the cup and stylised flowers bearing a similar style to Crown Ducal.

THOS C. WILD & SONS LTD
St Mary's Works, Longton

Originally known as Thomas C. Wild & Co from 1896, based at the Albert Works (renamed to commemorate the birth of Prince Albert, later George VI, in 1895), Royal Albert was founded in 1917. Three years later, following the death of his father, Thomas Clarke Wild took control of the company and later his two sons joined him, both becoming directors in 1914. In 1905 they traded as Royal Albert Crown China. From the early days of production of their high quality bone china wares they built up a strong export market in countries such as

Africa, New Zealand and Australia. One of the earliest and best selling patterns was *Longton Derby.*

By the late '20s patterns such as *June,* depicting a printed hawthorn motif with blue border, decorated on the *Cecil* shape, and another depicting a crinoline lady among hollyhocks were typical. In 1930 the *Royal* shape was decorated with a futuristic pattern (7557). A new art deco shape range, which may include the *Ascot* and *Alton* shapes, was illustrated in the *Pottery Gazette* on 2 October 1933 (p.1205) decorated with a stylish art deco pattern of abstract flowers and linear motifs.

In 1934 the well-known designer Harold Holdcroft joined the company as Design Director and under his direction shapes became more rococo in style and patterns were much bolder, in line with current taste. As well as a number of nursery patterns, he created a mixture of traditional patterns such as the hand-painted *Dog Rose* and printed *Chelsea Bird* and many contemporary patterns including one featuring a central abstract floral motif in white and gold on a black background from the mid-'30s. He may also have designed the new modern styled *Apex* shape from 1935.

Plate 28.32. Royal Albert (Thos C. Wild) bone china coffee set decorated with an over-glaze printed pattern and stylised flowers, c.1934. Height 7⅜in. (10.3cm).

Other patterns in the modern style noted in the trade press included *Hydrangea, Harmony* and *Embassy,* whilst the transfer-printed pattern *Sampler* had the effect of decorated fabric that was achieved due to the improved quality of prints that were exclusive to them. The company was well known for their Royal Albert Crown Derby style china tea and breakfast sets. In 1964 the company became part of the Allied English Potteries, merging with Royal Doulton in 1972.

WOOD AND SONS
Trent and New Wharf Potteries, Burslem

This well-known family business, with a long history, was established in 1865. From 1910 they traded as Wood and Sons producing a wide range of domestic, toilet and hotel wares of a high quality. They also supplied blank wares to a number of other companies. Beryl Green Ware, launched in the '30s, is probably their best known range.

During the early part of the twentieth century Harry Wood was the driving force behind the success of the company, employing a number of designers and artists including Frederick Rhead from 1912. Rhead designed some of the most popular patterns, such as *Yuan* from 1916, and introduced tube-lined decoration for a number of patterns such as *Trellis* and *Elers.* The company

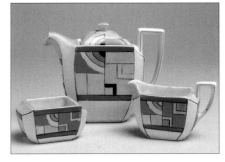

Plate 28.33. A Wood and Sons Cube shape part tea set decorated with a hand-painted pattern. c.1933. Height of teapot 5in. (12.5cm).

bought a small factory that they named Bursley Ltd in order to develop decorative wares. Charlotte Rhead joined Woods and her designs such as *Persian* and *Seed Poppy* proved popular. Later Bursley patterns were inspired by art deco and often mistaken for designs by Susie Cooper (Plate 28.33). A designer, Dora Tenant, is known to have produced a number of art deco patterns for Bursley Ware with her name included on the backstamp (Plate 28.34).

In 1930 John Butler, who had previously been an important designer at A.J. Wilkinson Ltd, took the position of Art Director at Wood and Sons although little information is available on what he

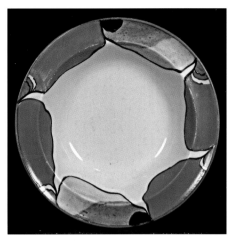

Plate 28.34. A Bursley earthenware bowl decorated with a stylised hand-painted pattern designed by Dora Tenant, 1930.

did during this short time before his tragic death in 1935. Eddie Sambrookes took charge of the artistic side of production and was probably responsible for a series of art deco inspired patterns such as *Summer Days*, a printed floral and tree pattern.[42]

At the same time Woods commissioned Susie Cooper to create a number of patterns including *Academy*, *Cavendish*, *Cromer* and *Charnwood* applied to the *Wren* shape that she designed as well.[43] She also modified *Wren* to create the *Jay* shape, exclusive to Woods. These shapes were later modified and renamed after the Second World War.

1. *Pottery Gazette*, 2 February 1931, p.165.
2. Ibid., 1 June 1935, p.733.
3. Illustrated in S. Lunt, *Age of Jazz British Art Deco Ceramics*, National Museums Liverpool, 2005, p.121.
4. *Pottery Gazette*, 1 August 1934, p.933.
5. Ibid., 1 September 1919, p.942.
6. Ibid., 1 March 1932, p.339.
7. Ibid., 2 May 1935, p.617.
8. Ibid., 1 October 1936, p.1361.
9. Ibid., 1 February 1934, p.187.
10. Ibid., 2 November 1936, p.1479.
11. Ibid., 1 February 1933, p.187.
12. Ibid., 1 July 1933, p.819.
13. Ibid., 1 August 1932, p.989.
14. *Pottery and Glass Record*, March 1934, p.60.
15. Ibid., March 1935, p.63.
16. *Pottery Gazette*, 1 April 1936, p.483.
17. Ibid., 1 June 1932, p.695.
18. Ibid., 1 November 1928, p.1751.
19. Ibid., 1 April 1920, p.485.
20. Ibid., 1 August 1933, p.947.
21. *Pottery and Glass Record*, March 1935, p.61.
22. Ibid., September 1937, p.258.
23. *Pottery Gazette*, 1 June 1933, p.693.
24. Ibid., 1 November 1929, p.1737.
25. Ibid., 2 January 1928, p.11.
26. Ibid., 1 April 1931, p.515.
27. Ibid., 1 September 1932, p.1101.
28. Ibid., 2 Sept 1935, p.1103.
29. Ibid., 1 June 1928, p.859.
30. Ibid., 2 October 1922, p.1509.
31. *Pottery and Glass Record*, March 1934, p.64.
32. Ibid., p.63.
33. Ibid., March 1935, p.65.
34. *Pottery Gazette*, 1 November 1930, p.1825.
35. *Pottery and Glass Record*, May 1937, p.116.
36. *Pottery Gazette*, 1 February 1935, p.211.
37. Ibid., 1 December 1933, p.1433.
38. Ibid., 1 February 1935, p.207.
39. Ibid., 2 April 1934, p.441.
40. Ibid., 1 July 1933, p.815.
41. Ibid., 1 September 1935, p.1082 and illustrated in the *Pottery and Glass Record*, March 1936, p.64.
42. Ibid., 1 April 1931, p.463.
43. Ibid., 1 February 1935, p.197.

Selected Bibliography

GENERAL

Anscombe, I., *Omega and After: Bloomsbury and the Decorative Arts*, Thames & Hudson, 1981

Ashworth, F., *Aynsley*, Shire Publications, 2002

Atterbury, P., *Cornish Ware*, Richard Dennis, 2001

Atterbury, P., Batkin., M. and Denker, E., *Twentieth Century Ceramics, A Collector's Guide to British and North American Factory Produced Ceramics*, Miller's, 1999

Batkin, M., *Gifts for Good Children, Part II, 1890-1990*, Richard Dennis, 1996

Batkin, M., *Wedgwood Ceramics 1846-1959 A New Appraisal*, Richard Dennis, 1982

Benton, C., Benton, T. and Wood, G., *Art Deco 1910-1939*, V&A Publications, 2003

Buddensieg, T., *Keramik in der Weimarer Republik 1919-1933*, exh. cat., Victoria & Albert Museum, London, 1986

Casey, A., *Starting to Collect 20th Century Ceramics*, Antique Collectors' Club, 2006

Casey, A., *20th Century Ceramic Designers in Britain*, Antique Collectors' Club, 2001

Cunningham, H., *Clarice Cliff and her Contemporaries*, Schiffer Publishing Ltd, 2000

Dufrene, M., *Authentic Art Deco Interiors from the 1925 Paris Exhibition*, Antique Collectors' Club, 1989

Fay-Halle, A., *Porcelaines de Sèvres au XXe siècle* (exh. cat.), Musée Nationale Céramique, Sèvres, 1987

Godden, G. *Encyclopaedia of British Porcelain Manufacturers*, Barrie & Jenkins, 1988

Godden, G., *Staffordshire Porcelain*, Harper Collins Publishers Ltd, 1983

Godden, G. *An Encyclopaedia of British Pottery and Porcelain Marks*, Hutchinson, rev. ed. 1972

Hannah, F., *Ceramics, Twentieth Century Design*, Bell and Hyman, 1986

Hawkins, J., and Hollis, M. (eds.) *Thirties: British Art and Design before the War*, Arts Council of Great Britain and Lund Humphries, 1979

Hillier, B., *Art Deco of the 20s and 30s*, Studio Vista, 1968

Kundryavteva, T., *Circling the Square, Avant Garde porcelain from Revolutionary Russia*, (exh. cat.), Somerset House, 2004-2005

Lunt, S., *Age of Jazz Art Deco Ceramics* (exh. cat.), National Museums, Liverpool, 2005

McCready, K., *Art Deco and Modernist Ceramics*, Thames and Hudson, 1995

Mawston, C., *British Art Deco Ceramics*, Schiffer Publishing, 2000

Rena, M., 'The English Pottery Industry', *The Studio*, July-December 1936

Spours, J., *Art Deco Tableware, British Domestic Ceramics 1925-1939*, Ward Lock, 1988

Stevenson, G., *The 1930s Home*, Shire Publications, 2000

Stevenson, G., *Art Deco Ceramics*, Shire Publications, 1998

Trethowan, H., 'Modern British Pottery Design', *The Studio*, July-December 1933

Periodicals

Crockery and Glass Journal (New York)

The Pottery Gazette and Glass Trade Review

Pottery Gazette and Glass Trade Review Diary and Directory

Pottery and Glass Record

The Studio Year Book

INDIVIDUAL FACTORIES

Burleigh

Bumpus, B., *Collecting Rhead Pottery, Charlotte, Frederick, Frederick Hurten*, Francis Joseph, 1999

Bumpus, B., *Charlotte Rhead, Potter & Designer*, Kevin Francis Publishing, 1987

Coupe, E., *Collecting Burleigh Jugs*, Letterbox Publishing, 1999

Coupe, E., *Collecting Burleigh Ware, A Photographic Guide to the Art Deco Tablewares of Burgess & Leigh*, Letterbox Publishing, 1998

McKeown, J., *Burleigh, The Story of a Pottery*, Richard Dennis, 2003

Crown Devon

Hill, S., *Crown Devon*, Jazz Publications, 1993

Crown Ducal

Bumpus, B., *Charlotte Rhead Pottery*, Francis Joseph Publishing, 1999

Grays Pottery

Joseph, F., *Collecting Susie Cooper*, Francis Joseph, 1994

Niblett, P., *Hand Painted Grays Pottery*, City Museum and Art Gallery, Stoke-on-Trent, 1982

Woodhouse, A., *Susie Cooper*, Trilby Books, 1992

Greta Pottery
Hudson-Wiedenmann, U. and Rudoe, J., 'Grete Marks, Artist Potter', *The Decorative Arts Society Journal* 1850 to the present, Journal 26, 2002

Maling
Moore, S., *Maling The Trademark of Excellence!*, Tyne and Wear Museum Service, 1989

Minton
Atterbury, P., and Batkin, M., A *Dictionary of Minton*, Antique Collectors' Club, 1990

Moorcroft
Atterbury, P., *Moorcroft: A Guide to Moorcroft Pottery, 1897-1993*, Richard Dennis, 1993

Myott Pottery
Pollitt, P., and Myott, A., *A History of Myott Pottery, Stoke-on-Trent, 1898-1991*, Anne Myott and Philip Pollitt, 2003

Paragon
Primary Sources
Births, Marriages and Deaths; last Will and Testament of Herbert James Aynsley, Somerset House
Commemorative Collectors' Society, consultative research paper on British commemoratives, The Archivist, Royal Doulton, Barlaston, Staffordshire
Correspondence, K. Cooper to former Paragon employees, 1989
Crow, G., *The Conquest of Ugliness*, Methuen, 1935
Hughes & Harbor, *Almanack* 1897, 1905 and 1907
Interview: James, G. (secretary to Hugh and Leslie Irving), 25 March 1999
Paragon China Sales Literature, Chamberlain King and Jones Ltd., Birmingham, nd (c.1932), The Archivist, Royal Doulton, Barlaston, Staffordshire
Paragon China Sales Literature, Nicholson, Elgin, nd (c.1933-4), Horace Barks Reference Library, Stoke-on-Trent
Paragon Family History, 30 October 1970, The Archivist, Royal Doulton, Barlaston, Staffordshire
Public Record Office, Kew Gardens, London (Board of Trade Registered Designs)
Star China/Paragon Pattern Books, The Archivist, Royal Doulton, Barlaston, Staffordshire
Other Printed Sources
Dale, R., *Louis Wain: The Man who Drew Cats*, Chris Beetles Ltd., 2000

Hallinan, L., *British Commemoratives*, Antique Collectors' Club, 1995
Hildyard, R., *European Ceramics*, V & A Publications, 1999
Hillier, M., *Chloë Preston and the Peek-a-Boos*, Richard Dennis, 1998
Horne, A., *The Dictionary of British Book Illustrators*, Antique Collectors' Club, 1994
May, J. and J., *Commemorative Pottery 1780-1900*, Heinemann, 1972
Parkin, M., *Louis Wain's Cats*, Thames & Hudson, 1983
Reade, B., *Louis Wain* (exh. cat.), Victoria and Albert Museum, 1972

Theses and Dissertations
Ashworth, F., *A Family of Potters. The Aynsleys of Longton as China Manufacturers and Entrepreneurs within their Community* (M. Phil. Thesis at Nottingham Trent University, May 2001)
Colbeck, E.M., *The Designer and the British Pottery Industry 1919-1939* (M. Phil. Thesis at the University of London, June 1983)

Poole
British Art & Design 1900-1960, Victoria & Albert Museum, 1984
Hawkins, J., *The Poole Potteries*, Barrie & Jenkins, 1980
Hayward, L., *Poole Pottery, Carter and Company and their Successors 1873-1995*, Richard Dennis, 1995

Royal Doulton
Atterbury, P., and Irvine, L., *The Doulton Story*, Royal Doulton, 1979
Eyles, D., *The Doulton Burslem Wares*, Barrie & Jenkins/Royal Doulton, 1980
Eyles, D., *Royal Doulton 1815-1965*, Hutchinson, 1965
Eyles, D., Irvine, L., and Baynton, V., *Royal Doulton Figures*, Royal Doulton and Richard Dennis (third ed.), 1993
Irvine, L., *The Doulton Lambeth Wares*, Richard Dennis, 2002
Irvine, L., *Royal Doulton Bunnykins Figures*, UK International Ceramics, 1996
Irvine, L., *Royal Doulton Bunnykins Collectors' Book*. Richard Dennis, 1993
Irvine, L., *Royal Doulton Series Ware* (five volumes), Richard Dennis 1980-98
Irvine, L., and Atterbury, P., with Skipwith, P., and contributors, *Gilbert Bayes, Sculptor 1872-1953*, Richard Dennis, 1998

Selected Bibliography

Irvine, L., and Dennis, R., *Royal Doulton Limited Edition Loving Cups and Jugs,* Richard Dennis, 1981

Lukins, J., *Collecting Royal Doulton Character and Toby Jugs,* Venta Books, 1994

McKeown, J., *Royal Doulton,* Shire Publications, reprinted 2004

McKeown, J., 'Tableware 1930s and '40s', articles in *Gallery,* the magazine of the Royal Doulton International Collectors' Club, Winter 1995 and Spring 1996

Niblett, K. (ed.), *The Legacy of Sir Henry Doulton,* exh. cat., Potteries Museum, 1997

Royal Winton

Busby, E., *Royal Winton Porcelain,* The Glass Press, 1998

Miller, M., *The Royal Winton Collectors' Handbook, from 1925,* Francis Joseph, 1998

Miller, M., *Collecting Royal Winton, Chintz,* Francis Joseph, 1996

Scott, S., *Charlton Standard Catalogue of Chintz,* Charlton Press, 1999

Shelley

Davenport, C., *Shelley Pottery, The Later Years, A Collector's Guide,* Heather Publications, Congleton, 1997

Hill, S., *The Shelley Style, A Collector's Guide,* Jazz Publications, 1990

Knight, R., and Hill, S., *Wileman, A Collector's Guide,* Jazz Publications, 1995

The Shelley Group, *The Shape Book, The Teaware Shapes of the Wileman and Shelley Potteries,* The Shelley Group, 2000

Watkins, C, Harvey, W. and Senft, R., *Shelley Potteries, The History and Production of a Staffordshire Family of Potters,* Barrie & Jenkins, 1980

Catalogues

Everyday Things, catalogue to the exhibition arranged by the Royal Institute of British Architects, London, 1936

Journals and Magazines

The Australian Shelley Collectors' Club newsletters, 1983-2007, Australia

The National Shelley China Club (USA) newsletters and magazines, 2000-2007, Seattle, USA

The Shelley Group newsletters and magazines, 1986-2007, Perton

The Shelley Standard (in-house magazine of Shelley Potteries Limited, formerly Wileman & Company), 1927-1931, Smedley Services, Stoke-on-Trent

Other Publications

Casey, Andrew, *The New Shelley Standard, A Reassessment of the work of Eric Slater,* The Shelley Group, Perton, 2001

Rush, Kay, *The Search for Elsie Harding,* The Shelley Group, Perton, 2005 and 2006

Russell, Thomas, *How to Advertise a Chinaware Business,* reprint from *The Shelley Standard,* Smedley Services, Stoke-on-Trent, 1927

Selection of Shelley advertising leaflets from 1910 to 1940 in the authors' collection including:
Satisfied It's Shelley (c.1925), Smedley Services, Stoke-on-Trent
Shelley Dainty White China, advertising leaflet, 1929
The Silver Book (1931), Shelley Potteries Limited

Spode

Wilkinson, V., *Copeland,* Shire Publications, 2000

Susie Cooper

Casey, A., *Susie Cooper Ceramics: A Collector's Guide,* Jazz Publications, 1992

Casey, A. and Eatwell, A. (eds.), *Susie Cooper: A Pioneer of Modern Design,* Antique Collectors' Club, 2002

Eatwell, A., *Susie Cooper Productions,* V&A Publications, 1987

Woodhouse, A., *Susie Cooper,* Trilby Books, 1992

Josiah Wedgwood and Sons Ltd

Batkin, M., *Wedgwood Ceramics, 1846-1959: A New Appraisal,* Richard Dennis, 1982

Des Fontaines, U., *Wedgwood Fairyland Lustre,* Sotheby Parke Bernet, 1975

Reilly, R., *Wedgwood: The New Illustrated Dictionary,* Antique Collectors' Club, 1995

Catalogue of Bodies, Glazes and Shapes, Current for 1940-1950, Josiah Wedgwood and Sons Ltd

Wedgwood 1936 exhibition, Grafton Galleries, London, 1936

A.J. Wilkinson

Slater, G. and Brough, J., *Comprehensively Clarice Cliff,* Thames & Hudson, 2005

Wentworth-Shields, P. and Johnson, K., *Clarice Cliff,* L'Odeon, 1976

Woodward, Dr.P., *Clarice Cliff – An Exhibition of Ugly Ware* (cat.), Vardy Gallery, September 1999

Periodicals

The Home (Australian periodical)

Archival material

A.J. Wilkinson and Newport Pottery archival material – Stoke City Archives, Hanley

Acknowledgements

FIRST I SHOULD LIKE TO THANK all the contributors for their support and hard work in putting this book together and for writing such excellent illustrated essays on their specialist subjects. They kindly supplied a wide range of images and archive material and were so patient in answering my many questions as the book was being developed.

So many people have helped with the production of this book. I should like to thank Judy Rudoe from the British Museum and Ursula Wiedenmann, for allowing me to use their published work on the work of Grete Marks, Frances Marks, Duane Kahlhamer for guidance and background knowledge. For the Spode chapter I should like to thank Olwen Grant, Eileen and Rodney Hampson, and Marguerite Coles and I am grateful to the Cochrane and Pettit Archive for information on Carlton Ware.

Many other people who have helped include Ivan Monty, Chris Walker, Bryan Tismond, Octavia Antiques, York and Ann Rogers.

A special thanks to Sue Lunt, Curator of Decorative Art, National Museums, Liverpool for arranging permissions from private collectors to use images of art deco ceramics that featured in her excellent *Age of Jazz* exhibition and book; thank you also to David Moffat, Assistant Curator, for sorting out all the practical aspects of images. I should particularly like to thank the lenders of images: Beverley and Beth, 30 Church Street, London, Nick Jones from Gallery 1930 (susiecooper ceramics.com), Nick Berthoud and Moorcroft plc.

I should like to specially thank the Wedgwood Museum for allowing us to reproduce a range of photographs, archive material and backstamps. Thank you to Gaye Blake Roberts, Museum Curator, Lynn Miller, Information Office, and Sharon Gater. I should also like to thank the staff of the Potteries Museum, especially Miranda Goodby and Julia Knight, for allowing me access to research material, pointing me in the right direction for other areas of research and providing me with several images for the book. Chris Latimer and the staff of Stoke-on-Trent City Library were very supportive to me and the other authors with regards to gaining access to the period and archival material and the various *Pottery Gazettes*. They patiently gathered the many photocopies and advised on and kindly gave me permission to reproduce certain materials. Thanks also to the Manchester Central Library (Technical Reference Section).

I should like to thank Michael Jeffery in particular for his continued support and for providing many high quality images for several chapters from his excellent auctions of twentieth century decorative art at Woolley and Wallis Auctioneers in Salisbury. Also David Hare of Gardiner Houlgate Auctioneers of Bath kindly gave me permission to reproduce a Royal Winton image from one of his special sales. I should like to thank the owners of Maison Gerard in New York who were so helpful in supplying high quality images of French ceramics. Thanks also go to a number of specialists and private collectors and authors including Louise Irvine and Lynn Knight.

For a book such as this I was able to gain the professional services of a number of excellent photographers including Lance Cooper of Suffolk, Northern Counties Photographers in Burslem and Gary Leggett. The Spode images were kindly produced by Martin Greatbach, Laurence Coombes and Bill Coles. I should like to personally thank Chris Rushton for not only taking excellent photographs but also organising photographic sessions with a number of authors and their private collections. Many thanks to Stella Calvert-Smith of Christie's Images for organising a number of images for the book, as well as Bryan Tismond. Andrew Sanigar, Thames and Hudson, kindly organised a number of images for the A.J. Wilkinson chapter.

Clarice Cliff®, Bizarre®, Fantasque®, Bizooka® are trademarks of Josiah Wedgwood & Sons Limited of Barlaston, Stoke-on-Trent, England and are used with

Acknowledgements

the owner's kind permission. Wilkinson and Newport archive pattern book information, images and extracts are reproduced by the kind permission of Josiah Wedgwood & Sons Limited, Barlaston, Stoke-on-Trent, England (publication and all other rights reserved).

A.J. Wilkinson Ltd factory archival excerpts are reproduced by kind permission of Wedgwood Museum Trust, Barlaston.

Finally, thank you to Eric Knowles for so kindly agreeing to write the Foreword to this book.

Picture Credits

Frank Ashworth: 229
Horace Barks Reference Library, Stoke-on-Trent, 199 (right), 202 (right)
The Nick Berthoud Collection: 62, 63 (top)
Beverley and Beth: 94, 164
Brighton Museum and Art Galleries: 12
British Museum: 222
Anita Calvert: 233
Christie's Images Ltd: 38, 39, 42, 137
Richard Dennis: 68, 108-111
By kind permission of Ellesborough Ltd, Isle of Man, photography courtesy of Josiah Wedgwood & Sons Ltd: 160 (top and bottom right), 161 (top), 162
Gardiner Houlgate Auctioneers: 218 (bottom)
Clive Graham: 208 (top left and bottom right), 209 (bottom), 211
Louise Irvine: 66
Nick Jones, Gallery 1930: 153, 157, 158, 161 (bottom)
Lynn Knight: 134
Liverpool Museum: 62, 63 (top), 76, 77, 78 (top right), 94, 153, 157, 158, 161 (bottom), 164
Maison Gerard Ltd, New York: 13-14
Frances Marks: 224 (top right), 226 (bottom)
Colin Mawston: 32
Minton Archives, formerly Royal Doulton: 63 (bottom)
W. Moorcroft Ltd: 74, 75, 76, 77, 78 (right)
Steven Moore/Maling: 135, 136, 138-141
Myott Collectors' Club: 213, 214 (bottom) 215, 216 (bottom)

Harvey Pettit: 210 (bottom)
Potteries Museum: 152, 172-177, 187, 188 (top), 191, 192 (bottom left), 193, 217, 223, 224 (top left), 225, 226 (top left and right), 250 (bottom centre)
Robert Prescott-Walker: 29 (bottom)
Ann Rodgers: 218 (top)
Greg Slater: 30 (bottom), 114-129, 132, 243 (bottom), 251. 30, 125 (bottom), 127 (top), 128 and 129 are reproduced from *Comprehensively Clarice Cliff* by Greg Slater and Jonathan Brough, published by Thames & Hudson, 2005
Les Smith, Royal Doulton Museum: 67, 69, 70, 71, 72, 73 (right), copyright Royal Doulton (UK) Ltd
Southampton Solent University, Faculty of Media, Arts and Society Study Collection: 203
Spode Museum Trust, Stoke-on-Trent: 52-60
Greg Stevenson: 21-27
Stoke on Trent Libraries: 192 (top right), 194
Bryan Tismond, Octavia Antiques trading in the Red House Antique Centre, York: 219 (top)
Ian Turner: 232
Victoria and Albert Museum: 41
Josiah Wedgwood & Sons Ltd: 132. Foley is a registered trade mark. The rights belong to Josiah Wedgwood & Sons Ltd.
Courtesy of the Wedgwood Museum Trustees, Barlaston, Staffordshire, England: 35, 37, 40, 43-46, 47 top and bottom left), 48, 50 (bottom), 51 (bottom)
Woolley and Wallis Auctioneers: 15, 19, 20, 28, 32, 36, 47 (bottom right), 49, 50 (top), 51 (top), 98 (right), 100 (top right and bottom) 101, 103 (bottom), 133 (top), 165, 181 (bottom), 192 (top left), 206, 208 (top right), 209 (top left and right), 210 (top), 212, 221, 238 (right), 242, 246, 249

Every effort has been made to secure permission to reproduce the images contained within this book and I am grateful to the individuals and institutions who have assisted in this task. Any errors or omissions are entirely unintentional.

The Contributors

Andrew Casey

Andrew Casey is an author, lecturer and artist. Born in Leeds, he became interested in twentieth century decorative arts whilst studying art and design at the Leeds College of Art during the early eighties. He later gained a First Class Degree in Combined Studies (Design) from the University of East London. An accomplished artist with work in private and public collections, he is also a lecturer in art and design.

His interest in ceramics, particularly those by the designer Susie Cooper, led him to form the Susie Cooper Collectors' Group in 1990. His first book, *Susie Cooper Ceramics: A Collector's Guide,* was published in 1992. He has curated several exhibitions of art and decorative arts including one on 'Women Ceramic Designers of the Twentieth Century' at the Croydon Clock Tower, South London and 'Susie Cooper Productions' for Ipswich Museums and Galleries in 1989. For *20th Century Ceramic Designers in Britain,* published by the Antique Collectors' Club, Andrew Casey was awarded the prestigious Besterman/McColvin Gold Medal for the most outstanding work of reference published in 2001 given by the Chartered Institute of Library and Information Professionals (CILIP). For Susie Cooper's centenary Andrew Casey and Ann Eatwell edited the official book *Susie Cooper: A Pioneer of Modern Design,* published in 2002 by the Antique Collectors' Club. This was followed in 2006 by *Starting to Collect 20th Century Ceramics,* also published by the Antique Collectors' Club. He writes for several magazines and lectures across the country; in 2004 he was invited to lecture in Sydney, Australia, by the Ceramic Society of New South Wales.

Frank Ashworth

Frank Ashworth studied at Manchester and Cambridge Universities before qualifying as a Chartered Arts and Antiques Surveyor. He has lectured at Southampton Solent University since 1985, specialising in professional, degree and postgraduate courses on ceramics to prepare students for careers in the antiques and auctioneering profession. Frank has a long-standing interest in the Staffordshire ceramics industry, researching extensively the china firms of Longton. He has written various articles and publications, including *Aynsley China* in 2002. He was also editor of the *Journal* of the Paragon International Collectors' Club from 1998 until 2005. He is married with two grown-up children and lives in Hampshire.

Peter and Brenda Aspinall

Peter and Brenda Aspinall have been involved in buying and selling antiques for the last twenty-five years, exhibiting at many of the major antiques fairs throughout the country. They had always carried a large and varied stock of one of their favourite potteries, Fielding's Crown Devon, and made the acquaintance of many people who also loved and collected Fielding's products. Gradually they gravitated to displaying and selling only items made by this manufacturer. At a fair at Newark they met Alan Roberts who had been collecting Fielding's musical novelties for many years. They co-operated with Alan, by now a close friend, in the production of the book *Crown Devon Musical Novelties* which was written by Alan. Brenda and Peter also produced and marketed a video of Fielding's musical novelties. Finding themselves spending more and more time answering questions about the company and its products they decided, after much coercion from dedicated collectors, to establish a collectors' club and so in 1999 Fielding's Crown Devon Collectors' Club was launched; it is still going strong today.

In 2003, after a heart attack, Peter was advised to adopt a more sedentary lifestyle and Alan Roberts, who had been editor of the Club magazine, was persuaded to take over the running of the Club. Brenda and Peter ceased trading as antique dealers in 2003.

Paul Atterbury

Dr Paul Atterbury is a writer, lecturer, broadcaster and historian specialising in the art and design of the nineteenth and twentieth centuries. He has written or edited over thirty books, ranging from pottery and porcelain to railways and canals. His subjects include Minton, Moorcroft, Poole, Ruskin Pottery, Parian, Cornish Ware, twentieth century ceramics, the North of France and Branch Line Britain. In the late 1970s he was Historical Adviser to Royal Doulton, with responsibility for factory museums, and subsequently editor of *The Connoisseur.* Since 1990 he has been a member of the team of experts on BBC's Antiques Roadshow.

John Barter and Linda Ellis

John Barter and Linda Ellis, both separately and together, have been ardent collectors of Wileman and Shelley pottery and china since the 1980s. They are both active in research projects on British ceramics, especially art pottery, and they also collect art deco styled ceramics manufactured by the many major factories during the 1920s and 1930s. John is also very interested in style developments following the 1951 Festival of Britain. In 1986 Linda was one of the founder members of the

Shelley Group, the collectors' club for Shelley enthusiasts, which is now twenty-one years old. This group has become a charity, promoting knowledge about and interest in the products of the Shelley factory and its nearly two hundred year history. They have both supported the charity as Trustees for many years, Linda as Treasurer and John as Archivist.

Linda and John have contributed to a number of magazine articles and books about ceramics and have helped support various authors, including Andrew Casey, with specialist knowledge and background information about Wileman and Shelley and other manufacturers of ceramics. Both have given lectures and talks about ceramics and architecture to a range of domestic and overseas organisations, including the Shelley Group and the National Shelley China Club of the USA. They are also active in supporting national architecture preservation organisations, local history and heritage societies with particular emphasis on archival research.

Stella Beddoe

Stella Beddoe has been Keeper of Decorative Art at Brighton & Hove Museums since 1985. She has published widely on aspects of the decorative arts, in particular: with Jessica Rutherford, *Art Nouveau, Art Deco, The Twenties, The Thirties and Post-War Design, The Ceramic, Glass and Metalwork Collections at Brighton Museum,* Brighton, 1986; 'Art Deco in Britain: A Missed Opportunity' in *L'Art Deco en Europe: Tendances Décoratives,* exh.cat., Brussels, 1989; with Pat Halfpenny, *Circus & Sport: English Earthenware Figures 1740-1840,* exh. cat., Louisville, Kentucky, USA, 1990; 'Interior Decoration in France, 1900 onwards', *The Macmillan Dictionary of Art,* London, 1996; 'Art Deco Fans: Product Promotion' in *The Jazz Age,* Brighton, 1996. She reviews regularly for *Art Quarterly* (The Art Fund, London), *The Journal of Design History* (Oxford) and *Studies in the Decorative Arts* (Bard Center, New York).

Hilary Calvert

A chance purchase in the late 1980s was the start of Hilary's absorbing interest in British art pottery. One small piece of George Clews' Chameleon Ware grew to become a definitive collection and led her to research this previously undocumented pottery. The result was a book which was published by Schiffer in 1998 as *Chameleon Ware Art Pottery* which remains the only work on the subject. In recent years she has become interested in the pottery made by the Potters' Arts Guild at Compton in Surrey. Researching this tiny village industry made a welcome change from industrial art pottery and has resulted in a book published by the Watts Gallery, with which the pottery is associated. Hilary and her husband

are now retired and live with a houseful of pots in the Cambridgeshire fens.

Dan Dunlavey

Dan Dunlavey was a student in London when Britpop was at its height and a pint cost less than £1.50. Since then he has tried his hand at everything from finance to farming, but has settled on a career in publishing. His interest in antiques was first piqued while working as a writer and editor for a series of guide books and he quickly developed a lasting affection not just for the objects themselves but also for the colourful characters that populate salerooms and dealers' premises around the world. Despite a valiant effort to resist the collecting bug himself, Dan will admit to owning a few modern first editions and a couple of pieces of West German pottery. In an ideal world his house would be furnished with Ruhlmann, but unfortunately publishing pays neither lavishly nor promptly. He lives in Cambridgeshire with his partner and their pets.

Ann Eatwell

Ann Eatwell, an Assistant Curator in the Sculpture, Metalwork, Ceramics and Glass Department of the Victoria and Albert Museum, curated the major retrospective exhibition 'Susie Cooper Productions' in 1987 and wrote the accompanying book. She and Andrew Casey edited *Susie Cooper: A Pioneer of Modern Design,* published in 2002 by the Antique Collectors' Club, the official book for Susie Cooper's centenary. Ann contributed to the research and presentation of Channel 4's 'Pottery Ladies' and has researched and written widely on the history of ceramics and silver, including modern industrial ceramic production. Ann was the first person to publish an article on the 'Harrods Experiment' (in *Antique Collecting*). She is currently working on a jewellery project at the Victoria and Albert Museum.

Sharon Gater

Born and raised in the Potteries in a family involved in all aspects of the manufacture of ceramics, Sharon Gater graduated from Oxford Brookes with a degree in English Literature and History of Art. She intended to work with paintings but accepted the position of Museum Assistant at the Wedgwood Museum in 1978. Immediately captivated by the work of such twentieth century artists as Keith Murray and the Powells, she began to pursue the study of Wedgwood's modern history, including its social aspect. She obtained an M.A. in Victorian Studies and co-authored, with Dr. David Vincent, *Factory in a Garden,* an account of the move of the

Wedgwood factory from Etruria to Barlaston in 1940. She has lectured extensively at exhibitions and in the United States and has also contributed to numerous publications. Sharon is currently involved with the planning of the new Wedgwood Museum due to open in Spring 2008.

Miranda Goodby

Miranda Goodby has been Curator of Ceramics at the Potteries Museum & Art Gallery, Stoke-on-Trent, since 1995, and has a long-standing association with its collections. She has worked in museums since graduation and has a special interest in Staffordshire ceramics from the late eighteenth century onwards and in the social conditions of the potters. She has written on the moulding technology used by eighteenth century pottery factories, the work of the potters Enoch Wood and William Littler, and on the emigration of Staffordshire potters to the United States in the 1840s.

Miranda has lectured widely at home and in North America on subjects as varied as Josiah Wedgwood, 'everyday' ceramics in domestic use and working conditions in the early pottery industry. Her interest in the Empire Porcelain Company dates back to her childhood and the stories that her father told her of working there as a fourteen year old in 1940.

Clive Hillier

Clive Hillier lives with his wife and two children in Newcastle, Staffordshire, where he owns Louis Taylor Fine Art Auction Rooms in Hanley, Stoke-on-Trent, selling antiques, collectables, and specialising in ceramics. For many years Clive has had an avid interest in the art deco period and after buying his first piece of Grays in a small secondhand shop in Colwyn Bay became 'hooked' and has subsequently gone on to acquire an extensive collection. He has given many talks, written articles for numerous publications and is to be heard regularly on BBC Radio Stoke as their antiques expert.

Michael Jeffery

Michael Jeffery graduated from Warwick University and after ten years at Christie's joined Woolley and Wallis Auctioneers, setting up a twentieth century design department in 2003. He has developed this market with a series of specialist sales including auctions devoted to the Martin Brothers, Clarice Cliff, Poole Pottery and British Art and Design 1900-2000. Michael is a member of the Decorative Arts Society and has had numerous articles and reviews published on twentieth century design, particularly ceramics. He is a keen collector of the period.

Julie McKeown

Julie McKeown is a freelance writer and ceramic historian. A graduate in the History of Art, her first appointment was with the Gladstone Pottery Museum in Stoke-on-Trent. She subsequently worked as an historical researcher for ceramics manufacturers, including Minton and Spode. At Royal Doulton, where she was employed as curator of the Sir Henry Doulton Gallery, she wrote a popular short history of Royal Doulton (Shire 1997, 2004), later contributing a biography of the Doulton Lambeth artist Hannah Barlow to the *Oxford Dictionary of National Biography* (Oxford University Press 2004). Julie is also the author of *Burleigh, the Story of a Pottery* (Richard Dennis Publications 2003), which was awarded the *Antiques Trade Gazette* 'Book of the Year', and *English Ceramics: 250 Years of Collecting at Rode* (Philip Wilson Publishers 2006), a study of the major collection of English porcelain and pottery acquired by the Wilbraham family of Rode Hall in Cheshire. Her articles include 'The Burleigh Renaissance' and 'Peacocks and Pottery: Walter Crane at Rode' for *Antique Collecting* magazine (2004).

Helen Martin and Harvey Pettit

Helen Martin has had an interest in Carlton Ware and English ceramics since the 1980s. She has collected, researched and compiled data on Carlton Ware, ultimately becoming the leading specialist Carlton Ware dealer in the country. She and her then husband Keith ran Carlton Ware Collectors International, the collectors' club for Carlton Ware, producing the Club magazine and providing information for collectors. They also ran the very successful Annual Conference with the only specialist Carlton Ware Collectors' Fair in the world. Helen has written many articles on the subject and appeared on television. She continues her interest in Carlton Ware, helping the new Carlton Ware World Wide club compile their magazine, *The Carlton Comet,* with Harvey Pettit and selling from her website and the occasional fair. Helen also continues her research of Carlton Ware with Harvey who has been compiling the definitive reference work on Wiltshaw & Robinson (Carlton Ware).

Steven Moore

Steven's passion for collecting started as a child, beginning with curios begged or borrowed from his grandmother's attic. By the age of sixteen he had curated his first exhibition at Newcastle's Laing Art Gallery and had written his first book by twenty-one. After studying to be an archaeologist, he moved into antique dealing and writing. He is curator for C.T. Maling & Sons and Chairman of the Maling Collectors'

The Contributors

Society. He currently works as a freelance art and antiques consultant, writer and broadcaster.

Susan Scott

Susan Scott is a Canadian writer, researcher and collector who has specialised in twentieth century English ceramics for the past twenty years. She has written articles about Susie Cooper, Clarice Cliff and their contemporaries, about Moorcroft, Poole Pottery and other china factories, as well as about chintz ware. She has been a speaker on ceramics at conventions in England and the United States, as well as Canada, and for five years she was the co-organiser of 'Collecting the Twentieth Century Symposium' at the Royal Ontario Museum. For some years she wrote a 'hot collectibles' column for a Canadian home design publication. Her book, the *Charlton Standard Catalogue of Chintz*, was first published in 1997 and went to three editions. Many of the articles she has written for antiques publications in Canada and the United States including *Antique Showcase, Upper Canadian, New England Journal of Antiques, Antique Trader, and Collector's News* are antiques-focused travel stories.

Greg Slater

Greg Slater is a long time collector of both A.J. Wilkinson Ltd and Clarice Cliff pottery. He is the principal author of *Comprehensively Clarice Cliff* and is the editor of *The Agora*, a specialist publication for the discussion of art deco ceramics. Greg regularly contributes articles on A.J. Wilkinson Ltd and Clarice Cliff to the Australian publication, *Collectables Trader*.

Greg Stevenson

Dr Greg Stevenson is Honorary Research Fellow of the University of Wales (Lampeter). His PhD researched British ceramic design 1927-37. The author of *The 1930s Home* and *Art Deco Ceramics* (both published by Shire), Greg lives in West Wales where he manages a social enterprise company restoring historic buildings.

David Steventon

David Steventon is a direct descendant of John Steventon but has had no direct involvement in either the company or the pottery industry. He has an honours degree in Natural Sciences from Cambridge University and is a member of the Institute of Operations Management and of the Chartered Management Institute. He works in the software industry as a principal consultant for Oracle Corporation UK Ltd. It was not until middle age that he started taking an interest in Royal Venton Ware

production from the 1920s and 1930s, but he has collected over 1,000 representative pieces during the last ten years.

Sue Taylor

A librarian by profession, Sue Taylor's interest in ceramics led her to study part-time for an MA in the History of Ceramics at Staffordshire University. Her dissertation on Bullers' art pottery studio and its role in the British modernist movement led to other publications about this Stoke-on-Trent company. From 2000 to 2004 she worked in the ceramics section of the Potteries Museum & Art Gallery, Stoke-on-Trent, as a research and documentation assistant, cataloguing new acquisitions, redisplaying the twentieth century ceramics collection and working on a collaborative European ceramics exhibition and website. In 2004 she was awarded a grant from the Cumming Ceramic Research Foundation to support research into nineteenth century electrical porcelain manufacturers. After running several successful ceramics evening courses, Sue now delivers occasional lectures for local WEA organisations. She has written extensively on the subject of Bullers including *Bullers of Milton* published by Churnet Valley Books, 2003.

Ian Turner

Ian Turner was born in Birmingham and educated at the universities of Cambridge and Washington before qualifying as a Chartered Town Planner. He ended his planning career as Director of Planning for Derby City Council and then took early retirement to pursue his interests in twentieth century glass and ceramics. He was the joint author of *Ysart Glass*, Volo Editions Limited, London, 1990 and the author of *Candy Art Pottery*, Hillian Press, Melbourne, 2000. He is a past Chairman of the Glass Association. He sold his collection of Monart glass at Christie's in 2003 and now collects art pottery made as a sideline in the lesser known Potteries tile works. He contributes occasional articles to *Antique Collecting* and to publications of the Glass Association and the Northern Ceramics Society, and gives talks to other collectors. He lives in a former brewery in South Derbyshire.

Vega Wilkinson

Vega Wilkinson was born in West Yorkshire but moved to Staffordshire in the early 1970s where she began to study the art and history of the potteries. She has written the guidebook to the Spode Copeland collection at Trelissick, Cornwall, *Spode-Copeland-Spode: The Works and its People 1770-1970*, published by the Antique Collectors' Club and the Shire albums *Copeland* and, with Robert Devereux, *Porcelain Pastille Burners*. She is currently researching *The Forgotten Potteries*, to be published this autumn. She is married with two children.

Index

Page numbers in bold type refer to illustrations and captions